FIRST PRIZE COOKBOOK

Dimetra Makris
David Dax
Diane Powell

THE STEPHEN GREENE PRESS

BRATTLEBORO, VERMONT
LEXINGTON, MASSACHUSETTS

TO OUR NEW FRIENDS, THE COOKS

FIRST EDITION
Text copyright © 1982 by Dimetra Makris, David Dax, and Diane Powell
Illustrations copyright © 1982 by The Stephen Greene Press

This book was manufactured in the United States of America. It is designed by Irving Perkins Associates and published by The Stephen Greene Press, Fessenden Road, Brattleboro, Vermont 05301.

LIBRARY OF CONGRESS CATALOGING IN PUBLICATION DATA
Main entry under title:

First prize cookbook.

  Includes indexes.
  1. Cookery. I. Makris, Dimetra. II. Dax, David.
III. Powell, Diane.
TX715.F5317   641.5   81-22930
ISBN 0-8289-0467-7   AACR2

CONTENTS

———•———

ACKNOWLEDGMENTS

———————●———————

We wish to give a very special thank you to Ernestine Breisch Powell and to Mr. and Mrs. Nicholas Makris for their encouragement and support.

We especially appreciate Austin Lynn's enthusiasm and patience with this book. For their help we are grateful to Anne Krapp, Rosemary Fry Plakas of the Library of Congress, Morton Nitzberg, Senator Larry Pressler of South Dakota, Mrs. Joan Kennedy and Senator Edward Kennedy of Massachusetts and New York Representative Geraldine Ferraro and her district staff.

We appreciate the special efforts of Suzanne F. Edwards and the National Pineapple Cooking Classic office. Thanks also to Connie Parvis and the Delmarva Poultry Industries. At a time when we really needed help, Jean Stewart of New Orleans Magazine, Bob Gonko of the State Journal Register, Springfield, Illinois and Nina Rubel with the News-Gazette, Champaign, Illinois had the answers for us.

There were hundreds of persons who helped us along the way and we only wish we could thank each one individually. To the many home economists, those marvelous secretaries and administrators in Chamber of Commerce offices, to the 4-H leaders, cooperative extension offices, secretaries and fair managers of the state and county fairs, thank you for your encouraging notes and letters as well as your assistance. Just a few of these are: J. R. Spencer, Pattyann DesMarais, Jean Gibbs, Margaret Richmond, Ginny Trenary, Mildred Minor Gregory, Betsy H. Owens, Louise King, Marilyne Hubert, Sharlene Larsen, Deborah Wallis, Charles R. Smith, B. C. Lloyd, Debbie Moore, Janie Johnson, S. Ralph Andrews, Bob Record, Robert W. Walker, Helen E. Snyder, Miriam E. Gerhart, Lila Varn, Katherine Tucker, Trish Tanner, L. Olin Mills, Sandra K. Haldiman, James R. Salimbene, Norma A. Weber, Bob LeBlanc, Sam Theriot, Leona J. Dudzinski, Ramona Jamison, Melinda Smith, Frances Young, Barbara Johnson, Claire Sessions and Mary Kay Kuschel.

The patience of our friends, among them, Nicki Goldstein, Marina Doukas and Darlene Dew of Delaware, Ohio is greatly appreciated.

Finally to our INTV friends, Wendy Schacter, Leon Morse, Fred Gold and Herman W. Land, thank you.

FOREWORD

———————●———————

Would you like getting up before 5:00 A.M. to load your car with cakes and pies, biscuits, and breads? Or driving for hours to the fairgrounds to enter your work in competition with hundreds of other top cooks? All the cooks in this book have shared the rigors of competition. And they've all won awards for their efforts— some of them have won literally hundreds of fair ribbons! And many have cooked for more than sixty years. We have junior cooks and men and women, who have all won prizes at state fairs, county fairs, cook-offs, and competitions across the country.

This book is by and about your neighbors, successful, hardworking, careful achievers. We have come to think of our prizewinners as friends, for without exception, they are generous and interesting people sharing what they know and enjoy doing so well—cooking. All the cooks share their recipes in their own words, giving you hints and suggestions plus a little information about themselves. Some tell about their kitchens and how they learned to cook. Some share funny or disastrous cooking misadventures.

Our cooks are careful. They have to be, to become winners. The recipes included here are the culmination of years of effort and countless hours of precise experiment. How many people would make a hundred cookies to get a few perfect ones, or a dozen pies to get one that looks just right?

There are pages and pages of prizewinning cakes, bread, biscuits, pies, and cookies. But if you think fair winners are just cakes and pies—read on. There are meat, fish and poultry recipes: casseroles, ham recipes, stews and chilis, beef roll-ups, and more. There are international dishes as well.

For your sweet teeth there are plenty of candy and dessert recipes cakes, cookies, pies, special desserts, bonbons of all sorts from divinity to peanut brittle.

We have winners with preserved fruits—prizewinning butters and spreads— jams, jellies, juices, and pickles. There are also prizewinning recipes for canned vegetables and home canned meats.

Some of the recipes are simple, others complex. Many are old recipes, passed down through generations; others were invented by their winning cooks.

Here are the cooking champions, the culinary Gold Medal winners. Here are the folks who spend hours and hours and hours getting it right. These cooks have earned their recognition, and you can benefit by trying these recipes for yourself. We did and we guarantee—they work. Good food like this deserves more than blue ribbons, more than money—it deserves your hungry appreciation.

USING THIS BOOK

It is remarkable how clear and concise several hundred cooks can be in presenting their best recipes. Naturally, all these personalities don't use exactly the same terminology, but we have standardized the abbreviations used. Measurements vary. One cook will tell you to use a stick of butter, another will tell you to use ½ cup, a third will say 8 tablespoons. Most of the recipe ingredients are standard and readily available, but you may find a few that are hard to come by. Some cooks give step-by-step directions, but most simply describe the procedures they use while cooking.

At the back of the book, before the index, are a Table of Standard Weights and Measures and a Table of Metric Conversions. The index lists recipes by name, and food category. In addition, there is an index of states and names, listing the names of the cooks by state and town.

THANK YOU

Out of so many great cooks, not everyone could be included. Deciding which recipes to include or not include was extremely difficult and many hours were spent reading and re-reading the hundreds of recipes submitted. The selection was arbitrary on our part. Choices were made on the basis of regional diversity, recipe variety, and space limitation.

In other words, if your prizewinning layer cake isn't here it is not because it isn't every bite as good as the ones included. It is probably because we got to the others first. Some recipes are not first prize winners—this is because some were duplications of the first prize recipe, or were unique. Others were submitted by judges of cooking contests.

For all of you who shared your recipes and experiences with us and who are not in this book, we want to extend our special thanks.

NOTE: Biographical information about the cooks is marked

CHAPTER ONE

APPETIZERS

APPETIZERS

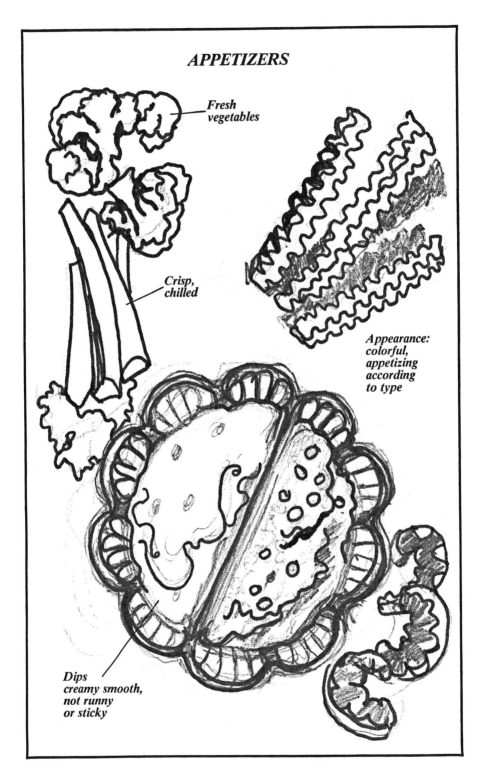

Fresh vegetables

Crisp, chilled

Appearance: colorful, appetizing according to type

Dips creamy smooth, not runny or sticky

COLEEN ADDY
ROSWELL, NEW MEXICO

FIRST PRIZE
EASTERN NEW MEXICO STATE FAIR
NEW MEXICO STATE FAIR

SPRING TIME DIP

½ cup red or green chili sauce
1 cup cottage cheese
1 cup sour cream
1 tsp. salt

1 T. sugar
¼ cup minced onions
¼ cup minced radishes
½ cup minced cucumbers

Blend first 5 ingredients well in blender. Remove to bowl and add minced vegetables. Serve with corn chips or tostadas.

"Coleen is recognized as the 'Candy Chef of the Pecos Valley.' Not only does she make prizewinning candies, she willingly shares her recipes and techniques for making them with everyone," says Jewell Limacher, Extension home economist. "If you listen to her and do what she says, you'll never have a failure. I know—she taught me."

Coleen married when she was fifteen, joined an Extension Club in 1929, and has been an active member ever since. In 1979, she was honored for her work at the national meeting in Albuquerque. A versatile cook, she shares her prize-winning appetizer here.

Try her Chicken Tortilla Pie (page 57), Mexican Corn (page 79), Garlic Pecans (page 355), and Hard Candy (page 355).

REESA BYRD
ENTERPRISE, ALABAMA

FIRST PRIZE
DAILY LEDGER NEWSPAPER
HOLIDAY COOKING BOOK

HOT BEEF DIP

1 2½-oz. jar dried beef
1 cup cold water
½ cup Parmesan cheese
¼ cup sour cream
¼ cup salad dressing or
mayonnaise

¼ cup chopped onion
1 8-oz. pkg. cream cheese
1 T. parsley flakes

Cut beef into small pieces. Combine beef and water as directed on jar and boil. Drain well. Mix remaining ingredients. Cook over very low heat until hot, stirring occasionally.

Serve with crackers, chunks of bread, or vegetable sticks—or Doritos or anything that's good with a dip.

Reesa, National Peanut Festival recipe queen, cooks for five every day in her pretty blue-and-white kitchen that "lets the outside in." She has developed several winning recipes, including Grand Prize in the National Peanut Festival ($250.00 and a trip to New York and Washington.)

Here are some of Reesa's helpful hints:

1. When trying a new recipe I always halve or third it, so if we don't care for it not much is wasted.
2. Bake and pressure cook and stop frying meats.
3. Cook seasoning with bouillon cubes, not grease.
4. Double recipes and freeze food for another meal—saves time and electricity.
5. I always cook ten pounds of hamburger and freeze what we don't eat. When I want to make spaghetti or tacos or whatever, the meat is already cooked and ready.

CAROLYN CHANEY
BATON ROUGE, LOUISIANA

SECOND PLACE
STATE TIMES AND *MORNING ADVOCATE* CONTEST
BATON ROUGE, LOUISIANA

STUFFED CUCUMBERS

6 small unpeeled cucumbers
12 anchovies
1 T. chopped fresh dill
1 T. chopped fresh chives

6 oz. cream cheese
2 T. sour cream
Salt and pepper to taste

Scrape cucumbers lengthwise with fork tines to make long grooves. Cut into 1-inch sections and hollow out seeds in center, leaving firm cucumber rings. Mash 12 anchovies and mix well with dill, chives, and cream cheese softened with sour cream. Season to taste with salt and pepper. Fill cucumber rings and chill in refrigerator for several hours.

TO SERVE

Place 1 teaspoon sour cream on top of each stuffed cucumber ring. Top cream with small piece of pimento or small olive. Garnish platter with lemon wedges and parsley.

NOTE: If fresh dill and/or fresh chives are unattainable, parsley can be substituted for the dill and finely chopped shallots for the chives.

SARDINE SNACKS

MIX TOGETHER

1 can sardines, mashed
    (discard liquid and remove
    bones)
¼ cup coarsely grated Romano
    cheese
¼ cup coarsely grated Cheddar
    cheese
3 T. Worcestershire
Leaves from heart of celery,
    chopped fine

2 tsp. dry onions
Dash ground cloves
1 heaping tsp. mustard
Salt
Plenty cayenne
Enough mayonnaise to make
    spreading consistency

Remove crusts from bread. Very lightly spread outer side of bread before spreading unbuttered side with sardine mix. Roll and secure with toothpicks. Place in 375-degree oven till toasted.

MOM'S CAPONATA

1 diced eggplant (unpeeled)
1 chopped medium onion
1 rib chopped celery
2 cloves chopped garlic
1 small chopped bell pepper
Small amount of oil
3 oz. tomato paste

¾ cup water
3 T. sugar
Salt and cayenne to taste
1 small jar sliced green olives
   (with or without pimento)
1 small bottle capers (liquid
   also)

Soak eggplant in salt water about ½ hour. Drain. Sauté onion, celery, garlic, and bell pepper in oil until soft. Add tomato paste. Cook well. Add water, sugar, salt, and cayenne. Cook till thick. Add olives, capers, and eggplant. Simmer 10 minutes.

Remove from heat, and let cool to room temperature. To serve, surround with hard crackers.

NOTE: This Caponata can also be added to a spaghetti sauce for a real taste treat.

This contest (the 1976 *State Times* and *Morning Advocate* contest) asked for old family recipes. I used the recipe my mother uses to make Caponata in volume to put in jars, and reduced it down to the amount shown above. The original recipe makes 6 pints of Caponata. The procedure is the same as above, but her original recipe is shown below.

CAPONATA—JARRING RECIPE

. 6 eggplants
2 T. vinegar
½ stalk celery
4 cups water
1 bell pepper
1 small jar olives

2 6-oz. cans tomato paste
1 cup sugar
2 large onions
1 small bottle capers (liquid
   also)
6 cloves chopped garlic

Use same cooking procedure as above. Process 15 minutes.

 Carolyn advises, "Try something different, even though it may be a flop. So what! You can't always succeed. But keep experimenting, and after a while you learn combinations that are always successful."

Try Carolyn's "Beef Spinach Frittata" (page 84), and her "Marinated Lamb Steaks" (page 29).

LELIA DALY
GILLINGHAM, WISCONSIN

FIRST PRIZE
RICHLAND COUNTY DAIRY BAKE-OFF

ONION CHEESE BREAD

½ cup chopped onion
2 T. butter
1 egg, beaten
½ cup milk
1½ cups biscuit mix
½ cup shredded Cheddar
   cheese
2 tsp. parsley flakes
½ cup shredded Cheddar
   cheese

Sauté onion in melted butter in a small skillet, until tender (do not brown). Set aside to cool. Combine egg and milk in bowl. Add biscuit mix, stirring just enough to moisten. Stir in cooked onion, ½ cup cheese, and parsley flakes. Spread batter in greased 8-inch square pan. Sprinkle with ½ cup cheese. Bake in 400-degree oven 20 minutes or until done. Serve warm.

Yield: 9 servings

Try Lelia's Home Comfort Donuts (page 175) and Cottage Cheese Chiffon Pie (page 276).

GEORGIA ANN EFFENBERGER
OCONTO FALLS, WISCONSIN

FIRST PRIZE
OCONTO COUNTY DAIRY MONTH
BAKE-OFF: DAIRY DRINK AND
CHEESE SNACK,
OCONTO, WISCONSIN

ORANGE BLOSSOM DRINK

¼–⅓ cup orange juice
1 tsp. sugar

2 drops almond flavoring
1 scoop vanilla ice cream

Place orange juice in large glass; add sugar and flavoring. Stir. Add ice cream. Add enough milk to fill the glass. Stir again.

Yield: 1 serving

TANGY CHEESE ROLL

1 lb. sharp Cheddar cheese, softened
1 8-oz. pkg. cream cheese, softened
Dash of Tabasco sauce
¼ cup salad dressing

2 T. Worcestershire sauce
¾ cup cut-up pecans
2 cloves garlic (optional)
Pinch of salt
Paprika

Dice cheese. Put in blender container with Tabasco sauce, dressing, Worcestershire sauce, and pecans. Process at high speed until smooth. Use a rubber spatula to help keep ingredients flowing to the processing blades. Add garlic and salt while blending. Shape mixture into a roll. Roll in paprika (or sprinkle on paprika) and refrigerate. Put sprigs of parsley around for color.

 Georgia Ann began cooking when she was a little girl on a farm. Now she cooks for her husband, two daughters, and seventeen-year-old Wayne, who also likes to cook and bake.

LORRAINE JACOBS
NAHUNTA, GEORGIA

FIRST PLACE
DISTRICT PEANUT FESTIVAL
NAHUNTA, GEORGIA

STUFFED CELERY

1 8-oz. pkg. cream cheese,
    softened
1 small can crushed pineapple
    (drained)
½ cup roasted chopped peanuts

½ cup crunchy peanut butter
    (or plain creamy)
½ cup brown sugar
½ cup fresh grated coconut

In a small saucepan heat the pineapple and brown sugar over low heat until sugar melts. Cool. Mix all ingredients together in a medium-size mixing bowl and let stand overnight to mix flavors. This can be made and stored in refrigerator for 4 or 5 days. The flavors are blended more and I like it better. Cut celery into bite-size pieces and soak in ice water for 2 or 3 hours or until good and crisp.

Yield: 3½ cups

Try Lorraine's Orange Peanut Butter Surprise Pie (page 287) and Fanci-Chicken Salad (page 104).

CHAPTER TWO

SOUPS/STEWS

SOUP AND STEWS

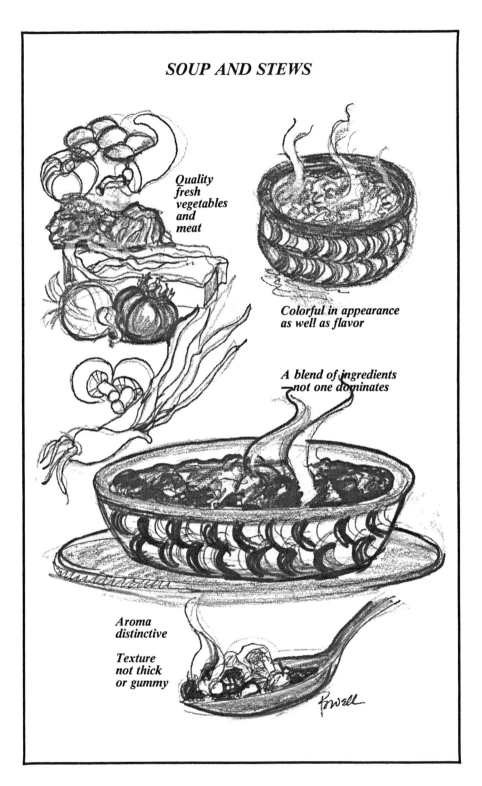

Quality
fresh
vegetables
and
meat

Colorful in appearance
as well as flavor

A blend of ingredients
not one dominates

Aroma
distinctive

Texture
not thick
or gummy

Powell

MAZO ECCLESTON
FOWLER, KANSAS

RABBIT CHILI

4 lbs. ground meat from cotton-
    tail rabbits (could use
    tame rabbits in this day
    and age)

2 lbs. onions chopped
1 gallon cold water

Cook above 3 ingredients for 2 hours (stir now and then).

1 lb. suet ground and fried (can grind fat off a roast or steaks to get suet)

Add following to fried suet:

2 T. paprika
1 T. vinegar
Box of cumin seed
½ T. black pepper

1 cup hot ketchup
1 T. oregano
Salt to taste

Add to cooked ground rabbit meat the seasoning and simmer. Can be frozen and added to beans when you want to serve it. I have made this when rabbits were more plentiful and froze it.

See Mazo's Canned Whole Tomatoes (page 88).

JO MCMILLON
BALLINGER, TEXAS

NELDA'S CHILI RECIPE

2 lbs. ground meat
2½ T. chili blend
2 cups water
1 tsp. ground cumin seeds

¼ tsp. garlic salt
2 tsp. salt
½ tsp. black pepper
1 can tomato sauce

Cook meat until it turns a gray in color, add all ingredients and cook on low heat for an hour or more (unless you are in a hurry for it—less cooking time is okay). If it seems too greasy, add 1 or 2 tablespoons of meal.

Jo told us she came up with this chili recipe when "I ate chili at my friend's house. She told me she didn't have a recipe. She just put in ingredients until it tasted right. I told her I needed a recipe and to come over and we'd make one. That's what we did and I've been using this recipe for 15 or 20 years."

VAL COWLEY
LOGAN, UTAH

FIRST PLACE, BEEF
MORGAN COUNTY FAIR
FIRST PLACE, BEEF
UTAH STATE FAIR

DUTCH OVEN STEW

½ lb. bacon
2 lbs. cubed T-Bone roast
1 lb. carrots
2 lbs. potatoes
3 green peppers

¾ lb. onions
2½ lbs. tomatoes (sauce or
    juice may be substi-
    tuted)
6 stalks celery

Fry bacon in pot to season. Add meat and onions and brown. Coarse-chop vegetables but save tomatoes and season with 1 teaspoon Tabasco, 1 tablespoon Worcestershire sauce, salt and pepper. Add tomatoes, cover, and simmer until done, about 45 minutes.

 Val Cowley reports that he made a Fry Bread and Cheese Centerpiece to serve with the Dutch Oven Stew at the 1977 Utah State Fair. "I try to use cheese in all of my cooking or as a side dish, as it compliments them and is nutritionally sound. It completes my meals," he says.

Val gives credit for his cooking skills to 4-H and to his mother. Twenty years of professional cooking experience (as a short-order cook, a buffet cook, and cooking for the Navy) probably helped Val devise this prize winning stew.

Now he works in a kitchen "well equipped to handle most anything I cook."

MARGIE E. GROVE
Moccasin, Montana

DISTRICT FIRST PLACE
COWBELLE'S BEEF COOK-OFF
JUDITH BASIN COUNTY

HEIRLOOM BEEF STEW

2 lbs. boneless beef round cut in 1-inch cubes
¼ tsp. pepper
1 cup chopped onion
2 cups water (add more if needed)
5 medium carrots, cut in 2-inch-long strips (2 cups)
6 medium potatoes, pared and cut in 1-inch cubes (4 cups)
2 tsp. dried marjoram leaves (if desired)

½ cup water
2 tsp. salt (1 salt, 1 season salt)
2 T. cooking oil
½ cup chopped celery
2 beef bouillon cubes
4 cups coarsely chopped cabbage
1 1-lb. can tomatoes, cut up
¼ cup flour

Season beef cubes with 1 teaspoon salt and pepper. Brown beef in hot oil in electric fry pan or dutch oven. Add onion and celery; sauté 5 minutes. Add two cups water and bouillon cubes. Cook, covered, 45 minutes.

Add vegetables, marjoram, and 1 teaspoon salt. Simmer covered, 30 minutes. Blend together flour and ½ cup water. Stir into simmering stew; cook 2 minutes.

Yield: 8 servings

Margie Grove learned to cook "by asking a lot of questions and by following directions." She says she follows "mother recipes" that is, how her mother says recipes, "from her head—not a book. A handful of that, a glass of this, a small bowl of something, and a spoonful of this."

MRS. CLOY HARVEY
STEPTOE, WASHINGTON

BLUE RIBBON, BEEF
WHITMAN COUNTY FAIR,
WASHINGTON

BEEF BURGER SOUP

1 lb. hamburger
2 pkgs. beef broth or 3 bouillon
  cubes
1 bay leaf
1 small onion, chopped

1 cup diced celery
2 cups diced carrots
1 cup diced potatoes
1 can stewed tomatoes
1 cup water

Brown beef, sprinkle beef broth on meat, add water, tomatoes, vegetables except potatoes, wait until other vegetables are done. You can use rice or macaroni, instead of potatoes for a change. Take bay leaf out before serving. Can cook all in heavy kettle or skillet.

Mrs. Cloy Harvey suggests serving this soup with a salad and rolls: "It makes a meal." She's been cooking since she was twelve, and now has three married children; she learned the basics from her mother and by "working out summers for farm wives."

"Don't be afraid to try different seasonings," she says. She also tells a story on herself. "Once I was showing how good I could make biscuits for Grandmother at her house. I used soda instead of baking powder. A dog wouldn't eat them."

MARGIE'S OYSTER SOUP
(Serves 10)

1 stick butter	Salt & red and white pepper
2 bunches chopped shallots	to taste
1 onion, chopped	4 doz. oysters
2 toes chopped garlic	2 qts. oyster liquor and water
1 celery heart, finely chopped	1 cup whipping cream
¾ cup flour	½ bunch chopped parsley

Sauté chopped shallots, garlic, and celery until tender. Stir in flour to make a smooth paste. Add oysters and oyster liquor. Bring to boil; add cream and parsley. *Do not boil.*

Yield: serves 10

 Although Warren LeRuth has not won a first prize he has judged more than 40 cooking contests. We thought you cooks might like to judge the judge! See his Broken Shrimp Jambalaya (page 43), Red Beans and Rice (page 92), Bibb Lettuce and Mushroom Salad with Vermouth Dressing (page 105), and Day-Old Beet and Onion Salad (page 105).

In addition to being in the deciding seat at cooking competitions, Warren is the owner-chef of Le Ruth's Restaurant (one of New Orleans' finest), and created the famous Green Goddess salad dressing for Seven Seasons.

He learned to cook "aboard ship, and in professional kitchens," and published his own cookbook, *Front Door, Back Door,** which may be obtained by writing to him.

**LeRuth's Front Door, Back Door Cookbook* by Warren LeRuth, 636 Franklin St., Gretna, LA. Copyright by W. LeRuth, 1975. (Printed by Tokay Press, New Orleans, Louisiana. 5 printings.)

CHAPTER THREE

MEATS/SEAFOOD

MEATS

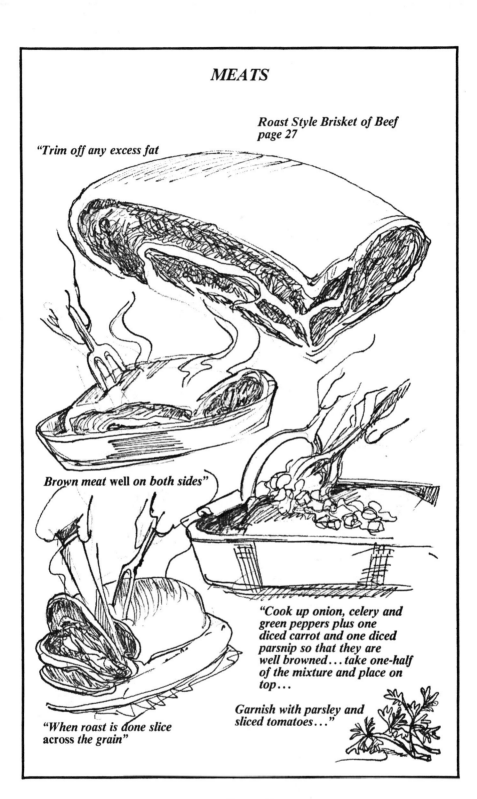

Roast Style Brisket of Beef
page 27

"Trim off any excess fat

Brown meat well on both sides"

"Cook up onion, celery and
green peppers plus one
diced carrot and one diced
parsnip so that they are
well browned...take one-half
of the mixture and place on
top...

Garnish with parsley and
sliced tomatoes..."

"When roast is done slice
across the grain"

JOYCE BANKS
BANCROFT, IDAHO

FIRST PLACE
IDAHO BEEF COOK-OFF

BRACIOLA

3 lbs. round steak
Soft butter
¼ tsp. garlic powder
6 T. Parmesan cheese
1 T. parsley
4 T. olive oil
2 T. flour

1 cup grape juice (red) or
    red wine
2 16-oz. cans tomato sauce
¼ tsp. basil
2 cups whole mushrooms
¼ tsp. oregano
Salt and pepper

Pound steak with mallet into thin slices, about ¼–½-inch thick, cut into about 16 pieces, salt and pepper, spread with softened butter, sprinkle with mixture of cheese, garlic powder, and parsley. Roll and tie with string at each end.

Brown quickly in hot olive oil, in large skillet, rolling back and forth to brown on all sides. Remove from the pan to a plate and set to one side.

To drippings add mushrooms, sauté gently for a minute, add flour, grape juice, tomato sauce, and seasonings, mix together.

Add beef rolls, cover, and cook very slowly for about 1½ hours or until tender.

Remove strings and serve in deep platter on top of wide egg noodles with a bowl of Parmesan cheese on the side.

Joyce Banks not only won First Place in the Idaho Beef Cook-Off with this Braciola recipe, she also won an all-expenses-paid trip to Columbus, Ohio.

Joyce began to cook when she was eight years old, and made her first cookies. Later she helped her mother and grandmother prepare meals, and eventually took home economics in high school. "This class did a lot toward expanding my food interests and my creativity in cooking," she says.

LEONA BESS
CHERRYVILLE, NORTH CAROLINA

APPLESAUCE-STUFFED FRANKFURTERS

½ cup soft breadcrumbs
3 T. melted butter or
    margarine
½ tsp. poultry seasoning

1 cup canned applesauce
8 frankfurters
8 bacon slices

Combine breadcrumbs, butter or margarine, and poultry seasoning. Cook applesauce, stirring occasionally, until most of the water has evaporated (7 minutes). Combine crumb mixture and applesauce. Split frankfurters almost through to bottom, lengthwise. Fill with applesauce mixture. Wrap 1 slice bacon around each frankfurter; fasten with toothpicks. Broil 8 minutes.

Yield: 4 servings

SOPHIE BURDEN
WICKENBURG, ARIZONA

DAD FLETCHER'S TAMALE PIE

Chop 1 onion, ½ green pepper (ortega green peppers are okay), 1 carrot, 3 stalks celery. Cook these until soft. Add 3 or 4 pounds of ground beef and cook whole into a paste.

Add 1 can of cream corn, 3 small cans of red chili sauce, chopped ripe olives, salt and pepper to taste, and a can of stewed tomatoes. Tomato sauce or paste makes it yummy—also oregano.

Optional, if you like to experiment: chili powder, taco sauce, hot sauce, chopped pork, rosemary, etc. Keep tasting it and adding things as you think of them.

Scald salted (½ teaspoon per cup) white corn meal and mix it until it is the right consistency to spread. Spread it over the bottom and sides of deep baking pan. Pour meat mixture in and cover or dot it with grated or chopped Cheddar cheese. Then cover it all with a crust of corn meal—I like it with corn meal all around it, but some like it just on top.

Bake slowly at 350 or 375 degrees for about an hour, remembering that the larger the pie the longer it takes.

"We went to a pot luck in Wickenburg along about 1928," says Sophie Burden, a Grand Champion cook. "One lady brought a tamale pie and my dad thought it was the best thing he'd ever tasted. So he told me to keep trying until I found out how to cook it. I asked the lady and she said, 'I wouldn't know anything about a recipe for that. You just keep putting good things together until you think it's good.' So I did—and this is what I finally came up with. Try it—you'll like it."

Sophie's Real Spanish Rice (page 81), Charros Beans (page 81), Strawberry-Rhubarb Salad (page 101), Tomato Aspic (page 101), Remuda Beer Biscuits (page 169), and Christmas Rum Squares (page 356) are winners too!

HAM CASSEROLE DELUXE

8 slices boiled ham
24 asparagus spears
8 slices Swiss cheese—4x4-incn slices

For best results, have ingredients at room temperature. Place cheese and asparagus on ham. Roll up; secure with toothpicks. Arrange in casserole dish and cover with the following sauce.

SAUCE

4 T. flour
1½ cups milk
1 T. butter

½ cup evaporated milk
Salt and pepper to taste

Mix well in saucepan. Cook until very thick. Pour over ham and bake in 350-degree oven until bubbly. During last 5 minutes sprinkle top with ½ cup grated cheese (Cheddar) and ¾ cup toasted almonds.

Yield: serves 8

MEXICAN TOSS-UP

1 lb. ground beef
½ tsp. salt

½ onion, chopped
½ green pepper, chopped

Cook above ingredients till done. Add to beef mixture the following and cook till thick:

1 can chili beans or kidney beans
½ cup catalina or French dressing
½ cup water

Break lettuce in salad bowl. Put 8 ounces crackerbarrel shredded cheese and 1 bunch green onions diced on top. Pour hot beef over salad and eat immediately. Beef mixture can be frozen.

"If you make a mistake first time, don't give up. Keep trying," advises Catherine Burger.

She told us about a mistake she made: "I quit school when I was sixteen—started working for a family with a new baby. I didn't know anything about cooking. Guess I had never heard of or eaten spaghetti or I would have known better. I was supposed to be making American Spaghetti. No one told me to drain the water off the spaghetti so I put it all together. The husband sat down to eat—took a helping and asked me what it was. They ate it. Never said a word about what I had done wrong. I didn't know either until she asked me to cook it again and told me to drain off the water."

Catherine says to serve her Mexican Toss-up with applesauce and bread and butter.

HOWARD B. CAMDEN, CPCU

WEST BLOOMFIELD, MICHIGAN

FIRST PRIZE
AMERICAN NATIONAL COWBELLES; AMERICAN NATIONAL CATTLE-MEN'S ASSOCIATION, DENVER, COLORADO

CAMDEN'S SUPER BARBECUED SPARE RIBS

2 slabs of meaty spare ribs	Barbecue seasoning salt
3 cups water	Paprika
1 cup (white) vinegar	Parsley
Camden's Barbecue Sauce	Garlic powder
Oranges	Pineapple

Trim the spare ribs of any excess fat. Put the ribs in a roasting pan and add the water and vinegar. Turn about every ½ hour. Marinate in this mixture for 2 to 4 hours. Take the ribs out and drain.

Sprinkle lightly on both sides with the garlic powder, paprika, and barbecue seasoning.

Place the ribs on the grill when the charcoal has a good gray covering. *Turn the ribs frequently* so as not to burn. Cooking time about 1 hour, or when the ribs appear to be thoroughly barbecued.

Brush on Camden's Barbecue Sauce or serve with the ribs, warmed. Garnish the platter with oranges, pineapple, or parsley.

Yield: 4 generous portions

CAMDEN'S BARBECUE SAUCE

1 bottle (28 oz.) Open Pit Barbecue Sauce, Original Flavor	½ cup brown sugar
	2 T. Lee & Perrins Worcester-shire Sauce
1 bottle (20 oz.) Heinz Catsup	4 T. Liquid Smoke
6 oz. Heinz 57 Steak Sauce	½ tsp. garlic powder
6 oz. A-1 Steak Sauce	
½ cup dry red wine, grape juice, or water	

Mix well, bring to a boil, and let simmer 30 minutes.

You can make it sweeter by adding more brown sugar, tarter by adding lemon juice or vinegar, and hotter by adding Tabasco.

The sauce will burn if you baste the meat with it from the beginning. Like most tomato- and sugar-based sauces, it should be added only during the last few minutes of cooking or else served warmed with the meat at the table.

Goes very well with pork. Will keep in the refrigerator for a long time.

Yield: About 2 quarts

FIRST PRIZE WINNER—BLUE RIBBON
NATIONAL BEEF COOK-OFF
AMERICAN NATIONAL COWBELLES
AMERICAN NATIONAL CATTLEMEN'S
ASSOCIATION, DENVER, COLORADO

ROAST STYLE BRISKET OF BEEF

1 6–8-lb. beef brisket	2 T. fresh dill leaves or
3 T. cooking oil	1 tsp. dried dill leaves
2 cups chopped onion	2 bay leaves cut in half
4 stalks celery, including leaves chopped up	2 cups dry red wine
	2 T. vinegar
2 rounded tsp. crumbled beef bouillon	2 1-lb. cans small whole potatoes *or* 2 lbs. fresh
1 large green pepper, chopped up	medium potatoes, quartered
2 cloves garlic or ½ tsp. garlic powder	10+1 carrots cut in half
	10+1 parsnips cut in half
1 tsp. paprika	½ bunch parsley
½ tsp. fresh milled pepper	2 ripe tomatoes

Trim off any excess fat and brown meat *well,* on both sides, in roasting pan or dutch oven.

Cook up onions, celery, and green peppers plus 1 diced carrot and 1 diced parsnip so that they are *well* browned. Fat side up, sprinkle the meat with the paprika, garlic, beef bouillon, and dill, and place the bay leaves around the top of the meat. Then take half the fried mixture and place on bottom of roast and the other half on top.

Put in dutch oven or roasting pan with a covered top. Add wine and vinegar. Put in 325-degree oven and cook for 3 to 3½ hours.

When the roast *appears almost done, add more liquid, if necessary.* Add the carrots, parsnips, and potatoes around the meat in the liquid and cook for approximately 30 minutes.

When the roast is done, remove from pan, wait 20 minutes, then slice the meat *across* the grain. Taste the meat and adjust the salt. Garnish with parsley and sliced tomatoes. Serve with the cooked vegetables and remaining juice.

Howard Camden has been cooking for many years. Though he told us he learned to cook "to survive" because the food was so poor at Michigan State, he has gone way beyond survival food. He not only won the Michigan Pork Contest (a $1000 prize and a trip) with these fantastic Barbecued Spare Ribs and a barbecue sauce, he also won the National Beef Cook-Off with his Beef Brisket recipe.

CAROLYN CHANEY
BATON ROUGE, LOUISIANA

FINALIST
NATIONAL PINEAPPLE COOKING
CLASSIC, HAWAII

MARINATED LAMB STEAKS

1 8¼-oz. can pineapple slices
¼ cup olive oil
3 T. Worcestershire sauce
2 T. ketchup
Juice of 1 lemon
2 T. brown sugar
1 tsp. mustard

2 cloves garlic, mashed
¼ tsp. mint
Crushed peppercorns (amount
  depending on individual
  taste)
4 lamb steaks, each 1-inch
  thick

Combine juice from can of pineapple slices with olive oil, Worcestershire, ketchup, lemon juice, brown sugar, mustard, garlic, and mint. Mix well. Marinate lamb steaks in this mixture overnight, or at least 4 hours. Turn to coat both sides. Remove from marinade. Press crushed peppercorns into both sides of steaks. Broil steaks to desired degree of doneness. Remove from broiler and keep warm. Heat pineapple slices in pan under broiler.

Place pineapple slice on each steak. Garnish with fresh mint leaves if available. Otherwise, use parsley sprigs.

Try Carolyn's Beef Spinach Frittata (page 84), Stuffed Cucumbers (page 5), Sardine Snacks (page 5), and Mom's Caponata (page 6).

LEISA COVOLO

MOUNTAIN VIEW, WYOMING

LEISA COVOLO'S LASAGNE

¾ lb. ground beef
½ cup chopped onions
2 cloves garlic, finely chopped
1½ tsp. salt
1 tsp. oregano
1 6-oz. can tomato paste
1 8-oz. can tomato sauce

¾ cup hot water
6 cooked lasagna noodles
1 egg
1½ cups cream-style cottage
   cheese
1 cup shredded Cheddar
   cheese

Preheat oven to 350 degrees. Crumble beef into a large skillet. Add onion and garlic. Cook over moderate heat, stirring as needed, until meat is lightly browned and onion is tender. Add seasonings, tomato paste, tomato sauce, and water. Simmer, stirring occasionally, for 5 minutes. Blend egg with cottage cheese.

Cover the bottom of a 7½x12x2-inch baking dish with an even layer of one-fourth of the tomato-meat sauce. Then make a layer using 3 noodles. Top noodles with a layer of one-fourth more of the tomato-meat sauce.

Add a layer of half the cottage cheese mixture and half the shredded cheese. Add another quarter of the tomato-meat sauce, then the remaining cottage and shredded cheese.

Spread with the 3 remaining noodles and then the remaining sauce. Bake uncovered for 30 minutes.

Yield: 6 servings

NOTE: Lasagne may be completely prepared and placed in the baking dish the day before use. Cover immediately with plastic wrap and refrigerate.

She recalls a mistake she made while giving a demonstration for a contest. "I licked my fingers," confesses Leisa. "It was embarrassing— a good thing the judge wasn't looking." Leisa Covolo is a 4-H prize winner, was Grand Champion at the County Fair, and won second place at the Wyoming state fair. She learned to cook "from 4-H projects and my mother," and now works in a kitchen "that I love to make the center of our activities."

BEATRICE M. DYER
FREEPORT, MAINE

TUNA CASSEROLE

1 medium-size can tuna fish (drain off liquid)
1 small onion
1 can cream of chicken (or cream of mushroom) soup
1 can milk
2 cups cooked noodles (wide)
Butter and salt to taste

Cover with cracker crumbs. Bake at 450 degrees for 20 minutes.

Yield: Serves 6

See her Date Balls (page 362).

BARBARA ESSER
MINOT, NORTH DAKOTA

SAUSAGE RECIPE

3 beef roasts, 10 lbs. each (lean)	4 T. salt
2 pork roasts, 10 lbs. each (semifat)	2 T. pepper
	1 T. ground sage
4 garlic cloves	½ cup boiling water

Put beef and pork roasts, salt, pepper, and sage through meat grinder, small blade. (Seasonings will be more thoroughly distributed if added while grinding.) Put garlic cloves in 5-inch cheesecloth squares, tie, then pound with mallet. Put in cup and pour the boiling water over cloves.

Discard cheesecloth and residue. Add the hot water to ground meat. Mix thoroughly but do not overmix, as that would make sausage too solid. Let set overnight to blend flavors.

Put sausage stuffer attachment on meat grinder. Thread with pork casings that have been soaked overnight in fresh water. Fill as many casings as there is meat or as many as you wish. Make remainder into patties and freeze. Prepare jars for canning, fill with sausage in circular motion, put length of sausage in center of jar. Process in pressure canner. Follow time and pressure that is right for your area.

DORIA GAUTHIER
TOPPENISH, WASHINGTON

FIRST PLACE
WASHINGTON STATE COOK-OFF
ALL-EXPENSE TRIP TO NATIONAL
BEEF COOK-OFF

MUSTARD BREAD WITH BEEF

2 lbs. beef, round, rump,
  or chuck
1 large onion, sliced
Fry mix
¼ cup oil
Salt, pepper, or seasoning salt
  to taste

2 slices bread (sour dough
  is best)
Prepared mustard
1½–2 cups water or broth
2–3 tsp. sugar
3 T. vinegar

Slice beef about 2x1x¼-inch, across grain, if possible. Season and dredge with fry mix, shake off excess. Add 1½ tablespoons oil to pan. When hot, add half of the meat and stir until brown. Remove to pressure cooker or dutch oven and proceed with other half of the meat, add more oil if needed.

Add remaining oil, onion, and seasoning spreading on top of the beef slices. Spread both sides of bread lightly with prepared mustard and cut into 1½-inch squares. Place on top of onion and beef, add water or broth, cover, and pressure cook for 15 minutes at 10 pounds. Reduce pressure. May be simmered in dutch oven until meat is tender. Using slotted spoon, remove immediately to a warm dish. Add vinegar and sugar to broth. Mix well and pour over meat.

Yield: 6 servings

BEEF POP-UP

1 lb. ground beef
Margarine
½ cup chopped onion
1 clove garlic
2 tsp. chili powder
1 tsp. each ground cumin and
  oregano
1 4-oz. can diced green chilies
1 tsp. seasoning salt or salt
  and pepper to taste

½ tsp. sugar
1 2-oz. can mushrooms,
  drained
2 eggs
1 cup milk
1 cup flour
½ tsp. salt
1½ T. margarine
½ cup Cheddar cheese,
  shredded

In a wide frying pan crumble and brown meat over medium heat. Drain fat into a quarter measuring cup and add sufficient margarine to fill. Return to pan and add onions, garlic, chili powder, cumin, oregano, and chilies, stirring until onion is soft. Add seasoning, salt, and sugar. Add drained mushrooms and keep warm.

Set oven at 400 degrees.

Place 1¼ tablespoons margarine in 9½-inch quiche dish or a 9- or 10-inch pie pan. Place in oven while it is heating to melt. In blender container combine eggs, milk, flour, and salt. Cover and blend about 30 seconds. Batter will be thin and smooth. Remove hot dish from oven, pour in batter, spread meat filling evenly over batter to within 1 inch of the edge.

Bake 20 minutes, then sprinkle cheese on top of meat filling. Bake an additional 15 minutes or until golden and puffy. Garnish with parsley.

ROULADE DE BOEUF

2 lbs. top round steak, cut
  ½-inch thick
1 tsp. seasoning salt
¾ cup celery (chopped fine)
¾ cup green onion (chopped
  fine)
24 slices (6 oz.) thin-sliced
  pressed cooked beef
1¼ cup Swiss cheese (grated)

¼ cup seasoned coating mix
¼ cup cooking oil
2 cups water
3 envelopes instant cream of
  chicken soup
1 4-oz. can sliced mushrooms
  and juice

BROWN GRAVY SAUCE

6 cups cooked rice, hot
½ cup margarine

⅓ cup cashew nuts
⅓ cup pimento

Cut beef in 12 4x5-inch pieces, pound with a flat mallet until flattened, sprinkle lightly on both sides with seasoning salt. Add some of the celery and onion on each piece of meat. Top with 2 slices smoked beef and some of the cheese. Roll beef firmly around filling and secure with small skewer or toothpicks. Dust lightly with seasoned coating mix, cook with oil in skillet until golden brown on all sides, 6 to 8 minutes. Remove and place on hot cooked rice, which has margarine, cashew nuts, and pimento added.

To skillet add water, envelopes of soup, mushrooms, and gravy sauce, and simmer until slightly thickened. Pour some gravy over meat rolls and serve the rest separately. Garnish with parsley and tomato wedges. Roulades freeze well.

Yield: serves 8 or more
Cost: about 75 cents per serving

Doria Gauthier won 27 blue ribbons at last year's fair. In addition to these winning beef recipes, she has received awards for yeast breads. And try Doria's delicious Dill Puffs (page 129).

Doria's five daughters and five grandchildren all "love coming back to the ranch." Her husband has lived on the ranch for 61 years and she has been there since they were married 39 years ago.

VIOLET GRICE
GILA BEND, ARIZONA

FIRST PRIZE
CHILI CONTEST
GILA BEND

BEEF SUMMER SAUSAGE

5 lbs. hamburger	1 T. smoked salt or 1 tsp.
2½ tsp. mustard seed or dry	liquid smoke
mustard	2 T. tender quick salt
2½ tsp. coarse ground pepper	2½ tsp. garlic salt

Mix, cover, and refrigerate for 3 days, remixing each day. The fourth day, form in 5 rolls 1½ inches round and 10 inches long. Place on broiler pan on rack on bottom of oven at 200 degrees for 2 hours. Reduce heat to 150 degrees, turn rolls every 2 hours for 6 hours. Sausage makes own casing. (You can add 1½ tsp. oregano and ½ tsp. Accent.)

Although she lives in Arizona, Violet is a transplanted West Virginian. She says of herself:

"I was born and raised in West Virginia. I was the oldest of eight kids and had to learn to do a lot of things at an early age. I baked my first cake at the age of seven. It was called a Poor Man's Cake and it came from an old Rumford Baking Powder cookbook. It belonged to my mother and I still have it.

"I remember when I was about eight years old my mother had to go out in the fields to hoe corn. I had to mind the younger ones and get dinner. She gave me a pound of dry pinto beans and said to pick out all the rocks and bad beans. She said when I washed the beans, if I hadn't gotten all the bad beans out they'd come to the top of the water, and for me to throw them away.

"What she didn't tell me was that when the beans started getting hot they'd all come to the top. You guessed it. When my mother came in for dinner all I had been cooking all morning was water. I'd thrown all the beans away.

"When I was thirteen I was married and started raising my own kids when I was fourteen. So I had to learn to cook for them too. I don't do as much as I used to since I've gotten arthritis in my hands so bad. I still do a lot of baking for the town people since we don't have a bakery here.

"All my kids are married now [Violet has ten], but they still come home for Mom to cook for them, and my grandchildren too. I have a wonderful husband who likes to cook too."

Try Vi's Grits and Cheese (page 90), and Barbecue Sauce (page 415).

HOMEMADE BEEF JERKY

At butchering time, take the flank steak and remove membrane and cut it into long, narrow strips of desired size. Dip pieces of meat into soy sauce, then salt and pepper it and lay on dehydrator trays. Dry at 100 to 125 degrees until done. Approximately 12 hours.

When my grandchildren want snacks or treats I give them jerky and fruit leather and dried fruits, etc., instead of sweets all the time.

EDITOR'S NOTE: See Nora Buskirk's recipe for Fruit Leather (page 408).

This is nice for family reunions, church picnics, etc.

BAR B Q BEEF
(Serves 100)

15 lbs. cubed stew meat	2–3 T. chili powder
10 lbs. hamburger	1 gal. tomato sauce
12 cups water	5 T. prepared mustard
1 cup soy sauce	2 T. savor salt
1 cup Worcestershire sauce	2 T. celery salt
4 oz. curry powder	2 T. garlic salt
1¼ cups vinegar	1 cup flour
⅔ cup brown sugar	18 finely chopped onions
1½ T. liquid smoke	½ cup shortening

In large pressure canner, cook stew meat with water and half of the 3 salts. Cook at 15 pounds pressure for 45 minutes. When cool, drain liquid and save. Shred meat. Fry hamburger with onions, and other half of 3 salts. Mix all ingredients (except flour) in large kettle (or use the pressure cooker with the lid off) and boil until blended. Be sure to stir often enough to keep from scorching. Brown flour in skillet in hot fat. When brown, add part of the meat broth to make gravy. Add the gravy to meat mixture last.

Recipe can be halved easily and then frozen in 4 plastic containers of approximately 3 pounds each for family use. Serve on crusty French roll.

ANN HILLMEYER
ALBUQUERQUE, NEW MEXICO

FIRST PRIZE
GREEN CHILI CONTEST—MEAT
NEW MEXICO STATE FAIR

POOR MAN'S FILET MIGNON

2 lbs. ground chuck	1 4-oz. can mushrooms
1½ tsp. salt	(stems and pieces),
¼ tsp. pepper	drained and chopped fine
1 tsp. chili powder	6 green onions, chopped fine
½ tsp. garlic powder (or to	(green part too)
taste)	4 slices Monterey jack cheese
1–2 T. Worcestershire sauce	4 T. chopped green chilies *or*
About 10 drops Tabasco sauce	jalapino pepper
(or to taste)	4 slices bacon

Divide beef, onion, mushroom, and seasonings mixture into 8 equal patties. Top 4 of the patties with a small slice of Monterey jack and a tablespoon of chopped green chili *or* 1 jalapino pepper. Top with remaining 4 patties and seal edges together well. Wrap each patty with a slice of bacon and secure well with a toothpick. Sprinkle tops with paprika. Broil or grill outdoors about 5 to 6 minutes on each side, making sure centers are done and cheese melted. Serve on platter with fresh parsley, cherry tomatoes, and fresh whole mushrooms. Garnish each patty with a fresh mushroom T-slice and a cherry tomato. Really is pretty to serve!

 Ann Hillmeyer told us that she learned to cook "from my dear Mother in her kitchen, from 4-H, and many nice friends and relatives."
She told us a story on herself: "I had a large bowl of cornbread stuffing (dry), mixed ready for our Thanksgiving turkey. My husband came in from the garage teasing about something that had made me angry. I threw the whole bowlful at him, missed as he shut the door. Needless to say, I had to do some fast rebaking for dinner." She adds, "We did make up!"

Ann's sunny, cheerful kitchen is "always full of good aromas." She contributes some good advice: "Always follow your recipes carefully, and *always* test new recipes before trying them out on guests."

TAMI HILLMEYER
ALBUQUERQUE, NEW MEXICO

BEST OF SHOW
JUNIOR BAKING SHOW
NEW MEXICO STATE FAIR

MEXICAN LASAGNE

In a large saucepan, sauté 1 large diced onion in 1 tablespoon oil. Add

2 large cans tomato sauce	2 bay leaves
2 small cans tomato paste	1 tsp. garlic powder
2–3 cups water	2 T. dry parsley
1 T. whole oregano	2 tsp. salt
1 tsp. sweet basil	¼ tsp. pepper

Simmer 2 hours on low heat. About ½ hour before sauce is done, cook 1 large package lasagne noodles according to directions. Drain.

Mix

1 lb. cottage cheese
2 slightly beaten eggs
1 T. dry parsley

Grate 1 pound Monterey jack cheese.
Roast 3–4 whole chilis, peel, remove seeds, and open for garnish. Set aside 1 cup chopped green chili.
In large greased baking dish, *beginning with sauce,* layer ingredients as follows until all is used:

Sauce	Cheese
Noodles	Chopped green chili
Cottage cheese mixture	

End with sauce, lots of cheese, and green chili strips. Sprinkle well with Parmesan cheese. Bake in 350-degree oven for 30–40 minutes. Let stand 10–15 minutes before serving.
Garnish with fresh parsley, black olives, and cherry tomatoes.

Tami, the prizewinning daughter of a prizewinning mother, Ann Hillmeyer, is one of our luckiest junior cooks. She told us that when she won the Junior Baking Contest at the New Mexico State Fair, "I had forgotten to put the vanilla in the batter and I had already poured the batter in the pans. I carefully took out the batter and folded in the vanilla. We cooled the cake in the freezer and I got my entry in 5 minutes before the deadline. The result—Best of Show."
This recipe won Best of Show in the Chili and Chili Casserole divisions of the New Mexico State Fair.

RUBY ISENHOWER
CALHOUN, TENNESSEE

LIVER VEGETABLE CASSEROLE WITH CHEESE

2 T. butter
12 chicken livers
3 T. flour
½ tsp. salt
¼ tsp. pepper
½ cup chopped onions
¾ cup chopped celery
2 cups cooked rice

1 can cream of mushroom
   soup
1 cup lima beans
1 cup milk
1 cup cottage cheese
1 cup grated American cheese
2 cups buttered breadcrumbs

Dredge liver in seasoned flour; brown in the melted butter. Remove from pan, and cook onions and celery in the butter until golden brown. Add liver, rice, soup, lima beans, and milk. Mix well. Heat to boiling. Stir in the cottage cheese and ⅔ cup grated cheese. Pour into buttered 2-quart casserole; top with buttered crumbs. Sprinkle with remaining grated cheese. Bake at 350 degrees for 20 minutes.

Yield: 6 servings

Ruby Isenhower actually did what we've all wanted to do—at least once! "I was baking a cake for my daughter, and I couldn't get the icing to get stiff. My daughter said, 'Mama, I don't want that old cake.' So I just threw it on the floor. However, I did make her another one later."

Ruby learned to cook "helping my mother and at the Backman Memorial Home in Farner, Tennessee. I was at the Post Exchange then when my husband was in the service." She cooks in a kitchen, "not too large, very convenient."

BETTY L. JONES
Malad City, Idaho

FIRST PLACE, BEEF
TRAILS END COWBELLES COOK-OFF
MALAD CITY, IDAHO

SPANISH STEAK

2 lbs. round steak, 1 inch thick	1 T. horseradish
¼ cup flour	1 cup canned tomatoes
1 tsp. salt	1 onion
¼ tsp. pepper	½ green pepper

Wipe off steak with damp cloth. Mix flour, salt, and pepper and rub into steak. Put steak on heat-resistant pan and brown on both sides. Remove from broiling oven and cool. Spread horseradish on top of steak. Pour tomatoes over steak on platter. Slice onion and green pepper; arrange slices on top of steak. Bake in moderate oven (350 degrees) for 1 hour or until done.

Betty Jones says her kitchen is "just ordinary—nothing fancy." She has been cooking for fifty years and told us that one of the worst things that can happen is "to start frying steaks—and the phone rings."

LANETTE LENHART
LAUREL, MONTANA

FIRST PLACE
COWBELLE COOK-OFF

FIRST PLACE
DISTRICT #9

MEXICALI BEEF PIE

6 slices bacon	1 tsp. salt
1 lb. ground beef	⅛ tsp. pepper
1 cup drained whole kernel	1 8-oz. can tomato sauce
corn	1 egg
¼ cup green pepper, chopped	¼ cup milk
fine	½ tsp. Worcestershire sauce
1 cup onion, chopped fine	1½ cups shredded Cheddar
¼ cup corn meal	cheese
½ tsp. oregano	4 stuffed olives, sliced
½ tsp. chili powder	

Fry bacon until crisp; break into large pieces. Chill ⅓ cup drippings until firm. Brown ground beef in large skillet; drain. Stir in corn, green pepper, onion, corn meal, oregano, chili powder, ½ teaspoon salt, pepper and tomato sauce. Prepare Pie Crust (below). Place meat mixture in pastry-lined pan. Bake at 425 degrees for 25 minutes. Combine egg, milk, remaining salt, mustard, Worcestershire sauce, and cheese. Spread on pie. Top with bacon and olives. Bake 5 minutes or until cheese melts. Let stand ten minutes before serving. If desired, serve with a tomato sauce.

Yield: 6 servings

PIE CRUST

1 cup flour
2 T. corn meal
⅓ cup firm bacon drippings or other shortening
3–4 T. cold water

Combine flour and corn meal. Cut in bacon drippings until mixture is the size of small peas. Sprinkle water over mixture, stirring with fork until dough holds together. Form into a ball. Flatten to ½ inch; smooth edge. Roll out on floured surface to a circle 1½ inches larger than inverted 9-inch piepan. Fit into pan. Fold edge to form a standing rim; flute.

2 lbs. round steak, cut into
   1-inch cubes
2 medium onions, sliced
1 bay leaf, if desired
1 10½-oz. can cream of
   chicken soup
1 10½-oz. can of onion soup

1 4-oz. can sliced mushrooms,
   drained
1 T. Worcestershire sauce
⅓ cup flour
1 10-oz. package frozen peas,
   thawed
4 green pepper rings

Place steak in 3-quart casserole; cover with onion slices. Add bay leaf. Combine soups, mushrooms, Worcestershire sauce, and flour. Pour over meat and onions. Cover. Bake at 350 degrees for 2 hours or until meat is tender. Remove from oven. Set oven at 400 degrees. Remove bay leaf. Place peas on top of casserole; place pepper rings in center. Drop dumplings by rounded teaspoonfuls around pepper rings. Cover. Bake for 20 to 25 minutes.

Yield: 6–8 servings

PARSLEY DUMPLINGS

1 egg
⅓ cup milk
2 T. minced parsley
2 T. cooking oil

1 cup flour
1½ tsp. baking powder
½ tsp. salt
¼ tsp. sage

Combine in small mixing bowl egg, milk, oil, parsley, and sage. Add flour, baking powder, and salt. Stir only until dry particles are moist.

An experienced cook, Lanette Lenhart has won blue ribbons with cookies, cakes, biscuits, brownies and rolls, jellies, and canned and frozen vegetables.

She told us about a hair-raising experience as she was preparing her prizewinning Mexicali Beef Pie for competition. She had to work on a very low table. She forgot her pastry cloth and had to roll out the dough on aluminum foil. There was a big crowd watching her every move as she transferred the dough to the pie pan. Did she make it? Yes, indeed.

WARREN F. LeRUTH
GRETNA, LOUISIANA

BROKEN SHRIMP JAMBALAYA

1½ lbs. broken shrimp (cooked)
1 cup peanut oil
4 chopped onions
5 toes garlic
2 bunches shallots
1 chopped bell pepper

2 T. paprika
Salt, red pepper, and black
   pepper
¼ lb. sliced smoked sausage
3 cups rice
5 cups water or shrimp stock

Heat oil, add onions, garlic, shallots, bell pepper, smoked sausage, paprika, salt, and pepper and sauté well. Add shrimp pieces, rice, and water or stock. Bring to boil, cover, and over very low heat steam for 20 to 25 minutes. Stir with fork and replace cover.

Yield: 6 servings

Warren's Oyster Soup (page 18), Red Beans and Rice (page 92), Bibb Lettuce and Mushroom Salad with Vermouth Dressing (page 105), and Day-Old Beet and Onion Salad (page 105) are mouthwatering too.

CRABMEAT ITALIANA

1 6-oz. pkg. Wakefield
   crabmeat
1 8½-oz. can artichoke hearts
   in brine
⅓ lb. fresh mushrooms, sliced
1 cup heavy cream
¼ lb. butter

⅓ lb. Italian Fontina or Bel
   Paese cheese
½ cup Parmesan cheese
½ lb. homemade fettuccine or
   commercial noodles
Salt and pepper

Melt butter in a large saucepan and add mushrooms. Cook until limp. Quarter artichokes and add to mushrooms. Add defrosted crabmeat and cream. Simmer gently and mix thoroughly. Grate cheese and add to sauce. While cooking the fettuccine, warm a large serving bowl in a low oven. Drain the fettuccine and toss with sauce in a serving bowl. Season with salt and pepper. Serve at once with Parmesan.

Yield: serves 4–6

Don Luria has been a finalist in the Pineapple Cooking Classic, a semifinalist in the National Chicken Cooking Classic (see Chili Hot Chicken, page 66), and a winner in the Wakefield Crabmeat Contest.
   "Don't take yourself or cooking too seriously—it's an art, not a science," he remarks. Donald's culinary career began when he was a teenager and his mother asked him to spy on the cook to try to figure out her recipes.

CLASSICAL STROGANOFF

1 lb. sirloin steak or beef
    tenderloin
½ lb. sliced mushrooms
½ cup minced onion
2 T. butter
1 10½-oz. can condensed beef
    bouillon

2 T. ketchup
1 small clove garlic, minced
1 T. salt
3 T. flour
1 cup dairy sour cream
Hot rice

Cut meat into bite-size pieces. In skillet cook and stir mushrooms and onion in butter until tender; remove. In same skillet brown meat lightly on all sides. Set aside. Add ⅔ cup bouillon, ketchup, garlic, and salt to skillet; stir to mix. Cover and simmer 15 minutes. Blend remaining bouillon and flour, stir into meat mixture. Add mushrooms and onion. Heat to boiling, stirring constantly; boil 1 minute. Stir in sour cream; heat. Serve over rice.

Yield: serves 4

VEAL SCALLOPINI

1 T. flour
½ tsp. salt
4 veal cutlets (about 1 lb.)
¼ cup salad oil
½ medium onion, chopped
1 16-oz. can tomatoes,
    chopped

1 3-oz. can (2/3 cup) sliced
    mushrooms with liquid*
1 T. snipped parsley
¼ tsp. garlic salt
¼ tsp. dried oregano, crushed
Hot buttered noodles

*If fresh mushrooms are used add with ½ cup beef bouillon or ½ cup red cooking wine.

Combine flour, salt, pepper; coat veal lightly with flour mixture. In medium skillet brown meat slowly in hot oil. Remove meat from skillet. Add onion to skillet and cook until tender but not brown. Add tomatoes, mushrooms with liquid, snipped parsley, garlic salt, and oregano. Stir to mix and then add cooked meat. Cover and simmer about 25 minutes, stirring occasionally. Arrange veal on hot buttered noodles; top with sauce and sprinkle top with additional snipped parsley.

Diane learned to cook "at home, from Mother." She shares one experience with other competition cooks: "While I was taking a dish to a food show, the dish turned over as I made a turn. I rearranged the dish before competition and won!"

See also her Pea Loafer (page 95).

JEANINE RICHARDSON
POMEROY, WASHINGTON

SWEDISH MEATBALLS

1 lb. hamburger	⅓ cup canned milk
¼ cup dehydrated onion	1 egg
3 T. instant rice	1 cup mashed potatoes
1 tsp. salt	

Break egg into large mixing bowl and beat lightly with fork. Mix in salt, rice, and onion. Mix in hamburger in chunks. Mix in milk. Make meatballs about 1 rounded tablespoon in size. Put in 400-degree oven for 20 minutes. For sauce cream of mushroom or celery soup works well.

Jeanine has been cooking for only two years—she gives credit to her mother and to 4-H leaders. Once, she told us, she made a cake and put in 1⅓ cup instead of ⅓ of oil. "The cake was in crumbles the minute I took it out of the pan."

BARBARA SCHMITZ
JEFFERSON CITY, MISSOURI

FIRST PLACE WINNER
MISSOURI BEEF COOK-OFF

ITALIAN BEEF PARMESAGNA

2 lbs. beef round steak,
  ¼–½-inch thick
⅓ cup olive oil
½ lb. mozzarella cheese, sliced
2 eggs, beaten with 2 T. milk

COATING

⅔ cup breadcrumbs
¼ tsp. garlic powder
¼ cup grated Parmesan cheese

SAUCE

1 medium onion, chopped
1 6-oz. can tomato paste
2 cups tomato juice or 1-lb.
  can whole tomatoes
½ tsp. oregano leaves (or more
  if desired)
1 tsp. sweet basil leaves (or
  more if desired)
1 tsp. salt
¼ tsp. pepper
⅛ tsp. garlic powder

NOTE: 1 jar of Italian cooking sauce may be substituted for the sauce mixture.

Preheat oven to 350 degrees. Place beef on board and pound thin. Trim off gristle and excess fat; cut into 8–10 pieces. Dip beef into beaten egg. Roll in crumb mixture. Brown beef on both sides in oil in skillet. Arrange in shallow baking pan or dish.

Cook onion in pan drippings in skillet over low heat until soft. Stir in remaining sauce ingredients. Simmer 5–15 minutes, stirring occasionally. Pour sauce over beef.

Bake at 350 degrees for 45 minutes, covered. Remove from oven and top with cheese slices; continue baking for 15 minutes, uncovered. Garnish with parsley.

Yield: serves 4–6

GEMMA SCIABICA
MODESTO, CALIFORNIA

STUFFED BEEF BALLS

2 lbs. top round sliced ¼-inch
   thick and cut into 4-inch
   squares
¼ cup fresh parsley or basil,
   chopped
¼ cup fresh chopped
   mushrooms
¼ cup shredded Provolone
¼ cup pine nuts or almonds,
   ground

½ cup raisins
6 T. olive oil
¼ cup grated Romano cheese
¼ cup red wine
2 cloves garlic
2 eggs
1 cup breadcrumbs

Mix chopped parsley or basil, cheeses, nuts, raisins, oil, and mushrooms in bowl. Spread 2–3 tablespoons filling on each square and roll carefully. Fasten each roll with poultry pins or toothpicks. Dip rolls in beaten eggs, then crumbs. Pour 4 tablespoons oil and mashed garlic in shallow baking pan. Add the rolls and bake 20 minutes at 375 degrees, then add wine and bake another 10 to 15 minutes.

NOTE: You can use veal or turkey for this recipe.

Gemma Sciabica, a winner in baking and canning contests, gives credit to her mother-in-law and to her mother for her cooking skills.

She says, "I am the happiest when I know my family is getting a well balanced meal, low in grease, salt, sugar, and starches. Above all, do not waste food. Try to keep to the natural foods instead of imitation or substitute ones. Use as much fresh fruits and vegetables as possible and do not overcook."

Gemma continues: "Try to use as little grease and salt as possible. For instance, when cooking pork sausage, just add a little water at the bottom of the pan when baking and serve after pouring off all the grease.

"Also, when frosting a cake, instead of using a thick, greasy, sugary frosting, spread with a thin layer. It will do and taste just as well; plus cutting off a lot of calories."

Try Gemma's Almond Sponge Wine Cake (page 262).

JOSEPHINE B. SEHI
BERKLEY, MICHIGAN

BEST COOK AWARD
STOKLEY VAN CAMP
DETROIT, MICHIGAN

VEAL CUTLETS WITH TOMATO SAUCE

Trim and wipe 6 veal cutlets, season with salt and pepper. Roll in breadcrumbs, then dip in 1 beaten egg diluted with 1 tablespoon salad oil, and dip again in breadcrumbs. Flatten them and sauté in butter, allowing 5 minutes for each side. Mix ½ pint of tomato sauce with 2 tablespoons of ketchup or tomato juice.

Simmer for 20 minutes and serve.

Josephine learned to cook from her mother, "a pinch of this and a handful of that." She works in an efficient kitchen with two ovens, an electric stove and a "model K5A KitchenAid dishwasher." She used to cook for six; now, with four daughters married, only two.

Her advice to other cooks: "Use well-known products, correct size pans, and correct temperature and timing."

PETRINA L. SLADE
HATTEESBURG, MISSISSIPPI

SECOND PLACE OVERALL
MISSISSIPPI STATE BEEF COOK-OFF

MOCK FILETS WITH SAUCE

MOCK FILETS

1 lb. ground chuck
1½ tsp. salt
½ tsp. pepper
½ tsp. garlic salt
1½ cup cooked rice
1 small onion, diced
8 strips bacon

SAUCE

1 10½-oz. can cream of
    mushroom soup
½ carton sour cream
1 pkg. dry onion soup mix
    (Do not mix with water)

For filets, combine all ingredients together and mix well. Make into patties about 3 inches wide and 1¼ inches thick. Wrap 1 strip of bacon around each and pin with a toothpick. Bake in a preheated oven at 350 degrees for approximately 20 minutes. Remove filets from broiler pan and place in casserole dish.

Combine mushroom soup, dry soup mix, and sour cream. Mix well. Pour over filets and finish baking about 15 to 20 minutes. Serve hot.

Yield: 8 servings
Cost: Around 70 cents per serving.

NOTE: Your cooking time may sometimes change with different ovens.

B B Q MOCK FILETS

2 lbs. ground chuck
1½ tsp. salt
½ tsp. pepper
½ tsp. garlic salt

1½ cups cooked rice
1 small onion, diced
8 strips bacon
Your favorite BBQ sauce

For filets, combine all ingredients and mix well. Make into patties 3 inches wide and 1¼ inches thick. Wrap one strip of bacon around each, and pin with a toothpick. Bake on a broiler pan in a preheated oven at 350 degrees for about 30 minutes. When they have baked about half of the cooking time put about 1 tablespoon of BBQ sauce over each and finish cooking. Serve hot.

Yield: 8 servings

"This recipe actually won first place in the State Cook-Off but had to be placed second because I used pork bacon instead of beef bacon. The judges told me they were afraid to send the recipe on to Regional because the judges there might discard it because of it not being 'all beef'."

Petrina goes on to describe her kitchen as "very country." She cooks for four people every day, unless "we have family in and then it's twelve to twenty-five."

MARY THOMPSON
LEWIS CENTER, OHIO

SWEET HAM LOAF

2 lbs. ground smoked ham	1½ lbs. ground lean pork
1 cup breadcrumbs	1 cup milk
2 eggs	¾ cup brown sugar
½ tsp. dry mustard	½ cup vinegar
1 cup water	Salt and pepper

Combine meat with crumbs and milk, break in eggs, and mix well. Shape into loaf and put in pan. In separate bowl make sauce of brown sugar, mustard, vinegar, water, salt, and pepper. Then pour over ham loaf. Bake 1½ hours at 350 degrees, basting frequently with the sauce.

Six to seven hundred fair ribbons are the result of 25 years of cooking and experimenting for Mary Thompson. She began cooking when she was nine. "Mother went to the barn and I got supper. I started experimenting at this time!" Now she cooks with her two daughters, Teresa and Barb. They enter fruits, preserves, jellies, pickles, and relish at the fair.

Mary made a cherry pie on television for Crisco in 1968, so maybe you've seen her at work in her modern farm kitchen.

She suggests using her Sweet Ham Loaf for big crowds. "We use this at Church Fall Dinner along with turkey."

SHARON WOOD
WOLFORD, NORTH DAKOTA

FIRST PRIZE
THE *NEWS* CONTEST
SAN ANTONIO, TEXAS

POLYNESIAN SWEET AND SOUR PORK WITH RICE

2 cans chunk pineapple (in
    its own juice)
1½ lbs. pork shoulder steak
    cut in 1-inch cubes
1–2 green peppers cut in strips
1 large onion sliced
2 T. oil
1 tsp. ginger

2 T. soy sauce
⅓ cup vinegar
⅓ cup brown sugar
2 T. cornstarch mixed in
    ¼ cup water
Steamed rice
Chow mein noodles

Drain and reserve juice from pineapple.

In medium skillet, brown meat in oil until golden. Add onion and pepper and sauté until just limp. Add vinegar, brown sugar, pineapple juice, ginger, and soy sauce and simmer ½ hour covered.

Add pineapple chunks and cornstarch mixture. Heat to a simmer and stir until thickened. Serve over steamed rice and top with chow mein noodles.

Try Sharon's Golden Chicken Curry (page 75).

CHAPTER FOUR

POULTRY

one broiler fryer...

Betty May's Chicken
page 60

...cut in parts,
sprinkle with salt
and pepper.

mix together egg,
marmalade, mustard
and garlic

Roll chicken in ground
peanuts.

Place in shallow baking dish, do not cover.

COLEEN ADDY
ROSWELL, NEW MEXICO

FIRST PRIZE
FOOD SHOW
ROSWELL, NEW MEXICO

CHICKEN TORTILLA PIE

1 pkg. tortillas, cut into narrow strips
1 2½- to 3-lb. chicken, cooked and boned
½ lb. Cheddar cheese, coarsely grated

SAUCE

½ cup green chili
1 can cream of chicken soup
1 can chicken stock broth (13¾ oz.) or from boiling the chicken
1 large onion sautéed in butter until limp

Mix all sauce ingredients together. In a greased baking dish, alternate layers of tortilla strips, chicken sauce, and cheese, and repeat until dish is full. Bake at 350 degrees for 30 to 45 minutes.

Coleen's Spring Time Dip (page 3), Mexican Corn (page 79), Garlic Pecans (page 355), and Hard Candy (page 355) are great too.

SARA C. BODELL
NEOLA, WEST VIRGINIA

FIRST PLACE, BLUE RIBBON
DELMARVA CHICKEN-COOKING
CONTEST, STATE OF VIRGINIA

CHICKEN BREASTS SUPREME

4 chicken breast halves, boned
2 slices old bread
Flour
Oil

1 small jar Armour's Dried Beef
1 T. parmesan cheese, grated
1 egg

Shred dried beef and bread in blender. Mix cheese with it. Roll skinned breasts in flour, dip in beaten egg, and coat with dried beef mixture—fry in ⅓ cup oil until nicely browned, and tender.

Cooking for a family of five, Sara Bodell learned the basics from her mother, and became more proficient with cookbooks. She works in a "small, convenient, and well-equipped kitchen."

LINDA NELSON
FRIENDSHIP, MAINE

SECOND PRIZE
STATE OF MAINE DAIRY
MONTH RECIPE CONTEST

CHICKEN CRUNCH

1 small onion, chopped
4 T. butter
4 T. flour
1½ cups chicken broth,
    well seasoned
1 cup milk
3 cups cooked chicken,
    chopped

1 cup celery, cut in small
    pieces
3 hard-cooked eggs, sliced
2 T. butter
8–10 crackers, crumbled
1 cup cheddar cheese,
    grated

Sauté onion in butter 2 minutes. Add flour, stirring well. Add chicken broth and milk. Stir until smooth. Add chicken, celery and eggs. Pour into buttered 8x12-inch baking pan and sprinkle with buttered cracker crumbs and cheddar cheese. Bake in 350-degree oven until cheese melts and top is lightly browned.

Yield: serves 6–8

Linda won an electric ice cream maker with her creative chicken recipe. She grew up in a large family with "many hands required to do the necessary cooking and baking."

BETTY MAY CALVERT
CLAYTON, DELAWARE

FIRST PRIZE
DELMARVA CHICKEN COOKING
CONTEST, DOVER, DELAWARE

BETTY MAY'S CHICKEN

1 broiler-fryer chicken, cut
    in parts
1 tsp. salt
¼ tsp. pepper
¾ cup flour

1 egg, beaten
1 cup orange marmalade
1 tsp. dry mustard
2 cloves garlic, crushed
1½ cups ground salted peanuts

Sprinkle salt and pepper on chicken. Place flour in bag. In shallow dish mix together egg, marmalade, mustard, and garlic. In another shallow dish place peanuts. Place chicken one piece at a time in bag and shake to coat, then dip in egg mixture, then roll in peanuts. Arrange chicken in single layer in large shallow baking pan. Bake 40 minutes at 375 degrees.

Yield: serves 4

NOTE: Peanuts must be *ground,* not chopped or crushed in blender. Also non-stick pan should *not* be used. If it is used the coating will stay in the pan instead of on the chicken. And don't let chicken pieces touch each other. Do not use cover over chicken.

A top prizewinner in the big time Delmarva Chicken Cooking Contest, Betty May Calvert won $500 in cash, approximately $300 in gifts, and an expenses-paid trip to Tampa, Florida for the National Cook-Off. She also won a silver bowl and a pewter trophy and tray.

She told us one of the most embarrassing things she did was to invite her neighbors over to see her prize—and forgot to buy refreshments.

DAN CURD
MADISON, WISCONSIN

FIRST PRIZE
WISCONSIN JOURNAL CONTEST
MADISON, WISCONSIN

Here is Dan's first-prize Cornish Chicken. Try his California Fruit Salad (page 102) and Coffee Rum Cookies (page 317), too.

CORNISH CHICKEN

6 cups cooked chicken (or turkey) roughly diced
Salt and pepper to taste
4 cups good chicken (or turkey) stock, degreased
2 small carrots, quartered
1 stalk celery with leaves
16 cloves garlic, unpeeled
4 peppercorns
¼ tsp. dried thyme
¼ tsp. dried oregano
4 sprigs parsley

2 T. butter
½ cup minced green onions
1 14-oz. can artichoke hearts, drained, rinsed, drained again, halved
¼ cup butter
¼ cup flour
1 egg yolk
½ cup heavy cream
1½ cups lightly packed coarsely grated mild Cheddar cheese

Preheat oven to 375 degrees. Salt and pepper the chicken and set aside.

Put the chicken stock, carrots, celery, garlic, peppercorns, thyme, oregano, and parsley in a heavy pan and simmer partially covered for 1 hour. Remove from heat and strain stock, reserving the carrot quarters and the garlic cloves. Return the strained stock to the pan and reduce over high heat until 2 cups remain. Remove from heat and purée in the reserved carrots and garlic cloves. Keep warm.

Melt 2 tablespoons butter in a skillet and lightly sauté the minced green onions. Set aside.

Melt the ¼ cup butter over low heat in a large heavy kettle (nonaluminum). Add the flour and stir for a minute or so—do not let the flour brown. Remove from heat and stir in the reserved 2 cups of stock. Return to heat and cook slowly until the mixture comes to a boil and thickens. Remove from heat. In a heat-proof bowl, beat the egg yolk and cream together until combined. Gradually, by driblets, beat in half of the hot sauce. Then beat the egg-cream-sauce mixture into the sauce. Return the pan to low heat and stir for a couple of minutes. Remove from heat.

Pour about ¼ cup of the sauce into the bottom of a buttered heatproof baking dish. Sprinkle with ¼ cup of the cheese. Mix the chicken with the sautéed green onions and cover the cheese in the baking dish with half the chicken mixture. Cover the chicken with ¼ cup of sauce and ¼ cup of the cheese. Top this layer with the artichokes. Cover with another ¼ cup of sauce and cheese. Then top with the remaining chicken, the remaining sauce, and the remaining cheese.

Despite the large quantity of garlic this dish does not have a strong taste. The garlic must be left unpeeled.

Bake at 375 degrees for 45 minutes or until hot and bubbly.

Yield: 6–8 servings

Dan has a gourmet kitchen. He uses a pasta machine as well as a strawberry huller, and has lots of very specialized equipment that he has collected from all over the world. In Wisconsin he is well known for his recipes and his cooking, and is called upon to help with extra special dinners. He told us about one of these occasions:

"I went to extra trouble to fix a meatless and fatless meal for Governor Jerry Brown—seafood and rice salad stuffed in a pineapple shell, homemade whole wheat bread, feta cheese, fresh strawberries with yogurt and mineral water."

Dan is extraordinarily capable as a cook and not afraid of big challenges. For example, when we talked to him, he was planning a party for 150 people; the invitation read, "Rafraichissements et hors d'oeuvres featuring the flavors of Provence, by Dan Curd." Sounds enticing, doesn't it?

BETTY EUBANKS
PENSACOLA, FLORIDA

FIRST PRIZE
DAIRY DIVISION
MAIN DISH COOKBOOK CONTEST

SOUR CREAM CHICKEN

Brown one cut-up chicken in small amount of oil. After chicken is brown, drain fat off and move chicken to one side of skillet. Put in 2 or 3 quartered potatoes, one bunch of green onions, and one can of cream of chicken (or cream of mushroom) soup. Cover with lid and either simmer until vegetables are done, or bake in oven until done (about 45 minutes). In either case a little water will have to be added in order to prevent sticking.

Before serving cover with sour cream.

Betty learned to cook from her mother and "a lady I lived with while going to business college." Like so many of us, her kitchen is convenient "but a little too small for storage."

She told us about a time she was entertaining "her husband's boss and his wife. She was an excellent cook. So I had prepared an oriental dish, hoping to impress, but the meal was spoiled by the gooey, sticky rice." All good cooks make mistakes once in a while.

EDITH JOHNSON
WILMINGTON, DELAWARE

FIRST PRIZE
DELMARVA CHICKEN-COOKING
CONTEST, DOVER, DELAWARE

CHICKEN TUTTI-FRUTTI

4 whole chicken breasts, halved and skinned	1 tsp. salt
½ cup oil	2 T. brown sugar
1 16-oz. can crushed pineapple	2 tsp. Accent
1 cup orange juice	2 tsp. soy sauce
	1 tsp. lemon-pepper seasoning

Brown chicken in 12-inch frypan with cover in oil. Sprinkle with lemon-pepper seasoning. Cover and simmer 20 minutes. Combine remaining ingredients, spoon over chicken, and cook covered for 30–40 minutes over low heat or until tender. Garnish with green grapes and maraschino cherries.

"My first meal after I was married was inedible," says prizewinning cook Edith Johnson. "I mistook a brown bag of soap for flour and had meatball gravy with a head on it." She learned to cook "by necessity when I got married," she says, and she thinks working in her green-and-yellow kitchen is like "cooking in a sunny garden."

The finalist from Delaware in the Delmarva Chicken-Cooking Contest, she won $300 for this first-prize recipe.

EARLINE JORDAN
ASHFORD, ALABAMA

GRAND PRIZE
NATIONAL PEANUT FESTIVAL
DOTHAN, ALABAMA

GRAND PRIZE GOLD COAST STEW

2 T. peanut oil
2 medium-size onions, cut
    into thin slices
2 medium-size green peppers,
    seeded and cut into thin
    strips
1 6-oz. can tomato paste
¾ cup peanut butter

3 cups chicken broth
1 tsp. salt
1 tsp. chili powder
1 tsp. sugar
½ tsp. nutmeg
4 cups diced cooked chicken
    or turkey

In a large saucepan, heat oil and sauté onions and green peppers for 5 minutes or until lightly browned and wilted. Stir in tomato paste, peanut butter, chicken broth, and seasonings. Stir constantly until sauce bubbles and thickens. Stir in chicken and simmer again until mixture is piping hot. Serve over hot cooked rice garnished with finely chopped peanuts.

Yield: 6–8 servings

 Earline Jordan says, "I was a twin daughter of a peanut farmer, and my sister and I learned to cook at an early age. While in our teens, we took over the cooking when our mother became seriously ill and died."
Now Earline is a Grand Prize winner. Her Gold Coast Stew won $275.00 and a four-day trip to New York City and Washington, D.C.

Earline has some interesting advice for us: "Do not be afraid to try the instant mixes and frozen products. They are great. I would not use them for years." And she told us a story:

"I was preparing a ham for a small dinner party, and put the ham back in the refrigerator instead of the oven. One and a half hours later, I went to the oven to check on the ham and it wasn't there. Dinner was sent in!"

DONALD S. LURIA
WASHINGTON, D.C.

FIRST PRIZE—REGIONAL
SEMIFINALIST
NATIONAL CHICKEN COOKING
CONTEST, WASHINGTON, D.C.

CHILI HOT CHICKEN

2 whole broiler-fryer chicken
   breasts, halved, boned,
   skinned, cut into bite-
   size pieces
3 T. flour
1½ T. paprika
2 T. chili powder
3 T. butter
1 T. cooking oil
1 cup raw rice

2 medium tomatoes, chopped
1 medium green pepper,
   chopped
1 medium onion, chopped
1 4-oz. jar pimentos, chopped
1 tsp. salt
¼ tsp. pepper
1½ cups water
1 avocado, chopped

In shallow dish, mix together flour, paprika, and 1 tablespoon of the chili powder. Add chicken, a few pieces at a time, dredging to coat lightly. In large frypan heat butter and oil to medium temperature. Add chicken and cook, turning, about 10 minutes or until brown on all sides. Stir in rice and sprinkle with ½ tablespoon of the chili powder. Cover and shake pan to distribute rice and chicken evenly. Place tomatoes, green pepper, onion, pimentos, salt, and pepper over chicken. Pour water evenly over vegetables in frypan. Add avocado and sprinkle with remaining ½ tablespoon chili powder. Bring to a boil. Cover and simmer over low heat about 35 minutes or until rice is done and fork can be inserted in chicken with ease.

Yield: 4 servings

Don also gave us his recipe for Crabmeat Italiana (page 44).

FAYNE LUTZ
Taos, New Mexico

FIRST PRIZE
NATIONAL CHICKEN COOKING
CONTEST, WINSTON-SALEM,
NORTH CAROLINA

HOT CHINESE CHICKEN SALAD

8 broiler-fryer chicken thighs, skinned, boned, cut into 1-inch chunks
¼ cup cornstarch
¼ cup corn oil
⅛ tsp. garlic powder
1 large ripe tomato, cut into chunks
1 4-oz. can water chestnuts, drained, sliced
1 4-oz. can sliced mushrooms, drained
1 bunch green onions, coarsely chopped
1 cup slant-sliced celery
1 tsp. Accent
¼ cup soy sauce
2 cups finely shredded iceberg lettuce

Roll chicken in cornstarch. Heat corn oil in frypan or wok over high heat. Add chicken chunks and quickly brown. Sprinkle with garlic powder. Add tomato, water chestnuts, mushrooms, onion, and celery. Stir. Sprinkle with flavor enhancer. Add soy sauce. Stir. Cover, reduce heat to simmer, and cook 5 minutes. Lightly toss chicken-vegetable mix with lettuce. Serve hot with rice.

Yield: 4 servings

Fayne takes her cooking seriously; she not only gives gourmet cooking lessons, she has put together her own cookbook. She has won prizes in the Knox Gelatin Contest, the Chex Cereal Contest, and many others. This $10,000 recipe is included with the permission of the National Broiler Council.

MARILYNN MANSFIELD
POTOMAC, MARYLAND

FIRST PRIZE
MARYLAND DELMARVA CHICKEN
COOKING CONTEST

TEN-MINUTE FRIED CHICKEN BREASTS

4 whole chicken breasts,
   skinned, boned, and
   halved
¼ cup flour
2 eggs, well beaten

1¼ Italian style flavored
   breadcrumbs
3 T. corn oil
3 T. margarine

Pound breasts lightly between waxed paper. Dust breasts with flour; dip in beaten egg; coat with breadcrumbs, pressing with hands to obtain a firm, even coating. Refrigerate chicken one-half hour.

Heat corn oil and margarine in large skillet. Sauté 4 pieces at a time, 5 minutes on each side or until golden brown and crisp. Keep first portions warm; prepare remaining breasts.

Yield: serves 8

 Marilynn Mansfield, who cooks for many people, "family, friends, neighbors, classmates," won $400 and an all-expenses-paid trip to Birmingham for her Ten-Minute Fried Chicken Breasts recipe.

GINGER MORTON
ATHENS, TEXAS

HONORABLE MENTION
ATHENS, TEXAS FAIR

CHICKEN BLACK-EYED PEAS SUPREME

6 chicken breasts
1 cup flour
2 tsp. salt
½ tsp. pepper
1 can condensed cream of
   chicken soup
3 cups bite-size celery

1½ cans black-eyed peas
½ cup light cream
2 T. pimento
2 cups breadcrumbs
2 T. melted butter
1 cup American cheese, diced
½ cup slivered almonds

Coat chicken with mixture of flour, salt, pepper, and paprika. Lightly brown chicken with butter. Put celery in ungreased casserole dish with browned chicken on top. Spoon drained black-eyed peas over chicken. Combine soup, cream, pimento, and cheese and pour over chicken. Cover with buttered crumbs. Spread almonds and bake at 350 degrees.

Ginger learned to cook from her foster mother. The family owned a restaurant and cooked home cooking for Texas A&M University. Now Ginger cooks regularly for four, but enjoys cooking for crowds of 100 or more.

She advises others to "experiment, and collect cookbooks and recipes from friends. And read directions before starting."

CAROL PFEIFFER
LEWES, DELAWARE

FIRST PRIZE
NATIONAL CHICKEN COOKING
CONTEST, BIRMINGHAM, ALABAMA

CHICKEN POT-AU-FEU

TO COOK CHICKEN

1 broiler-fryer chicken, quartered	1 tsp. salt
Giblets	2 envelopes instant chicken-flavored-broth mix
1 onion	3 sprigs parsley
1 carrot, sliced	2 ribs celery

Put chicken and giblets in 4-quart saucepan. Add water and remaining ingredients. Bring to a boil; cover tightly. Reduce heat and simmer 40 minutes or until tender. Remove from heat; strain broth. Refrigerate chicken and broth. When chicken is cool, remove meat from bones, cut into bite-size pieces. Skim fat from broth.

POT-AU-FEU

Reserved chicken broth	2 ribs celery, sliced
1 small cabbage, cut in eighths	1 cup frozen peas
8 small onions	Cut-up cooked chicken
4 carrots, pared, sliced	1 T. margarine

Heat reserved broth in saucepan. Add cabbage and onions and boil 20 minutes. Add carrots and celery and boil 10 minutes longer. Add peas, cut-up chicken, and margarine. Cook 5 minutes longer.

Yield: 4 servings

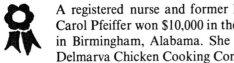 A registered nurse and former lieutenant commander in the Navy, Carol Pfeiffer won $10,000 in the National Chicken Cooking Contest in Birmingham, Alabama. She had already won First Prize in the Delmarva Chicken Cooking Contest at Dover, Delaware, which gave her a $300 prize and a round-trip all-expenses-paid trip to Birmingham.

Her prizewinning recipe was chosen unanimously by a panel headed by James Beard, internationally known cooking expert. She told us that she learned to cook "in my mother's home as a child." She also won a $150 bonus because her recipe was the best low-calorie chicken dish entered in the contest.

MABLE RHINEHART
MOULTON, ALABAMA

FIRST PRIZE, CASSEROLES
FEDERATED WOMAN'S CLUB

MABLE'S HOT CHICKEN SALAD

1 large hen, boiled, cut into
   bite-size pieces
4 cups chopped celery
4 T. lemon juice
4 chopped pimentos
1 cup mayonnaise

6 boiled eggs, chopped
1 cup sliced almonds
1 small onion, chopped
1 can cream of chicken soup
2 cups grated cheese
1 pkg. potato chips

Mix chicken with all other ingredients except cheese and potato chips; refrigerate overnight. Arrange in 9x12 casserole; sprinkle cheese and potato chips on top. Bake for 30 minutes at 350 degrees.

Yield: 18–20 servings

Mable began cooking for her father and seven brothers and sisters when she was ten. Now, after cooking for 68 years, she's still at it—cooking for clubs and parties.

CHICKEN ON PARADE

3 large chicken breasts, boned
 and cut in half
⅓ cup all-purpose flour
2 tsp. salt
¼ tsp. black pepper
¼ cup salad oil
¾ cup coarsely chopped onion
½ cup sliced celery

1 clove garlic, minced
1 10½-oz. can condensed
 cream of mushroom soup
¼ cup dry sherry
1 6-oz. can sliced mushrooms,
 drained
1 7-oz. package frozen
 Chinese pea pods, thawed

Coat chicken with flour; sprinkle with salt and pepper. Brown in hot salad oil in skillet. Remove chicken from skillet. In same skillet cook onion, celery, and garlic till just tender. Blend in soup and wine. Add mushrooms and water chestnuts. Bring to boiling. Return chicken to skillet. Cover; simmer 20 minutes. Add pea pods, cover, and simmer 10 minutes more. To serve, spoon some of the sauce over chicken. Pass remaining sauce.

Yield: 4 to 6 servings

This recipe for chicken breasts won $1000.00 and a large silver serving tray for Betty Robbins. She learned to cook quite young and she would cook while her mother made school clothes.

Her prizewinning dish may be prepared in an electric skillet. After browning the chicken and removing from the skillet and preparing the main ingredients, she pours the sauce into a 13½x8¾x1¾ pyrex dish, then returns the chicken; covers and bakes in the oven at 350 degrees for about 20 to 30 minutes. This makes the dish ready to serve from the oven. Betty advises: "Don't forget the pea pods. They make the dish."

MARIE SNOW
ASOTIN, WASHINGTON

ALMOND CHICKEN

2–4 chicken breasts
1 chicken bouillon cube

1 tsp. salt
Water

Boil until chicken is done. Let chicken cool and take it off the bones and break into small pieces. Dip chicken pieces in following batter mix and deep fry in oil until golden.

BATTER MIX

½ cup pancake flour
½ cup flour

Pinch of garlic salt
Water to make like pancakes

SAUCE

2 cups chicken broth
1 13-oz. can evaporated milk

1 T. sugar (optional)
Cornstarch to thicken

Bring to a boil and cook until thickened. (Stir continually; will burn easily.) Pour sauce over chicken. Sprinkle ¼ cup chopped or ground almonds.

Marie Snow "grew up in a farm family and helped my Mom cook for the crews." She also worked in a restaurant as a night-shift cook and pie baker. She told us about the time she got a new crock pot. "I put it to cooking and went off shopping. All day long I thought how nice it would be not to have to go home and fix supper. When I arrived home I had forgotten to turn it on. I still had to prepare dinner that night—but I learned to double-check!"

Try Marie Snow's Buttermilk Brownies (page 343).

HELEN T. WILLIAMS
DANVILLE, VIRGINIA

FIRST PRIZE
VIRGINIA CHICKEN-
COOKING CONTEST

MY-FAVORITE-THINGS CHICKEN

1 broiler-fryer chicken, cut in
   parts, skinned
⅔ cup flour
1½ tsp. Accent or other flavor
   enhancer
2 tsp. paprika
1 tsp. salt

⅓ cup corn oil
1 medium onion, sliced, rings
   separated
1 bell pepper, cut in rings
1 11-oz. can whole tomatoes
   (Italian)
¼ cup capers, drained

In bag mix together flour, flavor enhancer, paprika, and salt. Add chicken; shake to coat. Heat corn oil in frypan over medium heat. Add chicken and brown lightly on all sides. Add onion, pepper, tomatoes, and capers. Cover and cook on low heat about 40 minutes or until fork can be inserted with ease and sauce is thickened.

Yield: 4 servings

 "On my first trip to New York, about forty years ago," says Helen Williams, "I was served something in a salad that I could only describe as little pickled raisins, and I could not learn from the Italian waiter what I was eating. A few years ago at a friend's home, I was again served a salad containing the same delicious ingredient—capers! Once I learned what to ask for in the grocery store I stocked up and gorged."

When Helen was working on a recipe for the National Chicken Cooking Contest it was "a foregone conclusion that I would combine a few of my favorite things." She did, and won first prize in the Virginia Chicken-Cooking Contest—which earned her a trip to San Antonio, prize money, and a loving cup.

She began to cook "as a schoolgirl in the 1930s—then as a teacher, wife, and mother and now as a professional photographer and grandmother." She works in an enviable kitchen with plenty of cabinets, plenty of room, and a beautiful view of the western sky.

Helen adds this about her recipe: "It is easy to prepare, total time less than 1 hour, and requires only a minimum amount of attention; so I can completely prepare an entire company meal within an hour. The recipe can easily be doubled and cooked in an electric skillet—it freezes well and seems to have added flavor when reheated. I often carry some for lunch and enjoy it cold. It is an energy-saving recipe, as no oven heat is required; a low-cholesterol recipe, as chicken is skinned and corn oil is used. Most of all it is delicious and different."

SHARON WOOD
WOLFORD, NORTH DAKOTA

GOLDEN CHICKEN CURRY

Melt and cool ⅓ cup butter. Add ½ cup honey and mix well. Add ¼ cup prepared mustard and 1½–2 teaspoons curry powder. Dip chicken pieces of 3–4 pound cut-up fryer into sauce. Place in shallow baking 9x13 dish. Pour over any remaining sauce. Bake at 350 degrees for 1–1½ hours. Baste or turn halfway through.

Serve with steamed rice and green salad.

Sharon Wood is our "Media Prizewinner": her pork recipe won a newspaper competition and her Golden Chicken Curry and Hermit Cookies won first prize in a television contest.

She created her prizewinning Polynesian Sweet and Sour Pork with Rice recipe "after tasting a commercially prepared variety at a friend's. The recipe is now a family favorite," she says.

She wasn't always an expert, though. "My first pizza was like a sheet of rock, hard as nails." But Sharon has practiced and now her pizza is just fine.

Try Sharon's Polynesian Sweet and Sour Pork (page 53).

CHAPTER
FIVE

VEGETABLES

VEGETABLES

Use fresh ingredients,
judged on appearance,
flavor, originality

Vermont Vegetable
Cheese Casserole

Sauteed Green Beans
with Onions

COLEEN ADDY
ROSWELL, NEW MEXICO

MEXICAN CORN

1 T. cooking oil
1 onion, minced fine
3 cups corn, fresh, frozen, or
    canned
2 cups tomato purée

2 T. chili powder OR ½ cup
    green chilies, diced
2 T. butter
Salt and pepper to taste

Sauté onion in hot oil until golden yellow. Mix remaining ingredients. Add onion, mix well. Pour into a buttered casserole and bake 1 hour at 350 degrees.

Yield: serves 6

Try Coleen's Spring Time Dip (page 3), Chicken Tortilla Pie (page 57), Garlic Pecans (page 355), and Hard Candy (page 355), too.

TAMMIE BIERIG
OKEENE, OKLAHOMA

FIRST PRIZE
COUNTY CHEESE FESTIVAL
BLAIN COUNTY, OKLAHOMA

GOURMET POTATOES

6 medium potatoes
½ cup green onion, chopped
fine
2 cups shredded Cheddar
cheese

1 tsp. salt
¼ cup margarine
¼ tsp. pepper
1½ cups sour cream

Cook potatoes in skins. Cool, peel, and shred coarsely. In a saucepan, over low heat, combine cheese and margarine. Stir until almost melted. Remove from heat and blend in sour cream, onion, and seasonings. Fold in potatoes and turn into a buttered 2-quart casserole. Sprinkle with paprika. Bake uncovered in 350-degree oven for 30 minutes. Freezes well.

Try Tammie's Cherry Kuchen (page 385).

SOPHIE BURDEN
WICKENBURG, ARIZONA

REAL SPANISH RICE
(A Basque Recipe)

Brown more or less a cup of rice in butter, lightly, together with about 3 or 4 cloves of garlic, finely chopped.

When browned to light golden color, add 2 cans of consommé, 2 cans of beef bouillon and about 2 cans of water. However much you think will make it right. Cover and simmer lightly and gently.

While it is starting, cut up 2 pepperonis in small pieces, taking off skin. Add it.

Add large can of mushroom stems and pieces with juice. Chop 1½ cup of ripe olives and add them. For spicier taste use stuffed or Spanish olives.

You can use a can of tomatoes but if you do cut down on the water and use all the tomato juice. For color you can add a largish jar of pimento. Taste it for salt. You won't need pepper. Chopped parsley or parsley leaves look nice in it.

Simmer until it is about the right consistency—about ¾ of an hour probably.

For exactly measuring the liquid, go by the proportions on the rice box, only add about three-fourths of a cup more liquid, because it needs to be juicy. And of course figure the mushroom juice and all.

DANA'S CHARROS BEANS

Dana says, "Best served at the moment they are done, but they keep a long time frozen and I love them over and over."

3 slices bacon chopped small and fried	1 large tomato
2 tsp. salt	½ lb. pinto beans
½ sliced and chopped fresh onion	1 tsp. cumin
2 or 3 long green fresh chili peppers, or you can use canned jalapinos	½ cup olive oil

Cumin spice is a derivative of cilantro, in vegetable section if found at all in U.S. Use fresh cilantro if you can find it, but it is very strong, so use it sparingly.

Add beans to boiling water. Cook at low boil until nearly done (a bit more than 2¼ hours).

Boil tomato and chilis until skins peel off easily. Use all the chili you can salvage from skin—add all small "beans," as they contain the heat.

Chop chilis and tomato small.

To bacon add chili, onion, and tomato until all are started but not cooked up. When beans are nearly done, add salt, tomatoes, etc., and ½ cup olive oil. When beans are done, add cumin and boil for 1 minute.

Yield: serves 4–6

Sophie wrote us: "I learned to cook by pure necessity. I watched the camp cooks and learned from them—we had many cook-outs and I had to pitch in and help all I could. I think what I learned the most was one summer when I had a white gas two-burner stove and a crew of about 8 or 10 to cook for, and I just had to do it—no learning—just *do* it.

"I could not possibly describe my kitchen. It's nice, and I have an electric stove which I'm not crazy about. Most of my cooking has been on camp fires, and this stove often does me dirt.

"I've been cooking for 55 years. At the moment I cook for two, but I have cooked for 50 or 60 in my time.

"The only advice and hints I could offer are—Don't measure; taste, feel, and sniff. And keep experimenting."

Try Sophie's Tamale Pie (page 23), Real Spanish Rice (page 81), Charros Beans (page 81), Strawberry-Rhubarb Salad (page 101), Tomato Aspic (page 101), Remuda Beer Biscuits (page 169), and Christmas Rum Squares (page 356).

DEBORAH BUXTON
SOUTH LYNDEBORO,
NEW HAMPSHIRE

FIRST PRIZE
HILLSBORO COUNTY FAIR
NEW HAMPSHIRE

SAUTÉED GREEN BEANS WITH ONIONS

1½ lbs. green beans or 2 pkg.
   frozen beans
¾ cup chopped onions
4 T. butter or margarine
1 tsp. seasoned salt or veg-sal

⅛ tsp. freshly ground pepper
¼ cup tarragon or wine
   vinegar
2 T. minced parsley

Cook beans in salted water till tender but still firm. Drain well. Sauté onions in butter till soft and transparent. Mix in beans, salt, and pepper. Sauté 5 minutes. Sprinkle with vinegar and parsley.

Serve hot. The leftover beans are delicious in a tossed green salad!

Deborah told us about the time "I cooked a duck for a New Year's Eve dinner party. I cooked one duck for six adults! We filled up on cheese and vegetables—I've never lived it down."

Deborah began cooking with her sister; they would prepare dinner when their mother worked. She says, "I suppose my enjoyment began then—I love to experiment."

Try Debbie's Raisin Bran Muffins (page 171), and Sherbet Watermelon Surprise Dessert (page 386), too.

CAROLYN CHANEY
BATON ROUGE, LOUISIANA

HONORABLE MENTION
STATE TIMES AND *MORNING ADVOCATE* CONTEST
BATON ROUGE, LOUISIANA

BEEF-SPINACH FRITTATA

1 pkg. frozen spinach
1 lb. ground beef
¼ cup minced parsley
1 medium onion, diced
4 eggs, beaten
½ cup grated Cheddar cheese

Dash Worcestershire sauce
Pinch garlic powder
Pinch cayenne powder
Salt and pepper to taste
1 T. breadcrumbs

Thaw spinach. Sauté beef, parsley, and onion in heavy pot until slightly cooked. Remove from heat. Mix with remaining ingredients (except breadcrumbs). Place in greased 9-inch pie plate, or shallow casserole dish. Sprinkle with breadcrumbs. Bake in a preheated 350-degree oven for 35 minutes, or until set. Cut in wedges, or pieces.

See also Carolyn's Marinated Lamb Steaks (page 29), Stuffed Cucumbers (page 5), Sardine Snacks (page 5), and Mom's Caponata (page 6).

JOANNE CHESHIER
BALLINGER, TEXAS

FIRST PLACE
FIFTH ANNUAL PINTO BEAN
COOK-OFF, BALLINGER, TEXAS

BLUE RIBBON BEANS

Sort and wash 2 pounds pinto beans. Cover double with water in large pan and soak overnight. Discard soaking water—put beans in electric crock pot with 1 pound chopped salt pork and cover with water. Cover and cook on high 3 to 4 hours or until tender. Stir easily, if you must stir. When *tender,* add seasonings:

1 T. seasoning salt	¼ tsp. Tabasco sauce
1 T. Worcestershire sauce	1 tsp. onion powder
1 T. steak sauce	1 tsp. lemon pepper

The morning of the Pinto Bean Cook-Off, Joanne loaded her cooking gear, her uncooked beans, and her four-year-old son Jeff into the family car and backed out of the garage. On the way, the car stalled and she applied the accelerator and the brake at the same time. This tipped over her pot of water and beans. The floorboards were awash with beans. But she picked them up, washed them off, and cooked them and won first place, plus a sterling silver bowl.

Joanne says, *"Anyone* can cook. Just follow a recipe, learn by doing, and soon you'll have your own style."

ETHEL M. DAVIDS
LOUISVILLE, KENTUCKY

CANNED BEANS

Cut beans in 1-inch pieces. I heat in hot water before packing as they fit better in jars, pack to ½ inch from top. Add 1 teaspoon salt, cover with boiling water. Adjust jar lids. Process in pressure canner at 10 pounds (240 degrees). (Quart jars 25 minutes.) Remove when pressure goes down to zero. Cover so draft won't break jars.

"I started cooking in my Mom's kitchen," says Ethel Davids, "then read everything on cooking and canning. The effort and time really paid off." She is many times a prizewinner in "everything organic."

A cook for "fifty years—plus," Ethel says she has "all the necessary things" in her kitchen, including "a pressure canner (42 years old), food mill, strainers, etc.

"Just after being married, I thought I knew how to make noodles (watched my Mom for years). Only I used self-rising flour, adding water, more flour, more water, more flour, laying them to dry. Boiled my water, put in noodles. All over stove, enough for an army."

Although she only cooks for two now, on weekends Ethel welcomes her whole family of nine. About her Canned Beans she told us, "My boys would never eat canned beans from the store or in a restaurant. Now my 2 granddaughters say the same thing—I have to agree with them."

JANICE DeLONG
PEACH BOTTOM, PENNSYLVANIA

FIRST PRIZE
SOUTH LANCASTER COUNTY
COMMUNITY FAIR

HOMEMADE POTATO CHIPS

Fresh potatoes
Vegetable oil
Salt

Wash and peel the potatoes. Slice them as thin as a penny, and drop immediately into ice water to stop them from turning pink. Heat oil to 360 degrees. Dry the chips on paper towels and fry until golden brown and crisp. Remove, drain on paper towels, and salt lightly.

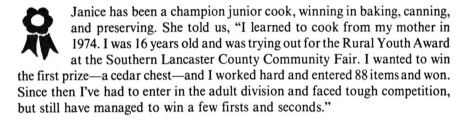

Janice has been a champion junior cook, winning in baking, canning, and preserving. She told us, "I learned to cook from my mother in 1974. I was 16 years old and was trying out for the Rural Youth Award at the Southern Lancaster County Community Fair. I wanted to win the first prize—a cedar chest—and I worked hard and entered 88 items and won. Since then I've had to enter in the adult division and faced tough competition, but still have managed to win a few firsts and seconds."

MAZO ECCLESTON
FOWLER, KANSAS

BLUE RIBBON, CANNING
MEADE COUNTY FAIR, GRAY COUNTY
FAIR, FORD COUNTY FAIR

CANNED WHOLE TOMATOES

Pick and put tomatoes in a box to ripen evenly in room out of sunlight.

When well ripened, scald ½ minute in boiling water. Plunge into deep cold water and skin and cut out cores. Place all that are same size in bowl and put them in wide-mouth jars. Do not smash in, but pack in solid. Take knife and run down sides and *drain out all seeds*. Strain juice and pour over tomatoes again and if any seeds are in jar do it again. (Judge notices this first thing when lifting up jar to see if in right canning jar, if clean, and if fill is right. If fill is wrong she will set it back no matter how pretty food in jar is.)

Add 1 teaspoon salt if you wish. Fill to neck of jar where it starts up on about ½ inch from top of jar. Put jars in hot water canner with hot water 1 inch over top of jars. Bring to boil and boil 40 minutes. Remove from water and set on board out of a draft. When they seal with popping sound put in refrigerator to cool rapidly. Turn upside down in 30 minutes. This keeps tomatoes from over-cooking and floating to top.

Now a senior cook, and mother of another of our prizewinners (Renae Eccleston), Mazo learned to cook as a girl. "I had to pack my two brothers' and sisters' lunch box. It was my job to keep cookies made. It was harder finding a place to hide them than making them as they would try to find them after I baked them to eat. Mom and I always canned together after school.

"I always helped in the kitchen. Stirring, tasting, chopping wood, taking out ashes and watching fire, churning and washing up the separator were some of my chores."

Mazo has won blue ribbons in all types of categories: candies, relishes, pickles, jellies, breads—including cracked wheat, whole wheat, apricot, quick bread, and piecrusts.

She cooks in a kitchen without countertops. Her work top is "my old deep-freeze, it has a black rubberized top, here I set the mixer to use in baking when I need it. Our refrigerator was new in 1963, has one-foot ice-cube compartment, the rest is refrigerator." Her stove has an extra large oven for baking whole meal or loaves and rolls of bread. She uses her table for work space.

Mazo Eccleston's Canned Whole Tomatoes have "taken a blue ribbon every year I take them to any fair. The secret of blue-ribbon canned tomatoes is to pack cores inside to middle of jar, use uniform color ripeness of tomatoes, and strain out seeds, as many as you can without crushing tomatoes. Then getting right fill of one-half inch from top of jar after processing. Cooling as quick as possible and turning upside down helps keep them from floating up from bottom. Don't overprocess in hot water. I don't take trouble to cool out ones I'm going to use. Store in covered box till fair time. Washing jars and putting on new screw lids impresses judge, too."

Try Mazo's delicious Rabbit Chili (page 13).

VIOLET GRICE
GILA BEND, ARIZONA

FIRST PRIZE
GILA BEND FOOD FAIR

GRITS AND CHEESE

1¼ cups quick-cooking grits	1 lb. cheese
6 cups salted water	3 eggs
2 sticks oleo	1 7-oz. can ortiga chilies

Cool grits in salted water until thick and done. Add butter and grated cheese, stir until melted. Cool slightly, then add eggs. Beat the eggs. Add chilies. Pour in greased pyrex dish. Bake 40 minutes at 350 degrees.

Freezes well.

Violet's Barbecue Sauce (page 415), and Beef Summer Sausage (page 35) are great, too!

MARY LOSSON
AHOSKIE, NORTH CAROLINA

FIRST PRIZE
COOK-A-PEANUT CONTEST
NORTH CAROLINA/VIRGINIA
PEANUT TRADE SHOW

PEANUT CASSEROLE DELIGHT

1 cup peanut butter	½ cup milk
2 cups mashed sweet potatoes	½ stick butter, melted
1 cup sugar	1 tsp. vanilla
2 eggs	½ tsp. salt

Mix all ingredients together until well blended. Pour into a buttered baking dish. Sprinkle with topping (below).

TOPPING

½ stick butter	½ cup self-rising flour
1 cup brown sugar	1 cup chopped peanuts

Melt ingredients in saucepan. Pour over casserole. Bake at 350 degrees for 30 minutes.

 "When I was a child, I was always trying to cook," says Mary, and she cooks for her children and grandchildren when they come to visit. She says it takes two things to make a good cook: "Time and good recipes."

WARREN F. LeRUTH
GRETNA, LOUISIANA

JUDGE OF COOKING CONTESTS

RED BEANS AND RICE

1 lb. red beans	Salt and pepper
3 qts. cold water	1 lb. ham trimmings with
4 chopped onions	skin on
4 toes garlic	2 lbs. smoked sausage

Pick over beans and wash thoroughly. Soak overnight. In order to have a creamy sauce, it is necessary to boil beans with onion, ham, and garlic. Boil over strong heat, using a heavy pot to avoid scorching. Check frequently. Use a rather tall pot so beans won't splash out while boiling. Some of the beans will break. When beans are tender add sausage, cut into 6-inch lengths. Continue to cook for 30 minutes. Add a little more water as necessary. Adjust seasoning. Serve over steamed rice that was seasoned with 1 or 2 bay leaves.

Margie's Oyster Soup (page 18), Broken Shrimp Jambalaya (page 43), Bibb Lettuce and Mushroom Salad with Vermouth Dressing (page 105), and Day-Old Beet and Onion Salad (page 105) are other offerings by cooking-contest judge and restaurateur LeRuth.

ELSIE LEYBA
ROSWELL, NEW MEXICO

FIRST PRIZE
ROSWELL FAIR

GREEN ENCHILADAS

1 cup green chilis, chopped
1 large onion, chopped
1 T. oil
1 T. flour
12 corn tortillas

½ cup Velveeta cheese, cubed
1 cup Longhorn cheese, grated
1 cup milk or water
1 cup sour cream
Salt to taste

Roast and peel chilis or used canned or frozen. Chop fine. Sauté some of the onion in the oil, add flour, and stir. Add liquid and chilis, stirring constantly. Add Velveeta cheese and stir until it melts, turn down heat, and add sour cream. Fry tortillas in oil for a few seconds, dip in chili mixture. Arrange on hot serving plate in layers—tortilla, onion and cheese, tortilla, onion and cheese, etc. May be topped with fried egg or served with a green salad.

CHILIS RELLENOS

6 green chilis
½ lb. Cheddar cheese—grated, cubed, or in strips
1 small onion

If fresh chili is used, peel chili, open slit below stem and remove seed. Leave stem on. Combine cheese and onion. Fill chili carefully to avoid breaking.

BATTER

4 eggs, separated
4 T. flour

¾ tsp. baking powder
¼ tsp. salt

Beat egg whites until stiff. Beat egg yolks until thick. Sift together dry ingredients. Blend well. Fold whites into yolks. Add dry ingredients. Blend well. Dip stuffed chili in batter, using large spoon, and fry in small amount of oil. Turn once. Remove to warm serving plate. Keep in warm oven until all chilis are cooked.

OPTIONAL. Using ground, cooked, well-seasoned meat for stuffing, place stuffed chilis in well-greased casserole. Pour batter over chilis and bake at 325 degrees for 45 minutes or until batter is done and lightly browned on top. Serve at once.

"My most horrible experience," says Elsie, "was when my husband brought home a turtle and I tried to bake it. I never had any experience with anything of that type, but they would never learn that from me (I thought, smugly) as I took the turtle from one of the fishermen, I took it from its shell, washed and scrubbed it well, and popped it in the oven. Yep, you guessed it, it exploded. What a horrible mess!"

Elsie now specializes in Mexican dishes, because "I like people to know what real home-cooked Mexican food tastes like."

DIANE MILNER
MURCHISON, TEXAS

SECOND PRIZE, MAIN DISH
ATHENS BLACK-EYED PEA JAMBOREE
ATHENS, TEXAS

PEA LOAFER

DOUGH

1 pkg. dry yeast
½ cup very warm water
1½ cups warm water
¼ cup sugar

½ tsp. salt
2 T. shortening
6 cups sifted all-purpose flour

Dissolve yeast in ½ cup very warm water. Stir in 1½ cups water, sugar, salt, shortening, and 3 cups of flour. Beat until smooth.

Mix in enough remaining flour to make dough easy to handle. Turn dough onto a lightly floured board; knead until smooth and elastic. Place in greased bowl; grease top. Cover; let rise in warm place until doubled, about 1 hour.

FILLING

Meanwhile, brown 1½ pounds pork sausage; drain and set aside.
Mix:

¼ cup bell pepper
½ cup ketchup
¼ tsp. cinnamon
2 cans black-eyed peas
1 tsp. garlic powder
2 T. Tabasco sauce

¼ tsp. nutmeg
1 tsp. salt
½ tsp. coarse pepper
½ can tomatoes, chopped
¼ tsp. oregano

Add 3 tablespoons flour and cook until thickened. Add cooked sausage. Cool. Punch down bread dough and roll in rectangle (about 12x16 inches). Spread mixture over dough. Sprinkle with Parmesan cheese, 2 bunches cut-up green onion, and Lawry's season-all seasoning. Roll up, starting with narrow end; grease top and put in large pan. Let rise 45 minutes. Cook slowly in 250-degree oven for 1 to 2 hours or until brown.

Try Diane's Classical Stroganoff (page 45) and Veal Scallopini (page 45).

LORENA PERLICK
SURING, WISCONSIN

NOODLES ROMANOFF

⅔–1 cup noodles
1 cup cottage cheese
¼ cup onion, finely chopped
1 clove garlic, finely cut
2 tsp. Worcestershire sauce
Dash Tabasco sauce or red
    pepper

½ tsp. salt
½ cup buttered breadcrumbs
½ cup grated Wisconsin
    Cheddar cheese

Cook noodles. Add cottage cheese, sour cream, onion, garlic, Worcestershire sauce, pepper, and salt and place in buttered 8-inch baking dish. Bake in oven at 350 degrees about 30 minutes.

Remove from oven and sprinkle with cheese and buttered breadcrumbs. Return to oven for 10 minutes.

I use 1 cup of noodles.

Yield: 6 servings

Lorena has won prizes with many kinds of dishes, from casseroles to cookies. She says, "To make foods look more attractive I always use a garnish. I never overcook foods, then they look and taste better."

She learned by helping her mother and she cooked in a restaurant for a few years. She has been cooking for 45 years.

BESSIE M. SECRIST
ALMA, WISCONSIN

SECOND PRIZE
DAIRY BAKE-OFF
BUFFALO COUNTY, WISCONSIN

PARIS POTATOES

5 cups potatoes
2 cups creamed cottage cheese
1 cup sour cream
2 T. butter
4 green onions, tops and all,
    cut fine

½ tsp. garlic (optional)
Salt and pepper to taste
1 cup grated Cheddar cheese
    (cornflakes can dress it up)

Precook potatoes in boiling water, salted, until *crispy* tender (do not over-cook). Drain and cut in ¼-inch cubes. Mix all ingredients except Cheddar cheese. Bake at 350 degrees in a 9x13-inch greased (with butter) pan for 20 minutes. Add Cheddar cheese and bake 10 minutes longer. Can be made ahead and refrigerated, but allow more cooking time in this event.

Bessie has lived on a farm all her life. She says, "We always have a big garden. I can and freeze and one year kept track—I put away eight hundred quarts of vegetables and fruits for winter use.

"I am a plain cook, no fancy stuff, because that's the way our family likes it." She came from a big family, and joined 4-H as a girl. She was a 4-H leader for "twenty-some years, besides raising a family of eight."

About her Paris Potatoes, Bessie says, "I have used this receipt on trips for people we visited. In February of this year we were in Texas for two weeks, and went to two pot-luck dinners, one church, and one for 'snow birds,' people from North, visiting down there, and took this potato dish. Many people asked for the receipt so now it's being cooked all over the U.S."

MARION URIE
CRAFTSBURY COMMON, VERMONT

MERIT AWARD
CASSEROLE USING VERMONT DAIRY
PRODUCTS, VERMONT FARM SHOW

VERMONT VEGETABLE CHEESE CASSEROLE

Make a white sauce, using 2 cups whole milk. Thicken with 3 tablespoons of flour and a bit of cold milk to make a paste. Add 2 tablespoons of butter. Add 1 cup shredded Cheddar cheese after removing from heat. Cube 2 slices home-made bread.

In a 2-quart casserole add in layers: 2 sliced hard-boiled eggs; 1 package frozen broccoli, partly cooked and drained; and 1 package (¼-pound crumbled) dried beef.

Top with ½ cup poultry dressing. Mix with 2 tablespoons of melted butter. Bake at 325 degrees for ½ hour or until bubbly and browned on top.

 One of our outstanding New England cooks, Marion Urie learned to cook from another prizewinner—her mother. Both of them were featured in *Yankee* magazine as "Great New England Cooks" (February 1978).

Her cozy nook of a kitchen is "where my happiest days are spent." Her happiness comes through in her recipes. She has been entering Farm Shows since 1960. In these shows the Merit Award is the highest prize, and she has won it four times.

She says of her Vegetable Cheese Casserole, "Serve with your favorite pickles and your meal is complete."

CHAPTER SIX

SALADS

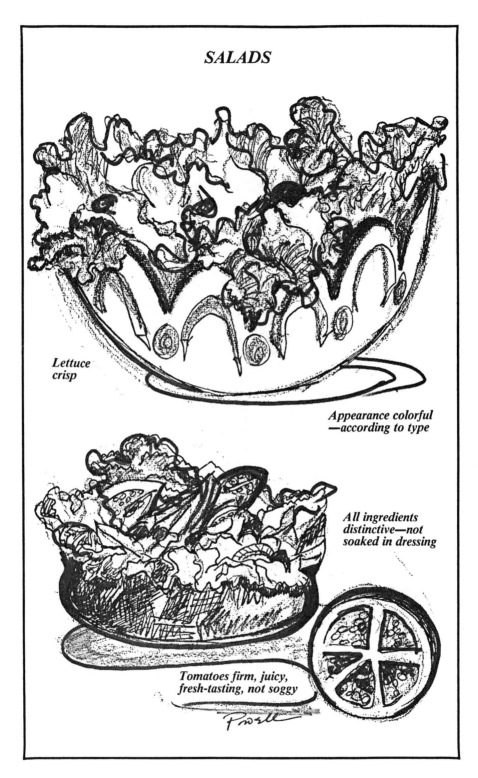

Lettuce
crisp

Appearance colorful
—according to type

All ingredients
distinctive—not
soaked in dressing

Tomatoes firm, juicy,
fresh-tasting, not soggy

Sophie Burden
Wickenburg, Arizona

STRAWBERRY-RHUBARB SALAD

2 small or 1 large pkg. strawberry jello
1 cup boiling water
½ cup cold water

Dissolve jello in hot water and add cold.

Cook rhubarb according to directions on package, or cook fresh rhubarb, and add to jello. Three-fourths of a cup rhubarb makes 2 servings.

Thaw the strawberries or hull the fresh ones. When jello is cool, add strawberries and pour into mold or small molds and chill.

FOR FRESH RHUBARB:

Mix ¼ cup sugar with ¾ cup water. Boil five minutes. Add rhubarb. Bring to a boil. Reduce heat and simmer about 5 minutes until tender.

NOTE: Once, not having any strawberry jello, I thawed the strawberries and used one-half cup of the juice to make strawberry gelatin. It was good.

TOMATO ASPIC

Sprinkle 1 envelope of unflavored gelatine on ¼ cup cold water. Let stand 5 minutes.

Bring 2 cups tomato juice to a boil. Sprinkle onion salt, celery salt, Accent, lemon pepper, a touch of marjoram, a squirt of lemon juice, and about a tablespoon of vinegar. Mix with the gelatine and stir well.

Turn into a mold, or small ones, and chill. Serve with avocado and lettuce or however you want it.

Great with lobster or crabmeat and watercress!

Sophie's Tamale Pie (page 23), Real Spanish Rice (page 81), Charros Beans (page 81), Remuda Beer Biscuits (page 169), and Christmas Rum Squares (page 356) are all great too.

DAN CURD
MADISON, WISCONSIN

FIRST PLACE, SALADS
WISCONSIN STATE JOURNAL CONTEST
MADISON, WISCONSIN

CALIFORNIA FRUIT SALAD

SALAD

1 head Romaine lettuce, washed, dried, and broken up
1 head of bronze leaf or leaf lettuce, washed, dried, and broken up
1 pint strawberries, hulled and sliced in half
1 cup seedless white grapes
1 large ripe avocado, sliced
½ cup walnuts, roughly broken
1 T. chopped fresh mint (½ tsp. dried)

Toss all ingredients with enough dressing to coat.

DRESSING (½ cup)

6 T. oil
2 T. wine vinegar
1 clove garlic, crushed
1 T. honey
½ tsp. salt
½ tsp. paprika
½ tsp. dry mustard
¼ tsp. tarragon
¼ tsp. thyme
¼ tsp. oregano
⅛ tsp. freshly ground black pepper

Put all ingredients in glass jar and shake. Let stand several hours before using.

Yield: 6–8 servings

Dan's Cornish Chicken (page 61) and Coffee Rum Cookies (page 317) are worth a try too!

CARROT FRUIT SALAD

2 cups grated carrots
1 cup pineapple chunks,
    drained
1 cup coconut

½ cup pecans
½ cup raisins (optional)
¼ cup maraschino cherries

Mix all together in a salad bowl.

DRESSING

½ cup oil
⅓ cup or more sugar
¼ tsp. each mustard and
    vinegar

1 cup cream
Pinch of salt

Shake in jar and pour over salad.

Sarah has a wonderful kitchen—big, with 28 feet of cabinets, built-ins, appliances (including a "trash-masher"), and a microwave. It's the microwave that has gotten her into trouble. Once she used the wrong bowl for a company casserole—and the bottom fell out on the floor in front of her guests. Another time she had popcorn in a bag in the microwave. The bag caught on fire, and when she opened the door the corn popped all over the kitchen.

A creative cook, Sarah tries different things, such as spaghetti sauce made with weiners instead of hamburger; sauerkraut porkchops and dumplings; hamburger balls with dressing inside and mushroom gravy; self-filling cupcakes, using cream cheese; and many more. She also paints, sews, knits, and does other needle work, but she says, "Cooking is one art I love."

LORRAINE JACOBS
NAHUNTA, GEORGIA

FANCI-CHICKEN SALAD

4 cups cold, cut-up chicken
(cook chicken in water
seasoned with chicken
bouillon granules for
extra flavor)
2 T. lemon juice
1 cup mayonnaise
1 tsp. salt
½ tsp. Accent
2 cups chopped celery

½ cup chopped bell pepper
4 hard-cooked eggs, chopped
¾ can cream of chicken soup
(undiluted)
1 small onion, chopped fine
1 pimento, chopped fine
1 cup grated Cheddar cheese
1½ cups crushed potato chips
⅔ cup chopped roasted
peanuts

In a large mixing bowl, combine all ingredients except cheese, potato chips, and peanuts. Place in a large (3-quart) rectangular dish. Top with cheese, potato chips, and peanuts. Let stand all day or overnight in refrigerator to mix flavors. Bake at 400 degrees for 20 minutes or until heated through and through.

Yield: 8 servings

NOTE: This recipe can be used as a casserole or as a main dish. It is very tasty.

Try Lorraine's Orange Peanut Butter Pie (page 287) and Stuffed Celery (page 9).

WARREN F. LeRUTH
GRETNA, LOUISIANA

JUDGE OF COOKING CONTESTS

BIBB LETTUCE AND MUSHROOM SALAD WITH VERMOUTH DRESSING

2 heads Bibb lettuce
1 cup sliced fresh mushrooms
⅓ cup salad oil

2 T. dry vermouth
¼ tsp. salt

Break cleaned lettuce to desired size. Arrange sliced fresh mushrooms over lettuce. Pour over dressing and gently toss.

Yield: serves 4

NOTE: LeRuth created this recipe for Les Amis du Vin because they wanted to have wine with salad without having the acidity from vinegar or lemon spoil the flavor of a delicate wine.

DAY-OLD BEET AND ONION SALAD

2 14-oz. cans sliced beets
2 sliced onions
½ cup olive oil
¼ cup vinegar
2 T. sugar

1 tsp. salt
¼ tsp. black pepper
¼ bunch parsley, coarsely
  chopped

Discard juice from one can of beets. Drain juice from the other can into a bowl. Add vinegar, sugar, salt, and pepper—mix. Add oil, sliced beets and onions and mix. Cover and chill overnight. Before serving add coarsely chopped parsley and serve.

Yield: serves 6

NOTE: "We normally serve beet and onion salad whenever we have red beans. When you soak the beans the night before it is your reminder to make the beet salad," says LeRuth.

See Warren's Oyster Soup (page 18), Broken Shrimp Jambalaya (page 43), and Red Beans and Rice (page 92).

DELIA VIEIRA
CARVER, MASSACHUSETTS

FIRST PRIZE
MASSACHUSETTS CRANBERRY
FESTIVAL

CRA-APPLE MOLD

2 3-oz. pkgs. raspberry
flavored gelatin
2 cups boiling water
1 16-oz. can (2 cups) whole
cranberry sauce

1 8½-oz. can (1 cup) applesauce
½ cup port wine
¼ cup chopped walnuts

Dissolve gelatin in boiling water. Stir in cranberry sauce, applesauce and wine. Chill till partially set; fold in chopped nuts. Pour into 6½-cup mold. Chill till firm, 5 to 6 hours or overnight.

Yield: 10 to 12 servings

Delia told us her children once added chocolate eggs to a batch of Easter stuffing she was making, "which was a surprise to me," she said.

This prizewinning New England cook has invented cake and bread recipes using cranberries as well as this blue ribbon salad.

LINDA MARTIN
ATHENS, TEXAS

FIRST PLACE, SALAD
BLACK-EYED PEA JAMBOREE
ATHENS, TEXAS

PEAS 'N' HAM HOT SALAD

3½ cups cooked ham, cut in
  strips
1½ cups celery, diagonally cut
⅓ cup diced green pepper
1 medium onion, chopped
1 small can water chestnuts

3½ cups cooked black-eyed
  peas, drained
1¼ cups mayonnaise
1½ tsp. lemon juice
⅓ cup crushed potato chips
8 lettuce cups

Combine all ingredients (except potato chips and lettuce) and mix lightly. Turn into a greased 1½-quart baking dish. Top with potato chips. Bake at 350 degrees for 25 minutes. Serve hot in lettuce cups. Also delicious served cold.

Yield: serves 8

"I started cooking at the age of seven with my Mom," says Linda, who cooks every day for her family of four. Once she made a beautiful "homemade apple pie, and took it out of the oven and was going to put it on the window sill to cool. It flipped! It's funny now, but wasn't then."

Linda won $250.00 for this blue-ribbon salad.

ALVINA LUTTIG MERRY
Yuba, Wisconsin

LIME PARTY SALAD

Combine ½ pound marshmallows (about 32 large ones) with 1½ cups milk. Place in top of double boiler until marshmallows are melted. Add 2 3-ounce packages of lime jello and stir until dissolved. Add 1 8-ounce package of cream cheese. Stir until well dissolved and add 1 8-ounce can of undrained crushed pineapple and 1 cup of cream or Cool Whip. Stir into jello mixture and add ¼ cup mayonnaise. Add ½ cup nuts if desired. Pour into 1-quart mold and let set overnight. In morning unmold and garnish with strawberries.

Try Alvina's Strawberry Cheese Pie (page 292).

MILDRED K. PYLES
CRESCENT CITY, CALIFORNIA

FIRST PRIZE
DEL MONTE COUNTY FAIR
CALIFORNIA

FRENCH SALAD DRESSING

1 medium grated onion
1 clove garlic, minced
⅓ cup chopped chives
½ cup sugar
¼ cup cider vinegar
½ cup salad oil

½ cup ketchup
Juice of 1 lemon
1 tsp. paprika
1 tsp. salt
¼ T. pepper

Take "four career girls fresh from college in one apartment. One 'cook' per week and one *hard-and-fast* rule—one new recipe per week!" That's the way Mildred learned.

She grew up on the family dairy, and told us about using cream when a recipe called for milk: "Everything fell, from gingerbread to cakes!"

ELIZABETH ROCKWELL
ENCINITAS, CALIFORNIA

DIVISIONAL WINNER
NATIONAL PINEAPPLE COOKING
CLASSIC, HONOLULU, HAWAII

CHILLED PINEAPPLE PAELLA

3 cups warm cooked rice,
    rinsed
½ tsp. curry powder
1 1-lb., 4-oz. can pineapple
    chunks
2 T. syrup from pineapple
    chunks
1¼ cups mayonnaise
⅓ cup minced green onion
⅓ cup finely chopped bell
    pepper

¼ tsp. garlic powder
1 6-oz. pkg. frozen cooked
    shrimp, peeled and
    deveined
1 T. lemon juice
1¼ cups frozen peas
1½ cups ¾-inch cubes cooked
    ham

Sprinkle rice with curry powder. Spoon off 2 tablespoons syrup from pineapple and add to rice, along with mayonnaise, onion, green pepper, and garlic powder. Mix well, cover, and chill at least 1 hour. Thaw shrimp and cut in halves lengthwise. Sprinkle with lemon juice. Add water to peas as package directs and bring to a boil. Drain at once, setting aside ¼ cup for garnish. Drain pineapple and set aside a few chunks for garnish. Combine shrimp, remaining peas, and pineapple and ham. Chill. About half an hour before serving, drain any liquid from shrimp-pineapple mixture and combine mixture with rice. Spoon into serving bowl lined with lettuce. Garnish with peas and pineapple chunks. Refrigerate until serving time.

Yield: 6 servings (about 8½ cups)

NOTE: You may omit the shrimp and the total effect is much the same.

Elizabeth Rockwell won a trip to Hawaii and $10,000 for her salad recipe. She says, "I like to improvise, and never follow any recipe to the letter."

When she had just started making her salad, she told us, using the "marvelously sharp knives," they provide at the contest, she cut herself. "There was a nurse there, but I felt like an idiot."

KERI ROSEBROOK

OKLAHOMA CITY, OKLAHOMA

FIRST PLACE, SALAD WITH MEAT
STATE FAIR OF OKLAHOMA
OKLAHOMA CITY, OKLAHOMA

SEVEN-LAYER SALAD

Layer ingredients in clear glass bowl as listed:

Iceberg lettuce torn small
    2 chopped green peppers
    1 red onion, sliced very thin
    1 pkg. frozen peas, thawed
Dressing—2 cups mayonnaise plus 2 T. sugar
    6–8 oz. sharp Cheddar cheese, grated
8–10 slices crisp bacon, crumbled

Yield: 8–10 servings

NOTE: Depending on the occasion you can adjust the amounts to fill a punch bowl and serve 20 or more.

 This salad won a blue ribbon "the first time I entered anything in the fair," says Keri. Salads are her specialty. She says, "I like lots of vegetables, especially sprouts, which I grow in jars in my kitchen sink. Radish sprouts are colorful and snappy and sunflower seed sprouts add a nutty flavor."

Once when she was making this seven-layer salad, she told us, "I had forgotten to thaw out my peas. I put them in my salad spinner with a little hot water in the bottom, and began spinning it. I opened the lid too soon and the centrifugal force threw the peas all over the kitchen."

She goes on to say, "My friend Becky gave me this recipe initially, but I improvised on it and changed it a little to make it my own. There are many layered recipes floating around—at one luncheon there were four different ones, and everyone agreed this one was the best."

JACKIE SANDBLOM
BOULDER, COLORADO

FIRST PRIZE
SAVORY SEASON RECIPE CONTEST

BANANA SALAD

4 large bananas, cut in half	1 egg, beaten
1 can peanuts	1 cup milk
½ cup sugar	1 T. mustard
3 T. flour	3 T. sweet pickle juice

Spread peanuts between two dishtowels and crush with a rolling pin (the towels will absorb the excess oil). Set aside.

Mix the sugar and flour together in the corner of a large skillet. Add the beaten egg, milk, mustard, and sweet pickle juice. Cook and stir over medium heat until the custard is thickened. Remove from heat and cool. Roll bananas in custard and then in crushed peanuts. Place 2 banana halves on each of 4 lettuce-lined salad plates to serve.

Try her Banana-Blueberry Bread (page 199), and her Strawberry-Yogurt Bread (page 199).

Barbara Truesdale
Vale, North Carolina

FIRST PLACE
LOW-CALORIE CATEGORY,
APPLE DISH CONTEST,
APPLE FESTIVAL, LINCOLN
COUNTY, NORTH CAROLINA

JELLIED APPLE NUT SALAD

1 1-oz. pkg. lemon-flavored
    gelatin
1 cup boiling water
¾ cup cold water
1 T. lemon juice

⅛ tsp. salt
½ cup celery, finely chopped
1½ cups apples, chopped
¼ cup chopped pecans
Salad greens

Dissolve gelatin in boiling water. Add cold water, lemon juice, and salt. Chill until slightly thickened. Stir in remaining ingredients (except salad greens); pour into a 1-quart mold or an 8x8x2-inch pan. Chill until firm. Serve on salad greens.

Calories per serving: 105 (⅔ cup)

JOYCE WENTHOLD
OKLAHOMA CITY, OKLAHOMA

SUPER SALAD SANDWICH

Pita bread
½ tsp. mayonnaise
6 slices cucumber
¼ firm tomato
¼ onion
¼ sliced green pepper

Lettuce leaves
3 fresh mushrooms, thinly
    sliced
⅛ large apple
1 kosher dill pickle
Seasoned salt

Wash all vegetables and slice into thin pieces. Spread mayonnaise on both sides of pocket. Fill with mixture of vegetables, sprinkling each layer with seasoned salt. Only 140 calories per sandwich.

See Joyce's Chocolate Peanut Delight (page 301).

CHAPTER SEVEN

YEAST BREADS

YEAST BREAD

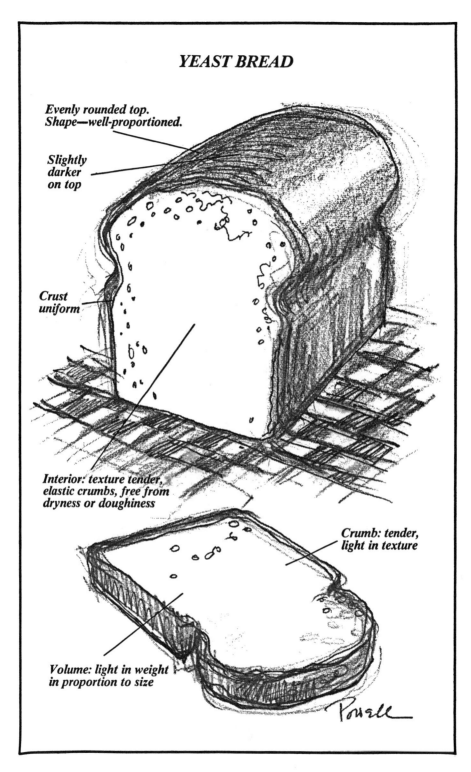

Evenly rounded top.
Shape—well-proportioned.

Slightly
darker
on top

Crust
uniform

Interior: texture tender,
elastic crumbs, free from
dryness or doughiness

Crumb: tender,
light in texture

Volume: light in weight
in proportion to size

Powell

IONE M. ANDERSON
GRAFTON, NORTH DAKOTA

FIRST PLACE, RYE BREAD
NORTH DAKOTA STATE FAIR

SWEDISH LIMPA
(Rye Bread)

---

1 T. fennel seeds
1 T. anise seed
1½ cups warm water
  (105–115 degrees)
2 pkgs. yeast
¼ cup molasses

¼ cup sugar
1 T. salt
2 T. grated orange rind
2½ cups sifted rye flour
2 T. softened shortening
2½–3 cups sifted bread flour

Crush fennel and anise seeds in small bowl until fine. Measure warm water into large mixing bowl. Sprinkle in yeast. Stir to dissolve. Add molasses, sugar, salt, orange rind, anise, and fennel. Stir in flour and shortening; beat until smooth and elastic, about 5 minutes. Place in greased bowl. Turn dough over to bring greased side up or brush top with softened shortening. Cover with damp towel. Let rise in warm place (85 degrees) free from draft for about 1½ hours or until doubled in bulk. Punch dough down. Turn onto board. Cut dough in half. Shape each half into slightly flattened oval; place on greased baking sheet; cover with damp towel. Let rise in warm place one hour or until doubled in bulk. Make three ¼-inch-deep slashes in top of each loaf. Bake in moderate oven (375 degrees) 30–35 minutes. Cool on wire racks.

PENNY ARNETT
LOUISVILLE, KENTUCKY

OLD MILWAUKEE RYE BREAD

1 envelope active dry yeast
1½ cups very warm water
   (105–115 degrees)
2 cups whole rye flour
2 T. caraway seeds
1 envelope active dry yeast
1 cup very warm water
   (105–115 degrees)
¼ cup molasses

1 egg, room temperature
1 T. salt
1 cup whole rye flour
5½–6 cups sifted all-purpose
   flour
3 T. vegetable shortening
1 egg
1 T. milk

Bake at 375 degrees for 40 minutes.

Yield: 2 or 3 loaves

SPONGE PREPARATION: 1–3 days

Dissolve 1 envelope of the yeast in the 1½ cups very warm water in a large bowl. Stir in the 2 cups rye flour and 1 tablespoon caraway seeds. (This is called the sponge.) Cover the bowl snugly with plastic wrap so the sponge loses none of the moisture that condenses on the plastic and drops back in the mixture. The sponge, which resembles a wet mash that is too thick to pour and too thin to knead, can be used anytime after 12 hours, although the longer it stands the better the flavor—up to 3 days.

BAKE DAY PREPARATION: 20 minutes

Uncover the sponge bowl, sprinkle on the remaining envelope of yeast, and add the remaining warm water. Blend well with 25 strokes of a wooden spoon. Add molasses, remaining caraway seeds, egg, salt, remaining rye flour, and about 2 cups of the all-purpose flour. Beat until smooth, about 100 strokes. Add shortening. Stir in the remaining flour, first with the spoon and then by hand. The dough should clean the side of the bowl, although it will be sticky because of the rye flour.

KNEADING: 5 minutes

Turn the dough out on a floured countertop. Knead it about 200 times or until the dough is smooth, about 5 minutes. The dough must be firm. It may sag slightly if lifted for a moment or two, but should not collapse. If it does collapse, knead in more flour.

FIRST RISING: 1 hour, 10 minutes

Return the dough to the large bowl; pat top with butter or shortening and replace plastic wrap. Leave in warm place (80–85 degrees) for about 1 hour, or until doubled in volume. Punch dough down and let rise 10 minutes.

SHAPING: 20 minutes

Turn dough out onto work surface to make 2 round loaves: divide dough in half. Shape each half into a smooth ball and place on greased cookie sheets.

SECOND RISING: 40 minutes

Cover the loaves with waxed paper supported on glass tumblers so paper does not touch dough. Return to warm place for about 40 minutes or until loaves have doubled.

BAKING: 40 minutes

Carefully make 3 or 4 slashes on the top of each loaf with a sharp razor. Brush the loaves with the remaining egg mixed with the milk for a shiny crust. Sprinkle the wet glaze with caraway seeds and kosher salt. Bake the loaves in a moderate oven (375 degrees) for about 40 minutes or until they sound hollow when thumped on the bottom.

FINAL STEP

Remove loaves to wire rack. Cool completely. Will keep for at least a week or more. Freeze well.

Try daughter Alyssa's Pina Colada Cake (page 211).

DOUGLAS J. BERGMEIER
DEWITT, NEBRASKA

WHITE YEAST BREAD

2 pkgs. active dry yeast
½ cup warm water
1¾ cup lukewarm milk or potato water
7–7¼ cups sifted flour
3 T. sugar
1 T. salt
2 T. soft shortening stirred into scalded milk or potato water

Dissolve yeast in warm water. Add cooled milk, half flour, sugar, salt, and shortening. Beat till smooth, mix in enough of remaining flour until dough cleans bowl. Turn onto a lightly floured board. Cover and let rest 10 to 15 minutes. Then knead until smooth and blistered. Cover and let rise till doubled in bulk. Punch down again, and let rise 30 minutes. Divide in 2 parts. Shape into loaves. Grease top of loaf. Cover and let rise 50 to 60 minutes. Bake at 400 degrees for 25 to 30 minutes.

Yield: 2 loaves

Douglas learned cooking in "Mom's kitchen and baking in the Youth Division for the March of Dimes Cake Auction."

Once he was "baking my State Fair Bread entry and the kitchen oven was full. So I ran down the basement steps with the raised bread, taking all the rise out. It looked like a dried-up prune."

Prizewinner Douglas has two hints for others: "Get cooking utensils and ingredients together before starting," and "Accurately measure ingredients."

CAROL BRADEN
SHEPHERDSVILLE, KENTUCKY

FIRST PLACE, RAISIN BREAD
KENTUCKY STATE FAIR

CINNAMON RAISIN BREAD

2 pkgs. active dry yeast	6–7 cups flour
½ cup warm water (105–115 degrees)	1 cup raisins
	¼ cup sugar
1¾ cups warm water	2 tsp. cinnamon
3 T. sugar	2 T. water
1 T. salt	Butter, softened
2 T. shortening	

Dissolve yeast in ½ cup warm water. Stir in 1¾ cups warm water, sugar, salt, and 3½ cups flour. Beat until smooth. Mix raisins and enough remaining flour to make dough easy to handle.

Turn dough onto lightly floured surface; knead until smooth and elastic, about 10 minutes. Place in greasing bowl; turn greased side up. Cover; let rise in warm place until doubled, about 1 hour.

Punch down dough, divide into halves. Roll each half into rectangle, 18x9 inches. Mix ¼ cup sugar and the cinnamon. Sprinkle each half with butter and half of the sugar mixture. Roll up, beginning at short side—with side of hand, press each end to seal; fold each end to seal; fold ends under. Place seam side down in greased 9x5x3 or 8½x4½x2½-inch loaf pan. Brush lightly with butter. Let rise until doubled, about 1 hour.

Heat oven to 425 degrees. Bake until golden brown and loaves sound hollow when tapped, 25–30 minutes. Remove from pans. Brush loaves with butter. Cool on wire racks.

Yield: 2 loaves

 Carol says her kitchen is "a mess but efficient. It's U-shaped and a nice size. Close to the chairs so my sons (two and three) can 'help' me."

She cooks for four every day, and has been cooking "ever since I can remember."

ANN CAMPBELL
LAWRENCEBURG, TENNESSEE

BLUE RIBBON
MIDDLE TENNESSEE FAIR

TWO-HOUR ROLLS

1 pkg. yeast	½ cup boiling water
½ cup shortening	½ cup cold water
⅓ cup sugar	1 egg
1½ tsp. salt	3½–4½ cups all-purpose flour

Place sugar, salt, and shortening in bowl. Pour boiling water over mixture, then cold water. Mix well. Dissolve yeast in ¼ cup warm water, add beaten egg, and add to other ingredients. Add flour. Roll out on floured area ¼- to ½-inch thick. Cut into rolls with biscuit cutter and place on greased cookie sheet. Let rise 2 hours. Cook at 375 degrees for 15 minutes.

This recipe makes about 2 dozen rolls. I make half in rolls and use the other half to make cinnamon rolls. Roll remaining dough ½ to ¼ inch thick, dot well with margarine or butter, sprinkle with sugar, then cinnamon. Roll dough lengthwise and cut into 2-inch slices and place in greased pan. Let rise 2 hours. Delicious served hot. I don't really measure my sugar, butter, or cinnamon, but about ½–¾ cup sugar, ½–¾ stick margarine, and 2–2½ teaspoons cinnamon seem right.

NOTE: I use corn oil; Crisco does well also. These are real nice to have. They can be made up and forgotten while your other meal is cooking. As in all yeast bread, they rise much faster in hot weather. They should always be placed in a place free from draft and covered.

BRENDA DETTEN
PONCA CITY, OKLAHOMA

JUNIOR GRAND CHAMPION
BAKING, OKLAHOMA STATE FAIR
OKLAHOMA CITY, OKLAHOMA

BASIC WHITE DOUGH

2 cups milk
1 pkg. active dry yeast
¼ cup lukewarm water
2 T. sugar

2 tsp. salt
1 T. shortening
6 cups all-purpose flour, sifted

Scald milk; do not burn or boil.

Soften yeast in lukewarm water. (I like to run hot water over measuring cup until warm, then put water in. This keeps the yeast warm until the milk is scalded and shortening has melted. A warmed mixing bowl keeps the dough warm.)

Now pour the scalded milk over the sugar, salt, and shortening measured in a mixing bowl. (I use a stainless steel bowl.) Stir till shortening is almost all melted. Be sure the milk mixture has cooled to lukewarm before adding the dissolved yeast, so as not to kill yeast.

Stir in the sifted flour one cup at a time. Mix thoroughly before adding next cup.

Turn out on a pastry cloth. (A pastry cloth makes for easy clean-up, and the dough tends to not stick as much.) Knead the dough until it is smooth and satiny, elasticlike. This takes approximately 8–12 minutes. (I knead the dough until it feels right, till I think it's done. Your finger will leave a hole in the dough when you have kneaded long enough. I like to take my madness out when I knead. And I think it works!) Remember not to work too much flour.

Let rise free of draft about 1–1½ hours, until doubled in bulk. Grease the bowl you're letting it rise in. Turn dough into bowl, turn over to grease on top. (This helps prevent a "crust" from forming on top.) Cover with a warm dampened cloth.

After rising, roll out half the dough and then roll "up" as you would cinnamon rolls. Pinch ends together. Curl the ends under and place carefully in greased loaf pan. (I use glass pans. You can see the color of the bottom of the loaf to see if it's done.) Cover with a warm damp cloth and let rise again about 45 minutes. Be careful not to let the sides of the dough run over the sides of the pan. Bake until golden brown, about 35 minutes. (If the top gets browner than the bottom place a piece of aluminum foil over the top.)

Take out of oven and immediately out of pans, cool on wire racks.

Brenda is a fifteen-year-old freshman in high school, as well as being the Junior Grand Champion of the fair. She and her family live on a "diversified farm in the north central part of Oklahoma." She says, "We are a large family, seven people, and everyone has their own job; mine happens to be cooking. I like to make bread, which also makes my family happy."

RENAE ECCLESTON
FOWLER, KANSAS

WHOLE WHEAT COTTAGE CHEESE ROLLS

3¾–4 cups whole wheat flour
    (or ½ white & ½ whole
    wheat)
2 pkgs. yeast
½ tsp. soda
1½ cups cream-style cottage
    cheese

½ cup water
¼ cup honey or brown
    sugar
2 T. butter
2 tsp. salt

Stir yeast and soda in flour, combine with other ingredients and heat to just 115 degrees (butter need not melt at this). Beat 2 eggs thoroughly. Add liquid to flour and beat ½ minute on Slow. Scrape bowl and beat 3 minutes on High.

By hand stir in enough more flour to make a stiff dough. Turn out on a floured surface and knead 8 minutes. Cover in greased bowl. Let rise till doubled. Punch down and form into rolls. Let rise. Bake at 375 degrees for 15 minutes.

HOME-STYLE BROWN ENGLISH MUFFINS

4–4½ cups white flour
1 pkg. yeast
½ cup whole wheat flour
½ cup wheat germ
½ cup quick-cooking
    oatmeal
1 cup nonfat dry milk
    solids

3 T. sugar
2 tsp. salt
2 cups warm water
¼ cup oil
½ cup corn meal

Mix 2 cups flour, yeast, whole wheat flour, wheat germ, oats, milk solids, sugar, and salt together. Add warm water (120 degrees). Add oil. Blend at low speed on mixer until moistened. Beat 3 minutes at medium speed.

By hand, gradually stir in remaining flour to a firm dough. Knead on floured board until smooth and elastic (5 minutes). Place in bowl, turn to oil top. Cover. Let rise in warm place until doubled, about 40 minutes. (I put it in oven with a pan of hot water under shelf.) Punch down and place on corn-mealed surface. Roll out ½-inch thick. Cut with 3-inch round cutter. Place on corn-mealed covered board or waxed paper to rise again until doubled, about 30 minutes. Bake corn-mealed side down in oiled electric skillet at 200 degrees for 8–10 minutes. Turn over and bake second side 8–10 minutes so each side is same color or brownness and center is done. Check for doneness, as some electric skillets differ. Cool, wrap, and freeze. Thaw in plastic bag overnight before exhibiting at fair, so moisture doesn't escape from muffins. In morning place in plastic bag on paper plate to exhibit. I like to make these about a week from fair time.

NOTE: Renae says these muffins are "good toasted, split and served with creamed meat or toast and served with butter and jelly."

Try Renae's Coca-Cola Cupcakes (page 389), too.

HAMBURGER BUNS

3½ cups milk, scalded
1 T. salt
¾ cup shortening
½ cup sugar
2 eggs, beaten

Flour for elastic dough (9-plus cups)
2 pkgs. dry yeast
1 cup warm water

Add salt, shortening, and sugar to the hot milk. Cool to lukewarm. Add yeast softened in warm water. Add beaten eggs. Stir in flour to make a rather soft dough. Stir the dough a lot to create elasticity—the more you stir it, the better it will be. Knead as you would bread dough. Put in a warm place to rise to double in bulk. Pinch off small balls, 3 inches in diameter. Place on a cookie sheet, moisten fingers with warm water and flatten buns. Rise again until about doubled in size. This dough may also be shaped into your favorite dinner roll. Bake at 400 degrees for about 10 minutes or until done.

Yield: 4 dozen

Helen Ediger is a lucky woman. Her warm, cozy kitchen is just right for sharing a "morning roll and coffee with my friends." She had it built to her specifications. Here she cooks for banquets and church dinners, Farm Bureau suppers, and farm sales.

Her Hamburger Buns recipe is an old Dutch recipe given to her by an "old crippled lady who lived next door to my husband's parents." Whenever they visited the aroma of warm bread would make mouths water. Helen says, "One day I asked this dear lady if we could have her recipe to enjoy. Little did she know that her recipe would become a family favorite. Her recipe and her memory have been fondly passed on to my children."

DORIS EWY
HALSTEAD, KANSAS

SWEEPSTAKES, REFRIGERATOR ROLLS, KANSAS STATE FAIR

SWEEPSTAKES, BREAD AND BUTTER PICKLES, HARVEY COUNTY FAIR

FIRST PRIZE, CHEESE DINNER ROLLS, HARVEY COUNTY FAIR KANSAS WHEAT COMMISSION

KANSAS REFRIGERATOR ROLLS

1 cup mashed potatoes
   (instant potato flakes can
   be used)
1 cup milk
½ cup shortening or butter
½ cup sugar

1½ tsp. salt
2 beaten eggs
1 pkg. (or 1 T.) dry yeast
¼ cup lukewarm water
5–6 cups flour

Melt butter, add milk, and cool to lukewarm in large mixing bowl. Add sugar, salt, eggs, and 2 cups of the flour. Dissolve yeast in warm water and add to first mixture. Beat thoroughly with electric mixer.

Gradually add enough of remaining flour to make stiff dough, mixing by hand or with a large spoon. Turn out on floured pastry cloth and knead until smooth, adding a little flour as needed to keep it from sticking.

Put back into bowl. Cover tightly. Refrigerate. When ready to use, work dough down and shape in any desired shape. Place on greased pan. Let rise until light. Bake at 375 degrees for about 20 minutes or until light brown.

"When I was growing up," said Doris Ewy, "I didn't much care for housework. I had three older sisters and an aunt living with us so I usually helped with the outdoor chores and field work instead of cooking. But, when I got married, that all changed. My husband was used to good cooking at home. So it was 'sink or swim' for me. I had a lot of flops but he never criticized or complained—he just wasn't very hungry that particular meal."

Doris told us about her worst cooking mistake: "My sister brought some sand from New Mexico to use in making bookends. She set the jar full on the pantry shelf. I thought it was white corn meal and tried to make corn bread out of it."

She cooks for three every day, "but with five married children and lots of grandchildren close by—hardly a week goes by without a houseful of people to cook for at least one day. Before our children were big enough to help out on the farm, there were always hired hands to cook for and then in season—there would be harvest crews of from 10 to 30 extra men to cook for three times a day."

KAREN EIFERT
WAUKOMIS, OKLAHOMA

FIRST PLACE, BREAD
WAUKOMIS COUNTY FAIR

FIRST PLACE, BREAD
RESERVE GRAND CHAMPION
OKLAHOMA WHEATHEART
BREAD-BAKING CONTEST

WHOLE WHEAT BREAD

2 pkgs. dry yeast	6 T. sugar
1 cup warm water	2 T. salt
3½ cups milk	5 cups whole wheat flour
¼ cup shortening	About 9 cups white flour

Dissolve the dry yeast in warm water (85 degrees). Stir in enough flour to make a thin paste. Let stand until yeast starts to rise, about 15 minutes. In a saucepan put milk, shortening, sugar, and salt, then place on a burner on low heat until shortening melts. Remove from fire and cool to lukewarm, then pour this mixture over the yeast paste. Stir in 5 cups whole wheat flour, then add enough white flour to make the dough easy to handle. (Do not make whole wheat dough too stiff, because the whole wheat flour swells.) Then pour on a floured board and knead for about 10 minutes. Leave the dough on the board for about 15 minutes, covering it first with your mixing bowl. Knead again for about 2 minutes. Place in a well-greased mixing bowl and cover with a damp cloth. Keep this in a warm place for 1½ hours or until it has risen to double the original size. Divide it into 3 equal parts and place in greased bread pans. Let stand for 30 minutes, then bake at 400 degrees for 30 minutes or until golden brown. Remove from pans and brush with butter.

My Mom's the finest cook on earth
And she told me long ago
That bread is no good unless you add
Some loving to the dough.

Karen is a sixteen-year-old Champion bread baker, and she put this rhyme on the *outside* of an envelope to us. She told us about herself, "I guess it could be said that I have grown up cooking with the help of my mother and three sisters and yes, sometimes even from Dad. We have a rather small, not too modern, farm kitchen so I have learned how to give and take with the rest of my family while cooking. I also enjoy the competitiveness of baking. This year I received Champion on my bread demonstration at the 4-H county contest."

She entered the Oklahoma Wheatheart Baking Contest on the county level in four categories—and received first place in each. "My whole wheat loaf was chosen as Grand Champion and I was honored with a trophy and a silver tray as well as a chance to send my bread on to the state contest, where I received first place and Reserve Grand Champion."

Her Whole Wheat Bread recipe, she says, "has been passed down in our family through the generations."

DORIA GAUTHIER
TOPENISH, WASHINGTON

BLUE RIBBON
WASHINGTON STATE FAIR
WASHINGTON STATE WHEAT
GROWER'S AWARD

DILL PUFFS

2 pkgs. dry yeast
½ cup warm water
2 cups cottage cheese
4 T. sugar
2 T. dry minced onion
  (dehydrated)

4 tsp. dill weed
2 tsp. salt
½ tsp. soda
2 eggs
4⅔ cups flour

Dissolve yeast in warm water. Heat cottage cheese until lukewarm. Stir in sugar, onion, dill weed, salt, and soda. Add yeast. Stir in eggs, then 2 cups flour. Add remaining flour more or less to make moderately stiff dough. Beat and cover. Let rise until double in bulk. Stir down. Divide into greased muffin pans. Bake at 350 degrees for 25 minutes. Brush tops with butter or margarine while still warm.

Yield: 2 dozen rolls

Try Doria's Mustard Bread with Beef (page 33), Beef Pop Up (page 33), and Roulade de Boeuf (page 34).

HAZEL GODFREY
CRESCENT, OKLAHOMA

FIRST PRIZE
LOGAN COUNTY FAIR
OKLAHOMA STATE FAIR

RAISED DOUGHNUTS

1 cup scalded milk
1 tsp. salt
¾ cup sugar
2 T. shortening
1 tsp. grated nutmeg

1 yeast cake, softened in
   ¼ cup warm water
3¼–4 cups flour
1 egg

Add scalded milk to salt, sugar, and fat. When lukewarm add the softened yeast. Add 1½ cups flour. Allow the sponge to stand in a warm place until it is so light that it will face at the slightest touch. Add the egg, nutmeg, and remainder of flour and knead. The dough should be softer than bread dough.

Cover and set in warm place to rise. Toss on lightly floured board and roll ¾-inch thick. Cut with a doughnut cutter and place on sheet pan. Let rise until doubled in bulk.

Fry in deep fat (360 to 370 degrees) 2 to 3 minutes. When frying, put the raised side of the doughnuts down in the fat. The heat will cause the top side to rise by the time the doughnuts are ready to turn.

Place only as many doughnuts as the fryer can allow, leaving room for them to float as they cook. When golden brown, use a fork to turn over the doughnut. Remove with a fork, and drain on paper towels. When completed, the doughnuts may be dipped in a thin icing or dusted with powdered sugar or granulated sugar to which cinnamon has been added. Place sugar in a brown paper bag and drop one or two doughnuts at a time and gently shake to coat.

Try Hazel's Pineapple Pie (page 281), Orange Raisin Pie (page 281) and Most Wonderful Toffee (page 367).

EVELYN GOOSEN
COLE CAMP, MISSOURI

WHITE BREAD
(Old-Fashioned Kind)

(Takes at least 7–8 hours)

    5 cups liquid (I use 3 cups water and 2 cups *unsalted* potato water)
    (Make sure temperature is 110 to 115 degrees.)

Add
    1 T. sugar; then add
    1 pkg. yeast
    Let set at least 5 minutes, then stir.

Measure 6 cups flour into sifter and sift into the liquid mixture. Beat well until tiny bubbles appear beneath the surface. Add 3 teaspoons salt and 3 tablespoons melted lard or shortening and mix well.

Measure 6½ cups flour into sifter and sift into the sponge batter. Work flour in with your hands; if you see any moist spots add a little more flour. Knead well for at least 10 minutes. It works well to let dough rest for 10 minutes or so. Then knead again until smooth and elastic. It's a good sign that the consistency is perfect if the dough "squeaks" when you finish kneading it. (Sometimes it won't do me the favor.)

Grease large container and place dough in same, greasing dough well. Cover and let rise in warm place, such as the oven with the light on.

I put a pan of hot water on rack beneath the dough when the room temperature is cool. Let rise until doubled; this may take 1½ to 2 hours. Work dough down and grease and let rise again for at least an hour or more.

Divide into 5 portions, shape into loaves, and place in 5 well-greased pans. Grease tops of loaves well. Place in warm place, such as a draft-free oven, and let rise until dough is light. This usually takes at least 2 hours.

Bake in a 350- to 375-degree oven around 40 minutes or until nicely browned. Immediately remove from pans and brush top with shortening or butter.

 "This recipe comes from my husband's grandma," says Evelyn, "she taught her daughter how to bake—who naturally is my mother-in-law. I learned the art of baking from her." After 31 years of marriage and raising four children, she's had lots of experience.

Evelyn says, "If anything takes practice, it is bread baking." Her advice on baking the old-fashioned bread is:

Proper water temperature.

Add *enough* flour before you begin to knead.

Cover dough with shortening and waxed paper or towel.
Let raise in warm place, such as the oven with the oven light on.
Give dough *enough time* to raise.
Be very sure to give at least 2 hours raising time after the loaves are formed.
This is the secret of "light-as-a-feather" bread.

You cannot bake good bread and "rush it."

ELIZABETH HERNANDES
ANCHORAGE, ALASKA

BUTTER ROLLS

Mix as you would for pie crust.

4 cups flour	½ cup sugar
1 cup shortening	½ tsp. salt

Dissolve dry yeast in ¼ cup warm milk. Beat 2 eggs, mix the yeast with 1 cup milk and add to first mixture. Cover and set in cool place overnight. Next morning divide into flour balls. Roll out like pizza and spread melted butter on it. Nuts may be added if desired. Cut as you would pizza and roll, starting at wide edge. Place on cookie sheet and let rise in warm place for 1½ hours. Bake at 350 degrees for 15 minutes or until golden brown—20 minutes.

Liz Hernandes specializes in yeast breads and pies. She says, "Being raised in fruit country, Yakima Valley, Washington, pies were just second nature."

Her advice to beginning cooks is to "start with your mother's time-tested recipes, the can't-fail type!" Liz is from a family of six and "since I was the eldest daughter I had the responsibility of cooking while my parents worked."

When we asked how many she cooks for, Liz said, "Eight—the Loan Department of Home Federal Savings and Loan in Anchorage where I work." She also told us about the first time she ever made bread: "It wouldn't stop rising. Even while baking, it rose so high it hit the top racks of the oven—I've been hooked on baking ever since."

Also try Liz's Alaskan Honey (page 392).

MARGIE McGLACHLIN

SEDGWICK, KANSAS

FIRST PLACE
BREAD BASKET
KANSAS STATE FAIR

CHEESE SESAME ROLLS

1 pkg. dry yeast	⅓ cup shortening
¼ cup warm water (110 degrees)	1 tsp. salt
	1 egg
1 tsp. sugar	2¾–3 cups flour
¾ cup milk (scalded)	1½ tsp. baking powder
2 T. sugar	

Dissolve yeast in warm water. Add 1 tsp. sugar to yeast mixture. Add shortening, 2 T. sugar, and salt to milk. Cool. Add ½ cup flour. Beat well. Add yeast mixture, egg, and ½ cup flour to which baking powder has been added. Beat again and add enough remaining flour to form a soft dough. Form into a ball. Let rest 10 minutes. Knead until smooth, adding more flour if necessary. Place in a lightly greased bowl, turning dough to grease entire surface. Cover and let rise until doubled in size. Divide into three equal parts. Let rest 5 minutes. Roll each ball into a 12-inch circle. Cut each circle into 12 wedges. Spread with butter and sprinkle with Parmesan cheese. Roll from outer edge to tip as for butterhorn rolls, and place tip of roll on baking sheet. Brush rolls with slightly beaten egg whites, sprinkle with sesame seeds which have been toasted slightly. Let rise until doubled. Bake at 400 degrees until golden brown (about 10 to 12 minutes).

Yield: 36 rolls

Try Margie's Lemon Lassie Cookies (page 333).

HERBERT D. MARZ
DETROIT, MICHIGAN

BLUE RIBBON, FIRST PRIZE
WHOLE WHEAT BREAD AND
RYE BREAD, MICHIGAN STATE FAIR

WHEAT BREAD

4 cups white flour
2½ cups whole wheat flour
1 T. salt
2 pkgs. instant dry yeast
3 T. shortening

½ cup honey
1 cup milk
1 cup water
1 egg

Mix together 1 cup white flour, all whole wheat flour, salt, and yeast. Heat honey, milk, and water to 120–130 degrees. Add shortening and let melt. Add liquid mixture to flour mixture and blend at low speed, adding egg. Gradually add more white flour until stiff.

Turn out and knead, using the rest of the flour if necessary. Use fingernail trick (jab finger into dough—if nail comes out clean it's ready to rise). Cover and let rise about 1 hour until doubled or until a finger hole punched in doesn't close up in a few minutes.

Punch down and shape into 2 loaves. Let rise about 30 minutes.

Preheat oven to 375 degrees. Bake 35–40 minutes until golden brown or until loaves sound hollow when tapped. Cool on rack. Brush on butter or oleo to soften crust.

RYE BREAD

3–4 cups white flour
3 cups rye flour (medium)
¼ cup sugar
1 T. salt

2 pkgs. active dry yeast
2¼ cups milk
¼ cup cooking oil
1 egg

Combine 2 cups white flour, sugar, salt, and yeast. Mix well.

Heat milk and oil to 120–130 degrees. (Never above 130 degrees, as it kills the yeast action to come.)

Stir together the heated liquid mixture with the flour mixture and beat well. Add egg during this mixing. (If you use an electric bread mixer, add the rye flour until the mixture follows the beaters—adding egg at this time.)

Turn out on a smooth surface and knead in rye (if any) and balance of white flour. Dough transforms from rough to smooth glob as you work. Stick finger into dough—if nail comes out clean it is ready to rise.

Let rise in greased covered pan or bowl until doubled in size. Keep warm— 80 to 85 degrees—for about an hour. Jab stiff finger into the dough—if the hole doesn't close it is through rising.

YEAST BREADS 135

Punch down and shape into 2 loaves. Let them rise until doubled—about 45 minutes.

Preheat oven to 350 degrees and bake 40–45 minutes or until loaves are golden brown and sound hollow when tapped. Cool on rack or else the loaves will sweat and get soggy on the bottom. Brush melted butter or oleo on top to soften crust if desired.

NOTE: Two teaspoons each of caraway and dill seeds make it a humdinger. I didn't use this in 1978; however, I do prefer the seeds in rye bread. Seeds go into mixture during the beating process.

Herbert Marz told us about himself as well as providing some helpful hints.

"Back in 1973, our local newspaper had an article on a retired army cook who baked bread just to have something to do. He gave away his loaves to neighbors, which proves the old adage, 'You don't have to eat it, just make it.' Out of curiosity I tried the recipe in that article and the bread came out terrible. So I took up the challenge and just kept changing the original recipe, adding mostly, until it became a smooth enjoyable hobby. As the work became more fun the taste seemed to improve.

"My daughter Anne Marie challenged me to enter the Michigan State Fair that year. I remember all the rushing to meet the August 1st deadline for entry. Although I took the easiest category, 'For Men Only,' I won a blue ribbon for white bread. Needless to say, our family was elated and I entered wheat bread in 1974, using a recipe I altered to suit my style of working. Behold! another blue ribbon.

"I plunged in on rye bread with a blue ribbon in mind. In 1975, 1976, and 1977 my rye bread prizewinning varied from zilch (zero) to a red ribbon (second place). In my diary through these years I noted a common denominator each day I baked—it was raining each time. It didn't take long to figure out the *lows* were prevalent weatherwise while I was wanting, praying, and wishing my rye dough would *rise* and look pretty.

"Therefore, in 1978 I made my entry to the fair on a bright sunny day and made six beautiful loaves of rye bread. I took the best two and froze them. At the fair that year, I captured that elusive blue ribbon. What made it even sweeter was that I had entered against the women of the state and won. I was very happy.

"Enclosed are the prizewinning recipes. As you know, the ingredients are the same everywhere—it's the baker who has the feel for good dough—who alters recipes to suit his particular talent, style, and preference."

HERB'S HELPFUL HINTS
FOR SUCCESSFUL BREAD BAKING

Bread rises best when the weather is sunny. I get two very different results in the natural rising of the yeast dough on a sunny day and a rainy day. So the aspiring to compete take note

Rye at best rises slowly so a pinch of yeast extra won't hurt. Using gluten flour substitute helps the heavy yeasts to rise. So you could substitute ½ cup of gluten flour for ½ cup of the *white* flour in any yeast bread recipe.

There is a high protein bromate flour on the market that makes a much better bread loaf than either the unbleached or the all-purpose flour.

I use a scale, rolling pin, and cutter to get two precisely even loaves. At fairs appearance means a great deal.

For uniformity, I flatten the dough to fit the pan and roll them like a cylinder (using a rolling pin). This also helps to make a neat preparation.

Eggs are usually kept refrigerated, so I place 1 egg in a cup of warm water for 15 minutes to take the chill off before adding to appropriate recipes.

CAROLE S. MORELOCK
GREENWOOD, INDIANA

HONEY OATMEAL BREAD

2 pkgs. dry yeast
½ cup warm water
1½ cups boiling water
1 cup quick-cooking
   rolled oats
½ cup honey
⅓ cup butter
1 T. salt

5½–6 cups all purpose sifted
   flour
2 beaten eggs
6–8 T. quick-cooking rolled
   oats
1 beaten egg white
1 T. water

Soften yeast in warm water. Combine boiling water, 1 cup rolled oats, honey, butter, and salt, cool to lukewarm. Stir in 2 cups flour and beat well. Add the softened yeast and 2 beaten eggs, and beat well again. Stir in enough of the remaining flour to make a soft dough. Turn out onto a lightly floured surface and knead until smooth and elastic, about 10 minutes, then shape into ball. Place into a greased bowl and turn over so that top of ball is greased. Cover and let rise in warm place until doubled (about 1½ hours). Punch down, turn out onto lightly floured surface, divide dough in half. Cover and let rest about 10 minutes. Grease 2 9x5-inch loaf pans with butter and sprinkle 2 tablespoons oats in each pan. Shape loaves and put in pans. Let rise till doubled (about 1 hour). Brush tops with mixture of beaten egg white and water, sprinkle tops with more oats. Bake at 375 degrees for 40 minutes. Cover with foil last 15 minutes to keep from browning too much. Remove from pans and cool on racks.

Yield: 2 loaves

 How do you get a good cook? Here is Carole Morelock's recipe: "You take one young girl, raised strictly city, who couldn't boil water, let alone cook a meal. Mix with one young man raised on the farm all his life, used to big meals, good food and a 4-H member in cooking, no less! Well, let me tell you, she had better learn fast in order to survive, especially when he cooks the meal for company and you have to admit your husband prepared the meal and baked the bread! So with a lot of tender loving care from one husband, a very understanding mother-in-law, and many mistakes, this city girl became a farm wife."

Now a Grand Champion cook, Carole Morelock adds this advice: "All children should be allowed to help in the kitchen at home, boys too! So that they will have some preparation for their future. It's just a matter of survival!"

Try Carole's Butter Crunch Nut Bread (page 190).

MRS. OSWALD MYRAN
WESSINGTON SPRINGS,
SOUTH DAKOTA

HONEY GRAHAM BREAD

7½ cups graham flour (or other
    dark flour)
5 cups white flour (more
    or less)
1 cup water (prefer potato
    water)

4 pkgs. yeast
2 T. salt
3½ cups lukewarm milk
1 cup honey
½ cup butter
¾ cup molasses

Scald milk, add honey, butter, molasses, salt, and potato water—stir in 2 cups white flour. Beat well. Add yeast dissolved in ½ cup warm water. Add graham flour and mix well. Add white flour to make moderately stiff dough. Knead well. Let rise till doubled in size. Let rise again and put in pans. Bake 50 minutes at 350 degrees.

Mrs. Myran has won many blue ribbons plus the coveted Home-makers Sweepstakes at the South Dakota State Fair.
    See her Watermelon Pickles (page 426), Beet Pickles (page 426), and Best-Ever Fudge (page 378), too.

SALLY PENNER
DAYTON, WASHINGTON

BREAD BAKING QUEEN
SPONSORED BY WASHINGTON
ASSOCIATION OF WHEATGROWERS
COLUMBIA COUNTY FAIR

HALF AND HALF BREAD
(Half Whole Wheat Flour and Half White)

2 T. yeast
1 tsp. sugar

1 cup warm water

Mix together and let stand till foamy (about 10 minutes).

½ cup shortening (or lard)
½ cup sugar or honey

2 cups milk
2 cups water

Heat to boiling, then cool to *lukewarm.*

2 tsp. salt
4 cups whole wheat flour

4–6 cups all-purpose flour

Pour lukewarm liquid into large bowl, add salt and whole wheat flour, mix, then add yeast mixture and enough white flour to make a soft dough. Turn out onto floured board, and knead till smooth and elastic, and no longer sticky, at least 5 minutes (when you can press your hand on the dough, count to 10, and lift your hand without the dough sticking, it's enough). Return dough to lightly greased bowl, grease top by turning dough in bowl, cover with a towel, and let rise in warm place till doubled in bulk, punch down, let rise again. Turn onto lightly floured board, form into buns and loaves, place into greased pans, brush tops with melted shortening, and let rise again. Bake buns for 20–25 minutes at 350 degrees, loaves for 50–60 minutes, till golden brown.

Yield: 15 hamburger buns and 2 1-pound loaves

 "A few years ago we purchased a Magic Mill Home Wheat Grinder, and started grinding our own wheat into flour. However, we do raise white wheat in this area, which doesn't have the gluten content of hard red wheat, so part of the time we purchase cleaned hard red from our feed mill, and grind that for the whole wheat flour."

Sally said she learned to cook by "marrying a farmer, raising four children, and boarding seasonal hired help our first 20 years of marriage. Cooked for 15 to 18 men in our wheat harvest crews. My mother and mother-in-law are both good cooks, so I received lots of helpful hints and good recipes from them, too."

Her cooking advice is to "get things done ahead of time as much as possible, don't leave too many things till the last minute, then be so rushed that you forget part of them." She also said she "can think of no other smell or taste that compares with fresh-baked yeast bread just out of the oven!" Agreed.

PAT PETERSON
BOISE, IDAHO

FIRST PLACE
CARIBOU COUNTY FAIR, IDAHO

WHOLE WHEAT BREAD

2 T. yeast
3 T. brown sugar

4 T. bran
5 cups warm water

Sprinkle yeast on top of water, add other ingredients, let stand. Then add 4 cups of whole wheat flour.

2 cups of sour dough starter
2 T. salt
6 T. oil

1 cup powdered milk
4 T. whey powder

Mix in 2 more cups whole wheat flour. Let stand 10 more minutes to soften and the wheat absorbs some of the moisture.

Add 3 to 4 cups white flour, knead, add whole wheat flour until you can work it. The mixture will be sticky so grease hands to work with dough. Bake at 350 degrees for 35 to 40 minutes.

Yield: 5 loaves

Pat also saves money by making her own Sour Dough Starter. She dissolves ½ teaspoon of dry yeast in ¾ cup of warm water or milk, then stirs in ¾ cup of whole wheat flour. This is covered and stored in a warm place. Make sure that there is an air hole in the cover so any gases can escape. The container must be high enough to hold the rising mixture. Allow 18 to 20 hours to develop. Pat prepared her starter one day in advance. This recipe is enough for two loaves, with about ¼ cup left over, to substitute for yeast in the next batch.

Ten years ago Pat started using whole wheat flour that she grinds at home for all her baking. She found that her baked goods, including her cookies, pies, breads and cakes not only tasted better—her family's health improved and she has saved a lot of money.

Pat uses an All Grain Mill, a hand-cranked grinder with a stone inside, so her flour is stone ground flour. Both whole wheat and stone ground flour are now available in most markets, but Pat believes home ground to be better tasting and more nutritious.

She uses her grinder three times a week and grinds 5 to 7 pounds of flour at a time. One hundred pounds of Turkey Red, a hard, winter wheat is about ten dollars and this is enough for three months baking.

Pat buys very little white flour or flour products. For example, she does not serve cereal. Her children get a hot breakfast every day of foods like French toast or waffles or coffee cake, all made from this flour.

The grinder produces flour as fine as face powder, fine enough to use in cakes and even pic crusts.

A side benefit, according to Pat, is that the family medical and pharmacy bills have gone down at least by half. She attributes this to the higher nutrient content and freshness of her home ground flour.

MARIE PUTTLITZ
UNDERHILL, VERMONT

GRAND PRIZE SWEEPSTAKES, YEAST DIVISION
CHAMPLAIN VALLEY FAIR

MARIE'S STOLLEN

1 cup raisins	1 cup butter
1 cup mixed candied fruit	2 T. active dry yeast
(soaked in ¼ cup of rum	¼ cup warm water
overnight)	2 eggs, beaten
¼ cup orange juice	1 tsp. grated lemon rind
¾ cup milk	5 cups sifted flour
½ cup sugar	1 cup chopped nuts
2 tsp. salt	

Combine fruits and orange juice in a bowl. Scald milk with sugar, salt, and ½ cup butter. Cool to lukewarm. Sprinkle yeast into water in large bowl till yeast dissolves, then stir in cooled milk mixture, eggs, and lemon rind. Beat in 2 cups of flour until smooth. Stir in fruit mixture and nuts.

Beat in just enough flour to make a stiff dough. Knead until smooth and elastic, adding just enough flour to keep dough from sticking. Place in greased large bowl. Cover with towel. Let rise until doubled. Punch down dough, knead a few times, and divide in half. Roll each into an oval 15x9 inches. Place on greased cookie sheet. Melt remaining ½ cup of butter in small saucepan and brush over each oval. Sprinkle with sugar. Fold in half lengthwise, cover, let rise again until doubled. Brush with part of remaining melted butter, bake in 350-degree oven for 30–35 minutes, or until golden brown and loaves give a hollow sound when tapped.

While hot, brush with remaining melted butter. Cool on wire rack, then sprinkle with powdered sugar.

Marie Puttlitz cooks in a modern contemporary kitchen equipped with a microwave oven and a Jennaire range as well as a conventional oven. When we asked how she learned to cook, she said, "Some at home, some things I learned from friends, but mostly trial and error."

In the first year of her marriage she cooked three pounds of spaghetti for just three people! Although she is Italian and had grown up eating Italian food, she had never cooked much because her relatives always helped.

SELMA RODENBERG
NAPOLEON, MISSOURI

BLUE RIBBON, BREAD
MISSOURI STATE FAIR

SELMA'S SUGAR 'N' SPICE BREAD

2 pkgs. dry yeast
½ cups warm water
½ cup butter or oleo
⅓ cup sugar
2 tsp. salt

1 cup milk, scalded
1 egg, beaten
½ cup Malt O Meal (plain)
4–4½ cups all-purpose flour

FILLING

2–3 T. butter
½ cup sugar

⅔ tsp. cinnamon
1 cup raisins (optional)

Never let the yeast get in contact with the lard until a little flour is added. The shortening coats the yeast and it is slower in rising. (Learned by doing.)

Soften yeast in warm water, set aside. Combine sugar, salt, and butter and lukewarm milk. Add egg, yeast, Malt O Meal, and 2 cups flour. Beat until smooth. Add rest of the flour to make a stiff dough.

Let rise till doubled in a warm place. Divide dough in half and roll each half into 7x12-inch rectangle on a floured board. Spread half the filling on each half. Sprinkle with cinnamon and sugar mixture. Put half the raisins on. Roll up like a jelly roll. Put in greased bread pan. Let rise until doubled. Bake at 375 degrees for 35–40 minutes. Put any kind of powdered sugar icing on top while hot.

Selma is a longtime prizewinner. She and her husband Alfred have won more than 6,000 ribbons—for flowers, quilting, and handwork as well as canning, baking, and cookies.

They started exhibiting in 1927 and "year by year went all out." Although Selma is now 78 (she's been cooking for 70 years) and has recently had eye surgery, she is planning lots of entries for this year.

DINNER ROLLS

1 cup milk, scalded
2 tsp. melted shortening
2 tsp. sugar
1 tsp. salt
1 cake fresh or 1 pkg.
    granular yeast

¼ cup lukewarm water
1 beaten egg
3½ cups flour

Mix by hand in 3-quart mixing bowl.

Combine milk, shortening, sugar, and salt. Cool to lukewarm. Add yeast softened in lukewarm water and then add egg. Gradually stir in flour to form soft dough. Beat vigorously. Cover and let rise in warm place until doubled in bulk, about 2 hours. Form into desired shapes and let rise until doubled. Bake in moderately hot oven (400 degrees) for 15–20 minutes or until a golden brown.

Yield: 3 dozen rolls

Try Betty's Fried Cakes (page 260).

KAREN SCHAAN
MINOT, NORTH DAKOTA

KAREN'S SWEET DOUGH BUNS

1½ cups lukewarm milk
½ cup white sugar
2 tsp. salt
2 pkgs. (or 5 T.) softened
    yeast

½ cup lukewarm water
2 eggs
½ cup oil
7–7½ cups flour

Heat milk to lukewarm. Add sugar and salt. Cool. Soften yeast in lukewarm water for 5 minutes. Stir well before adding to mixture. Add eggs, oil, and 3 cups flour, mixing well. Continue adding flour and mixing well. (When too hard to mix in flour with the spoon, turn out on lightly floured board and let rest for 10 minutes.) Knead in balance of flour or until smooth and elastic. Place in greased bowl after making into a round ball, with the greased side up. Cover with a cloth and let rise in a warm place (85 degrees) until doubled, about 1½ hours. Punch down and let rise again until amost doubled (about 30 minutes). Divide dough for buns or sweet rolls. Shape and let rise. Bake at 375 degrees for 12–15 minutes.

Karen Schaan is fourteen years old and has been cooking since she was six. She started out helping her mother and then learned through 4-H.

She enjoys trying out new recipes and has also taken top honors with her Prize Gingersnaps.

CONNIE SIMPSON
PUEBLO, COLORADO

BUTTERHORNS AND CRESCENTS

Soften 1 package active dry yeast in ¼ cup warm water (110 degrees). Combine ¾ cup milk, scalded, ½ cup shortening, ½ cup sugar, and 2 teaspoons salt; cool to lukewarm. Add 1 cup sifted all-purpose flour. Add yeast and 3 eggs; beat well.

Stir in 3½–3¾ cups flour, sifted. Add enough to make a soft dough. Knead on lightly floured surface 5–8 minutes.

Place dough in greased bowl, turning once to grease surface; cover and let rise till doubled (about 2½ hours). Turn out on lightly floured surface. Divide dough into thirds, roll each third into a 12-inch circle. Cut into wedges. Beginning at wide end roll to point—place pinched point down, curve for crescents. Bake at 350 degrees for 10–12 minutes, on top rack. (NOTE: These directions are for high-altitude cooking.)

Connie Simpson won the Queen of the Kitchen Award (and a microwave oven) at the Colorado State Fair. In order to be an entrant "You had to enter 12 categories and place in 10 of them." Connie entered 14 categories and placed in all 14! The Queen of the Kitchen was selected on the basis of total points won: blue ribbon, 3 points; red, 2 points; and white, 1 point.

How did Connie learn to cook? Not as a girl, as so many of our winners did. "After I was married I had to learn to cook so I bought my first recipe book and began to learn 'from scratch.'"

Her kitchen is efficient—she designed it "after living in two that weren't designed by women who cooked." Connie's kitchen has plenty of counter space, double ovens, Jennaire range, and lots of storage.

She told us of one mistake that we can all sympathize with: "I left some hamburger to cook on what I thought was low, I turned it too high by mistake. We came back from the neighbors to find a house filled with smoke, the cast-iron skillet was bowed in the middle, the hamburger disintegrated, yellow film on everything in the kitchen and dining room, but worst of all, an awful smell! It's funny now, but wasn't at the time, because it took all the next day to clean walls, ceiling, furniture, curtains, and the smell wasn't gone for two weeks."

Although Connie has only been competing for four years she has won an amazing number of prizes and ribbons. "Four years ago I got interested in the fair and cake decorating. I wanted to enter for the money and sugar I might win. My husband was all for it but he said he didn't want me to be too upset if I didn't win anything. That first year I won 7 ribbons out of 20 items entered. I was so excited. 1976 was a special year because of the Centennial and Bi-Centennial celebrations. Colorado was 100 years old. They had special categories, I won two first-place medals, one for Corncob Jelly, and one for Homemade Soap."

About her recipe for Butterhorns and Crescents, Connie says, "This recipe never has failed. I've won a blue and red ribbon on these. They are very good and almost melt in your mouth."

JOY SLAUBAUGH
WOLFORD, NORTH DAKOTA

CARAMEL ROLLS AND FANCY DINNER BUNS

1 qt. milk, scalded and cooled to lukewarm
2 cakes yeast dissolved in ¼ cup warm water (let rise
    to fill cup)
4 tsp. salt
3 beaten eggs
1 cup oil or melted shortening
1 cup sugar
About 12 cups flour, or enough for soft dough

Mix. Knead 10 minutes. Let rise 1 hour, punch down. Rise 45 minutes. Shape into buns or for rolls spread dough, butter, then sugar and cinnamon the dough. Roll up and slice.

CARAMEL

1 cup brown sugar
1 stick margarine
¼ cup white syrup

¼ tsp. soda
Pinch of salt

Combine brown sugar, margarine, and white syrup. Cook 4 minutes. Stir in soda and salt. (Make sure all sugar crystals are melted.)

Pour caramel on bottom of pan, then put rolls in pan (usually 9-inch). Let buns or rolls rise 2 hours. Bake at 350–375 degrees for 12 to 15 minutes.

NOTE: I usually knead longer than 10 minutes. I also knead each bun a minute or two before placing on bun sheet. This is not necessary but makes for finer dough texture.

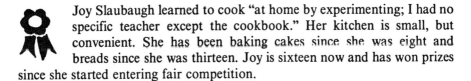

Joy Slaubaugh learned to cook "at home by experimenting; I had no specific teacher except the cookbook." Her kitchen is small, but convenient. She has been baking cakes since she was eight and breads since she was thirteen. Joy is sixteen now and has won prizes since she started entering fair competition.

JOSEPHINE SMITH
WICHITA, KANSAS

GOVERNOR'S COOKIE JAR
ARCHWAY COOKIE AWARD
(600 RIBBONS, 19 SWEEPSTAKES)

MRS. SMITH'S HOLIDAY BREAD

2 pkgs. active dry yeast	1 tsp. grated orange rind
¼ cup lukewarm water	1 T. salt
2 cups milk, scalded	¼ tsp. cardamon
⅔ cup margarine	2 eggs, beaten
⅔ cup granulated sugar	7–8 cups all-pure flour

Soften yeast in warm water; set aside. Combine milk, shortening, sugar, and salt, cool to lukewarm. Add softened yeast and eggs, mixing well. Gradually add flour, mixing thoroughly. Put out on floured surface and knead, adding enough flour until it is no longer sticky. Put in greased bowl and cover. Let rise until doubled in bulk. Punch down. Divide dough in half. Let rest for 5 minutes. Roll out each part to make a long, flat loaf 6 inches wide. Place on a greased cookie sheet. Spread filling down center of each loaf. Cut dough in small strips on each side almost to the filling; crisscross strips across filling. Let rise until doubled. Bake in 350-degree oven for 40 minutes.

FILLING

1 lb. chopped dates	½ cup chopped nuts
½ cup water	¼ cup maraschino cherries
¼ cup brown sugar	

Combine all ingredients and cook until thick, stirring. Cool.

Try her Tropical Fruit Cookies (page 341).

CINNAMON ROLLS

1 stick margarine
4 T. sugar
½ tsp. salt
1 cup scalded milk
1 pkg. active dry yeast

¼ cup lukewarm water
4 cups all-purpose sifted flour
1 egg, well beaten
Cinnamon

Add the margarine, sugar, and salt to the scalded milk. Stir until margarine has melted. When the milk has cooled to lukewarm, add the yeast dissolved in the ¼ cup lukewarm water, then stir all this together. Add 2 cups of flour and beat with spoon, then add one more cup flour and beat with spoon until your arm gets tired, then beat again until your arm gets tired. Now cover top of bowl with foil paper. Set in a warm place and let rise about one hour. Beat the dough again, then add the well-beaten egg and beat again.

Now add the fourth cup of flour, one-half cup at a time, and beat after each addition.

Now turn onto a floured board and knead until smooth. Be careful and don't get the dough too stiff (just so you can handle the dough).

Put the dough in a lightly greased bowl, cover, and let rise until doubled in bulk (about 40 minutes). Now punch down and let rest about 5 minutes, now pinch the dough in half and roll each half of dough out in a rectangular sheet and cut medium pieces of margarine and put around over the dough.

Sprinkle between a quarter and a half cup of sugar over the margarine on the dough, then take the cinnamon box and sprinkle around over the margarine and sugar. Now roll dough up like a jelly roll and cut in about 1-inch pieces, or a little thicker. I get 7 or 8 rolls out of half of the dough. Put them in a lightly greased pan and let rise until doubled in bulk (about 40 minutes). When you first put the rolls in the oven, have oven set at 375 degrees and let them bake until they start to brown, then turn oven to 350 degrees and let them finish browning. When you take them out of the oven, grease them with margarine while they are hot, then ice them with powdered sugar icing. While the rolls are hot, take them out of the pans and put on cooling racks.

PINEAPPLE-RAISIN TEA RING

A simple-to-shape coffee cake with filling of pineapple, raisins, cinnamon, and brown sugar.

Bake at 375 degrees for 20 to 25 minutes. Makes 2 tea rings.

SOFTEN:

2 packets active dry yeast (or 2 cakes compressed) in ¼ cup warm water

COMBINE:

½ cup sugar
¼ cup shortening
1 tsp. salt*
1 cup hot scalded milk in large mixing bowl. Cool to lukewarm.

STIR IN:

2 unbeaten eggs and softened yeast

ADD:

5–5½ cups sifted all-purpose flour gradually to form a stiff dough.

KNEAD:

on floured surface until smooth and satiny, 5 to 8 minutes. Place in greased bowl and cover in warm place (85 degrees)

LET RISE:

until doubled, 1 to 1½ hours.

DIVIDE:

dough in half. Roll out one portion on floured surface to 20x12-inch rectangle. Brush with melted butter. Spread with half the filling to within 1 inch of one long side and to edge of other sides.

COMBINE:

⅓ cup firmly packed brown sugar and 2 teaspoons cinnamon; sprinkle half over filling on dough.

SHAPE:

Roll as for jelly roll, starting with covered 20-inch edge, into a ring on greased baking sheet. With scissors, make cuts 1 inch apart through top of ring to 1 inch from bottom. Alternate cut slices, bringing one to the center and the next to the outside of the ring. Cover. Repeat entire process with remaining dough.

LET RISE:

in warm place until light, 45 to 60 minutes.

BAKE:

at 375 degrees for 20 to 25 minutes. While warm, frost with vanilla glaze. Garnish with chopped nuts and maraschino cherry halves.

*Omit salt with self-rising flour.

PINEAPPLE RAISIN FILLING

COMBINE IN SAUCEPAN:

1 No. 2 can crushed pineapple (1½ cups), well drained
¾ cup sugar
1 T. cornstarch
Cook over medium heat until thick. Add ½ cup raisins. Cool.

VANILLA GLAZE

1 cup sifted confectioners sugar
2 T. cream
½ tsp. vanilla
Blend and beat until of spreading consistency.

Minnie Snedeker still lives on the farm that was her own land allotment as a member of the official Choctaw Indian rolls. She is of Choctaw Indian and German heritage, and she "loves everything of quality and beauty." She is the mother of eight living children, the grandmother of twelve, and great-grandmother of seven.

Her daughter, Joyce Snedeker Thomas of Dallas, Texas, told us about her mother's accomplishment with so much loving pride that we want to share her words with you.

"Mom is eighty-one years young, a person who refuses to grow old, but accepts her years gracefully. She still plays 'tag' her own style with her grandchildren. Her natural creative ability is revealed in both cooking and ceramics.

"Born in Bokchito, Oklahoma, before statehood, she eventually moved to the area then known as Chicbasha Indian Territory; the original deed to this Indian land allotment is still in her possession. She married in the early 1900s and was widowed as a result of my father's heart attack in early 1966. Mom learned to cook from her mother and her aunts. She says that she has been cooking ever since she can remember.

"As a child, I can still remember her large country breakfasts with 'home grown' eggs, bacon or ham, fresh milk, and a large black pan full of fluffy, homemade biscuits which were made by making 'a well' in the bowl of flour and putting 'a pinch of this' and 'a dab of that'—and 'add enough milk and work in the flour until it looks about right'."

Joyce adds, "Following sufficient kneading on a floured surface, the biscuits were then pinched off, brushed on both sides with melted shortening, placed in the pan side by side, then popped into the hot oven. You have *never* tasted biscuits like those. Probably the most regal of her breadmaking was the four large loaves of homemade yeast bread made *every day* from everlasting yeast. This was started early in the morning, allowed to rise once in a large bowl, then made into loaves. The four loaves, after much kneading and turning, were placed into a large, blue granite flat-bottom pan; after rising sufficiently they were placed into the large oven heated by kerosene.

"The delicate aroma that filled the air had all of us primed for a contest to get the end slice or 'heel'; not only did we kids feast like royalty, her prize bronze turkeys were treated accordingly. A portion of their food was composed of leftover homemade light bread soaked in clabber milk. Mom said that nothing gave them the growth start like yeast bread.

"Her theory was proven in the hundreds of glistening feathers dancing in the autumn sun as the flock of several hundred beautiful, bronze birds were gathered for the market. Many, many of these were sold 'dressed and drawn' by my mother's skilled hand.

"Our winter food was prepared fresh from the garden, canned in one-half-gallon jars, and stored in our dirt cellar. Our family garden looked like a produce marketeer's, with an abundant variety of vegetables, always planted by the almanac signs.

"The only purchased grocery items were flour, sugar, and other staples. The remainder came from the good earth, the family toil and cattle and hogs produced on the farm. Cows produced enough milk; sides of beef hung from the windmill and chilled in the cold Oklahoma wind. Hams, side bacon, and pork shoulders were sugar cured and hung on large hooks on our back porch. Sausage was ground, seasoned, cooked, and canned.

"Our desserts were special, homemade pies, white coconut cake, plain chocolate cake, and best of all, homemade yeast cinnamon rolls that literally melted in your mouth.

"About midcentury, our farm was converted into a full dairy farm. It was in the late sixties, after retirement from dairy farming and after my father died, that my mother's artistic hands began to enter new areas. At the age of seventy she won the Oklahoma State Fair Sweepstakes in the Yeast Breads division. My mother has always placed on all entries entered since 1968, winning many ribbons and a variety of prizes. However, her greatest award comes from the light in the eyes of her children and grandchildren when a homemade cinnamon roll gradually melts into the inner being.

"Mom says that some of her secrets with yeast breads are:

1. The way the dough is handled. Overhandling makes for tough dough.
2. Use your own judgment in the amount of flour (most recipes call for too much).
3. Handle the dough with greased hands—never floured.
4. When using butter (on cinnamon rolls for example), *never* melt it, but place about the dough in small pieces so it will melt into the dough.
5. When shaping a tea ring: Take a pizza pan and cover with heavy foil. Then take a small stainless steel bowl and wrap it in foil. Put the bowl in the center of the pizza pan. Put the dough around the bowl and jam ends of the dough together. Cut the dough—then pull the sides of the foil up to make a pan."

In conclusion, Joyce adds, "Two of her children, myself included, are professional home economists, but we can't make yeast breads like *my Mom*."

STELLA TESSIN

SAGINAW, MICHIGAN

RYE BREAD

1½ cups hot water
1 T. sugar
1 T. salt
2 T. margarine
½ cup warm water
1 pkg. yeast
3 cups rye flour
2½ cups white flour

Measure hot water into a mixing bowl. Stir in sugar, salt, and margarine. Cool to lukewarm. Measure warm water in a small bowl. Sprinkle yeast. Stir to dissolve. Add yeast mixture and rye flour to lukewarm water mixture. Beat till smooth. Add 2 cups white flour and mix well. Add enough additional flour to make a soft dough. Turn onto lightly floured board and knead till smooth and elastic, about 8–10 minutes. Place in greased bowl, turning to grease all sides. Cover, let rise in warm place till doubled in bulk, about 45 minutes. Punch dough down. Divide in half. Shape into loaves, place in greased 9x5x3-inch loaf pans. Cover, let rise in warm place until doubled in size, about 40 minutes. Bake in hot oven (400 degrees) about 25 minutes.

Stella cooks for eight every day, and she has been cooking for 38 years. She works in a farm kitchen, and learned to cook "at home, from Mother, and from my own experience."

She advised others to "follow instructions, use good ingredients, fresh vegetables, fruits, for better flavor."

WILLIAM R. TULLY
LOUISVILLE, KENTUCKY

BATTER BREAD—CHEESE-BACON BREAD

1¼ cups warm (110–115
   degrees) water
1 pkg. active dry yeast
3 T. bacon drippings
3 strips of crisp bacon,
   crumbled
1½ tsp. salt
1 T. sugar

1 tsp. dry mustard
1 tsp. parsley flakes
Pinch each nutmeg and celery
   salt
5 oz. extra-sharp Cheddar
   cheese, grated
3 cups all-purpose flour

Mix all ingredients thoroughly and beat 300 vigorous strokes, scrape batter from sides of bowl, cover with damp cloth, and let rise until doubled in warm place.

Stir down by beating about 25 strokes. Spread evenly in greased loaf pan, pat down with floured hands till smooth.

Let rise again till batter is 1 inch from top of pan. Bake at 375 degrees for 45–50 minutes. Remove from oven 5 minutes before finished baking and sprinkle top with poppy seeds and grated Cheddar cheese. Return to oven till done. Remove and cool.

Try Bill's Coffee Cake (page 205).

RAISIN BREAD

6–6½ cups sifted all-purpose
    flour
1 pkg. active dry yeast
2¼ cups milk
½ cup sugar

½ cup shortening
2 tsp. salt
2 cups raisins (or 1 cup
    raisins and 1 cup nuts)

In mixer bowl, combine 3 cups of the flour and the yeast. In saucepan, heat together milk, sugar, shortening, and salt just till warm, stirring occasionally to melt shortening. Add to dry ingredients in mixer bowl. Beat at low speed of electric mixer for ½ minute, scraping sides of bowl constantly. Beat 3 minutes at high speed. By hand, stir in raisins and enough of the remaining flour to make a moderately stiff dough. Turn out on lightly floured surface; knead till smooth, about 5 minutes. Place in greased bowl, turning once to grease surface. Cover; let rise till doubled, about 1¼ hours. Punch down; divide dough in half. Cover and let rest 10 minutes. Shape in 2 loaves. Place in 2 greased 9x5x3-inch loaf pans. Cover and let rise till double, about 1 hour. Bake in 375-degree oven for 35–40 minutes. Remove from pans; cool. Frost with confectioners sugar icing.

Yield: 2 loaves

"I learned to bake myself, by trial and error. The first few times were not so good," says Sweepstakes winner Marie Vercauteren. Her kitchen is "always busy" with her baking and regular cooking for four.

FRENCH BREAD

2½ cups warm water	7 cups flour
2 pkgs. dry yeast	Corn meal
1 T. salt	1 egg white
1 T. salad oil	1 T. cold water
1 T. sugar	Poppy seeds

Add sugar to warm water in mixing bowl. Sprinkle in dry yeast and dissolve. Let stand 5 minutes, then add flour, salt, and oil. Beat until smooth and work with hands—dough will be sticky. Place in greased bowl, turning to grease top. Cover and let rise until doubled in bulk (about 1 hour). Divide dough in half and roll each half into a 15x10-inch oblong. Roll tightly like a jelly roll from the wide side, seal edges, and taper ends by rolling gently. Place loaves on greased baking sheet sprinkled with corn meal. Let rise until doubled. Slash 4 diagonal cuts in each loaf with sharp knife or razor blade. Bake in 450-degree oven for 25 minutes. Remove from oven, brush with egg white mixed with water. Sprinkle with poppy seeds, return to oven, and bake 5 minutes longer.

When she first started cooking, Blanche told us, "I didn't realize that beans had to be sorted, so I served company beans with rocks in them." She advises other cooks: "Don't be afraid to try new recipes and methods. The least amount of flour that you can add to bread and still have it workable will produce the best bread." Blanche knows—she has won a number of blue ribbons for her breads.

About this recipe she says, "It makes a French bread with a tender and crisp crust, and moist, soft texture inside."

BONNIE WIGGINS
SOUTH PORTLAND, MAINE

FIRST PRIZE, WHOLE
WHEAT BREAD
CUMBERLAND FAIR, MAINE

WHOLE WHEAT DINNER ROLLS

2 cups water	½ cup sugar
¾ cup shortening or oil	2 tsp. salt
2 T. molasses	2 pkgs. dry yeast
3¾–4½ cups all-purpose flour	2 eggs
3 cups whole wheat flour	

In small saucepan, heat first 3 ingredients until very warm (120–130 degrees). In large bowl, blend warm liquids, 2 cups all-purpose flour, 1 cup whole wheat flour, sugar, salt, yeast, and eggs at low speed until moistened. Beat 4 minutes at medium speed. By hand, stir in remaining whole wheat flour and enough all-purpose flour to form a stiff dough. Knead on floured surface until smooth and elastic, about 5 minutes. Place dough in greased bowl; turn greased side up, cover; let rise in warm place until light and doubled in size (45 minutes). Grease one 13x9-inch pan and one 8-inch-square pan. Punch down dough. Divide dough in 36 pieces. Shape into balls. Place in prepared pans. Cover and let rise in warm place until light and doubled in size (30–45 minutes). Bake at 375 degrees for 15–20 minutes until rolls sound hollow when lightly tapped. Remove from pans and brush with butter.

Bonnie has some good advice: "Be smarter, don't work harder—clean up as you go. You won't have a large mess after work."

Every good cook seems to have a special dish he or she wants to perfect. For Bonnie, pies are a problem. She can't seem to get the tender crust she wants. Yet her rolls are prizewinners, and most cooks think they are difficult to make.

FLOSSIE WILDER
LAWRENCEBURG, TENNESSEE

YEAST BREAD

2 pkgs. dry yeast
½ cup lukewarm water
2 cups buttermilk
3 T. sugar

4 T. cooking oil or melted
   shortening
6½ cups self-rising flour

Dissolve yeast in lukewarm water. Heat buttermilk, add sugar and shortening. When lukewarm add to yeast. Stir in 3 cups flour to make soft dough. Knead dough and put back in crock to rise an hour. Divide dough in half. Roll with rolling pin until air bubbles are broken up. Shape into loaves and bake at 350 degrees for 45 minutes.

 "I seldom use a recipe," says Flossie Wilder. "In fact I had to bake some yeast bread and measure ingredients for this recipe. This is an original recipe made with buttermilk. My mother taught me to make bread.

"We raised our own wheat and had good flour—but lately I can't make good bread from plain flour in the stores, so I came up with this buttermilk and self-rising flour."

Flossie is a champion cook who has "been entering different things in fairs practically all my life." (She's been cooking for 60 years.) She learned to cook "through observing my mother at an early age. I belonged to the 4-H clubs and Home Demonstration Club, and also had home ec in high school."

Flossie has another tip for us: "I've learned when making cooked icing to have the room warm and dry."

CHAPTER
EIGHT

NONYEAST BREADS, SPECIALTY BREADS, AND COFFEE CAKES

NONYEAST BREAD-MUFFINS

Shape: well-proportioned

Evenly rounded top,
cracking of top is OK

Texture: tender, light flavor
—all ingredients blended
in baking (not over-mixed)

Crumb: light
and cake-like

Powell

MARIE ARNOLD
SANTA ROSA, CALIFORNIA

ENGLISH MUFFIN BREAD

2½–3 cups all-purpose flour
1 pkg. active dry yeast
1¼ cups water

1 T. sugar
¾ tsp. salt
Corn meal

In large mixer bowl combine 1 cup of the flour and the yeast. In saucepan heat water, sugar, and salt till warm (115–120 degrees), stirring to dissolve sugar. Add to dry mixture in bowl. Beat at low speed with electric mixer for 1 minute, scraping bowl. Beat 3 minutes at high speed. By hand, stir in enough remaining flour to make a soft dough. Shape into ball.

Place in lightly greased bowl; turn once to grease surface. Cover; let rise 10 minutes. Grease a 1-quart casserole; sprinkle with corn meal. Place dough in casserole; sprinkle top with corn meal. Cover; let rise till doubled (30 to 45 minutes). Bake at 400 degrees for 40–45 minutes. Cover loosely with foil if top browns too quickly. Remove from dish; cool.

Yield: 1 loaf

Marie learned "from my mother at home, six years of cooking classes at school and—six years of marriage." Working in her modern, well-equipped kitchen, she cooks for four every day and is hoping to enter more recipes in the fair this year.

DORIS BARB
ELDORADO, KANSAS

FIRST PLACE, QUICK BRAN BREAD
KANSAS STATE FAIR

BRAN BREAD
(Quick)

1½ cups 100% bran cereal
½ cup chopped dates

2 T. grated orange rind
½ cup hot water

Combine the bran, dates and orange rind; add the hot water and blend.

CREAM TOGETHER:

½ stick butter or margarine and ½ cup firmly packed brown sugar. Add 1 large egg, slightly beaten. Sift together 1½ cups all-purpose flour, 1½ teaspoons soda, and ¼ teaspoon salt. Add the dry ingredients to creamed mixture, alternately with 1 cup buttermilk. Add this to the bran mixture. Bake in 2 small loaf pans (3x7 inches) at 350 degrees for 1 hour.

Try Doris's Butterscotch Oatmeal Chips (page 307).

ROSE NEWPOWER
ST. PAUL, MINNESOTA

TWIN TWIRL COFFEE CAKE

3 T. sugar
1 tsp. salt
3 T. shortening
¾ cup milk, scalded
1 pkg. dry yeast

¼ cup warm water
1 egg, beaten
About 3 cups of flour
2 T. grated orange rind
2 T. grated lemon rind

Add sugar, salt and shortening to milk, which has been scalded. Cool to lukewarm. Soften yeast in ¼ cup lukewarm water. Add to milk mixture when lukewarm. Add egg. Add half of flour and rind. Mix well. Add remaining flour, small amount at a time, mixing well after each addition. Put out on floured board and knead until smooth and satiny, about 5 minutes. Place in greased bowl. Cover and let rise in warm place until doubled in bulk (about 1½–2 hours). Punch down. Roll out on lightly floured board to a 13x10 inch rectangle. Brush lightly with melted butter and sprinkle generously with sugar and cinnamon. Starting at each end (long way of the dough) roll, as for a jelly roll until 2 rolls meet at center. Place on well greased baking sheet. With scissors, make deep cuts into outer sides of each roll of dough, about 2 inches apart. Turn or twist each slice, cut side up. Press down slightly. Cover and let rise until doubled. Bake at 375 degrees about 20–25 minutes until lightly browned.

When slightly cooled, frost sides of coffee cake with thin confectioner's sugar icing and fill center area with jam or jelly when cool.

Rose Newpower has won hundreds of ribbons in a cooking career that started when she was a young girl. She loves baking, and has set aside a section of her kitchen just for this.

Three years ago, Rose and her husband went to Bolivia, South America to visit their son who is a missionary priest in a remote little village high in the mountains. While there Rose made the Twin Twirl Coffee Cake several times. Her son has an Aymara Indian woman who cooks for him, and as Rose made the cake this woman would watch very closely. Since then the Aymara Indian cook has made the cake on special occasions and very successfully too. If she can do it—we can too.

ALICE BOWLES
EAGLE RIVER, ALASKA

JALAPENO CORN BREAD

1½ cups corn meal
1 tsp. baking soda
½ tsp. salt
¼ cup jalapeno peppers
2 eggs, slightly beaten

1 cup milk
½ cup bacon drippings
2 cups cream style corn
1 8-oz. pkg. Cheddar cheese,
    grated

Mix all items except cheese. Pour half the batter into 8x8-inch pan. Sprinkle half the cheese over batter. Pour rest of batter and top with cheese. Bake at 400 degrees for 30–40 minutes.

 Mexican cooking in Alaska? It sounds crazy, but Alice Bowles specializes in it. "Seems like I've always known how to cook," she says. "My kitchen is my incentive to love to cook. It has lots of counter space, lots of cupboards (built by my husband), lots of light."

Alice does cooking demonstrations on a local television show. Once, she forgot to take a can opener. She had to open a can of solids with a beer-can opener.

HELEN BROWN
DETROIT, MICHIGAN

FIRST PRIZE, BREAD
DATE NUT BREAD
MICHIGAN STATE FAIR

NEXT-DAY OATMEAL BREAD

2 eggs
1 cup granulated sugar
2 cups buttermilk
⅔ cup molasses
3 cups all-purpose flour
2 tsp. baking soda

1 tsp. baking powder
1 tsp. salt
1½ cups quick-cooking rolled oats
1½ cups chopped nuts
1½ cups chopped dates

Preheat oven to 350 degrees. Beat eggs until light and then gradually add the sugar. Blend in the buttermilk and molasses.

Blend together flour, soda, baking powder, and salt; add to mixture, beating only until blended.

Stir in oats, dates, and nuts. Divide batter into two greased 8x4x2-inch loaf pans. Bake 50 to 60 minutes or until cake tester inserted in center comes out clean. Cool 10 minutes, then turn out onto wire rack. Cool thoroughly.

Yield: 2 loaves

NOTE: Use willpower and resist the urge to cut into this moist, chewy bread right after it is baked. It improves with age.

A couple of weeks after the fair had ended I received a phone call from a complete stranger inquiring about this particular bread. She said that she had never seen that type of oatmeal quick bread and asked if I would be willing to give her the recipe. Score another point for the versatile oatmeal.

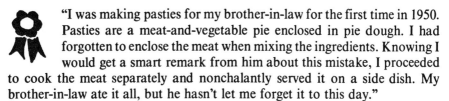 "I was making pasties for my brother-in-law for the first time in 1950. Pasties are a meat-and-vegetable pie enclosed in pie dough. I had forgotten to enclose the meat when mixing the ingredients. Knowing I would get a smart remark from him about this mistake, I proceeded to cook the meat separately and nonchalantly served it on a side dish. My brother-in-law ate it all, but he hasn't let me forget it to this day."

Helen began cooking when she got married. She says she used cookbooks mainly, "but was very happy to get tried-and-true recipes from friends."

BAKING POWDER BISCUITS

2 cups flour
3 tsp. baking powder
½ tsp. salt

¼ cup shortening
¾ cup milk

Mix first 3 ingredients. Cut in shortening. Add milk and mix. Knead on floured board. Roll out and cut. Bake at 450 degrees for 10 to 15 minutes.

Yield: enough for company

 "During fair time I'm busy preparing for entries. I once sent my husband out for dinner. When he asked why, I said 'Dinner? Can't cook dinner—I'm too busy cooking.'" Lee has won a total of 110 ribbons at county and state fairs since 1972.

She describes her kitchen as "full of love, good smells, and surprises." Lee is also a student. She returned to school five years ago and soon will become a registered nurse.

She says, "I enjoy all phases of cooking from meat and gravy to gourmet cooking. When asked to bring something, requests are for biscuits and jelly or corn chowder. Most all my recipes are my own. Some were my grandmother's first and have been adapted to my taste."

SOPHIE BURDEN
WICKENBURG, ARIZONA

REMUDA BEER BISCUITS

2 cups biscuit mix. Any amount of beer. (You can't measure the beer—and cold, warm, stale, or fresh, it's still great for biscuits.)

Mix the beer and biscuit mix to feel the way biscuits should. You can add grated cheese and that's wonderful—or you can add cheese and bacon pieces (not Bacon Bits, they just don't do it) or chopped onion, sausage, or whatever you can think of.

Dump the mixture out on a floured board. Don't roll it. Pat it to about ¼ or ½ inch thick. You can cut it with a biscuit cutter, or just pinch off pieces like dropped biscuits. Or you can pat it out quite thin and put marmalade or jelly or cinnamon and butter in the middle and put a lid on—it's all good and surprising.

Bake in a 475-degree oven or a real hot dutch oven if you are camping or picnicking. Put on a greased pan and brush with plenty of melted butter. Cook about 18 to 20 minutes. Serve hot with butter pats inside.

"The way I discovered my wonderful beer biscuits is that I took my ranch guests on an overnight camping trip. When we arrived and set up camp, I hollered, 'come get your cold wet beer!' All my guests had ulcers and had to have milk. So when it came to mixing up the biscuits—what could I do? Mix them with the extra beer of course—and they are still the best biscuits I can think of."

Here are six more winners from Sophie Burden: Dad Fletcher's Tamale Pie (page 23), Real Spanish Rice (page 81), Dana's Charros Beans (page 81), Strawberry-Rhubarb Salad (page 101), Tomato Aspic (page 101), Remuda Beer Biscuits (page 169), and Christmas Rum Squares (page 356).

MARLENA BURG
DES MOINES, IOWA

FIRST PLACE, QUICK BREADS
IOWA STATE FAIR

ZUCCHINI-CARROT BREAD

3 large eggs
1 cup oil
1½ cups sugar
1 tsp. vanilla
3 cups flour
1 tsp. cinnamon
1 tsp. salt

1 tsp. baking powder
1 tsp. soda
1 cup grated fresh zucchini
1 cup carrot baby food (the
     big jar is okay)
1 cup chopped dates or raisins
Nuts, if desired

Combine eggs, oil, sugar, and vanilla and beat together in large bowl. Sift together flour, cinnamon, salt, baking powder, and soda. Beat into egg mixture. Fold in rest of ingredients and pour into 2 greased loaf pans. Bake 50–60 minutes at 350 degrees.

NOTE: Only freshly grated zucchini works in recipe, not frozen. I always use raisins.

"Once I was baking for the State Fair," Marlena told us, "and had increased my number of entries over the previous year. Of course, I had to plan time off from work to do so—unfortunately, work was short-staffed for two weeks, which left me trying to bake after work! My plates of entries were getting slightly 'aged.' They looked okay the last time I saw them, but the judge had nothing but *mold* to judge on about three of the ten entries! I still get teased."

Marlena can laugh about this now, she has won so many ribbons and prizes with her cooking.

DEBORAH BUXTON

SOUTH LYNDEBORO,
NEW HAMPSHIRE

RAISIN BRAN MUFFINS

1½ cups unprocessed bran
½ cup flour
½ cup whole wheat flour
½ cup raisins
¼ cup nuts (chopped)
2 T. oil
1 tsp. vanilla

1 tsp. baking soda
1 tsp. cinnamon
1 tsp. nutmeg
1 egg
½ cup honey
¾ cup nonfat milk

Blend dry ingredients. Combine remaining ingredients and pour over dry ingredients. Stir till blended. Spoon into greased muffin tins.
Bake 12–15 minutes at 375 degrees.

Yield: about 12 muffins—at only 100 calories per muffin!

"*Very* bran-ny"—these are the best bran muffins I've tasted."

Debbie's Sautéed Green Beans with Onions are on page 83, and her Sherbet Watermelon Surprise Dessert is on page 386.

FAITH COLE
BROOKLYN, NEW YORK

DILL COTTAGE CHEESE BREAD

1 pkg. active dry yeast	2 tsp. dill seed
¼ cup warm water	1 tsp. salt
1 cup cream-style cottage	¼ tsp. baking soda
cheese	1 well-beaten egg
¼ cup shortening	2¼–2½ cups unbleached flour
2 T. sugar	Butter, melted
1 small onion, grated	Dill seed

Soften yeast in warm water. In saucepan, heat cottage cheese to lukewarm. Stir in shortening, sugar, dill, salt, baking soda, and softened yeast. Grate onion on a plate with medium section of cheese grater, saving all juice. Add to cottage cheese mixture, then beat in egg. Add flour, a little at a time, stirring to make a soft dough. Knead on a lightly floured surface till smooth and elastic, about 5 minutes.

Place in greased bowl, turning once to grease surface. Cover; let rise in a warm place for 1 hour. Punch down; cover. Let rest 10 minutes. Shape into loaf and place in greased 9x5x3-inch loaf pan. Cover; let rise again until almost doubled (30–45 minutes).

Bake in preheated 350-degree oven for 40 minutes. Remove from pan; brush with melted butter & sprinkle with additional dill seed.

Yield: 1 loaf

Faith was just a little girl at the end of World War II, but she still remembers the French chef her family took in during the war. He had been a Resistance fighter, captured by the Germans and held in a prison camp. After the Allies liberated France, he was able to join his wife, who was working as a cook for Faith's family.

"His arrival opened up new vistas for the entire family," says Faith. "Magical things began appearing on the table, and when my mother gave a party he outdid himself. Candy flowers were his specialty; he told us that his brother had been the second-best candy maker in Paris. I remember the day he made spun sugar (not the cottony stuff sold at carnivals) and the *entire* kitchen (which was very large) was covered in newspaper to prevent spattering. Being a little girl, I often hung around the kitchen and was introduced to steak tartare straight from the butcher's paper, limonade gazeuse (a form of sparkling beverage which sometimes erupted from the bottles like Mt. Vesuvius), and many more fascinating things.

"What I remember most particularly was watching him chop vegetables, or anything, for that matter. A very large chopping knife was used in a fan-shaped series of motions, using two hands, and to this day I can duplicate it exactly. It is by far the most effective and efficient method of chopping anything from parsley to potatoes. Beginning cooks please note: learn to chop properly (even if it's a small amount) and your time spent preparing will be considerably lessened, as will your aggravation. Did you ever try to chop carrots against the side of a pyrex 2-cup measure with a vegetable paring knife (as I once saw a relative of mine doing)?

"The second bit of advice for beginning or any stage of experience is use *fresh* ingredients wherever possible. No dehydrated parsley flakes—the real thing takes only seconds to prepare. Fresh mushrooms are a little more trouble than canned—but what a difference! Frozen fish fillets in those supermarket boxes often defrost to mush—better to walk those few extra blocks to the fish market.

"I cook for a family of four, and try to prepare unusual dishes as much as possible. However, teenagers occasionally rebel against things like stuffed artichokes, so good old hamburger comes in handy."

Faith has had a number of her recipes published, and this recipe is one of her prizewinners. About it she says, "It's strange that I won for a baked product, as I really don't specialize in this type of cooking. However, since I don't like sweet things but do like fairly spicy things, I've been making this bread for some time. As long as the yeast is good, it comes out fine every time."

LORA M. CREASMAN
DELANO, TENNESSEE

FIRST PLACE
POLK COUNTY FAIR

LORA'S CORN MEAL MUFFINS WITH CORN OIL

1 egg
1 cup milk
3 T. corn oil

2 cups self-rising corn meal
2 T. sugar

Heat oven to 425 degrees. Grease 12 medium-size muffin cups. (I use shortening and put just a sprinkling of corn meal in each cup.) Break egg in a bowl and beat with a fork; add milk and shortening. Stir in corn meal and sugar; mix just enough to blend. Fill muffin tin ⅔ cups full.

Bake 20 minutes. Serve hot with butter.

 Cooking in her pleasant country-style kitchen, Lora tells of learning to cook by "gathering recipes over the years and with the help of the Extension Service at club meetings." Since her two sons have left for college, Lora cooks for three.

She tells us about her recipe for Corn Meal Muffins with Corn Oil: "The recipe is made with white self-rising corn meal, which is readily available in the South. The difference in the taste is the corn oil used. With the addition of butter on the hot muffin, the taste is enhanced and the true corn flavor comes through. I use regular-size muffin tins (not teflon) with the shortening and a pinch of corn meal and they do not stick. The milk and egg produces a crispy golden-brown muffin."

HOME COMFORT DONUTS

2½ cups flour
¾ tsp. salt
½ tsp. nutmeg
2 tsp. baking soda

Sift together to mix well.

CREAM:

2½ T. shortening
½ cup sugar
2 beaten eggs

Add ½ cup milk alternately with flour to egg mixture to form a soft dough. Roll out. Cut with donut cutter. Fry in deep fat.

 About this recipe, Lelia says, "It is from a cookbook which came with the Home Comfort stove my father-in-law gave us as a wedding gift 52 years ago." She adds, "Wish we still had that stove."

Try Lelia's Cottage Cheese Chiffon Pie (page 276), and Onion Cheese Bread (page 7).

ELIZABETH HUGHES
PROVIDENCE, RHODE ISLAND

FIRST PRIZE
BAKERY SECTION CONTEST
NEW ENGLAND NATURAL FOODS
ASSOCIATION, WELLES, MAINE

RHODE ISLAND JONNY COOKIE

½ cup pure maple syrup
½ cup unsalted butter, melted
  (1 stick)
1 cup (sifted) stone-ground
  white corn meal (R.I.
  jonnycake meal)

1 tsp. Dr. Bronner's salt (now
  called, balanced protcin
  seasoning)
½ tsp. granulated kelp

While butter is slowly melting in pan, put dry ingredients (meal and seasonings) in (pre-heated) bowl. Stir.

Add syrup to melted butter. Stir. Pour liquid mixture into bowl of dry mixture.

Stir enough to mix. As quickly as possible "drop" the batter with a teaspoon or tablespoon, depending on your preference, and whether the batter is thick or thin. Bake in moderate oven (325 degrees) until edges are brown (20–30 minutes). The cookie sheet does not need to be greased.

Yield: about 30 cookies

HINT: The corn meal should not be ground too fine. It should not turn into flour.

HINT: Work quickly once the ingredients are combined.

NOTE: Elizabeth says, "This is my original recipe, and I won First Prize in a Bakery Section Contest sponsored by the New England Convention of the Natural Foods Association in Welles, Maine, for a cookie. The prize consisted of organically-grown produce (potatoes, carrots, fruit, etc.)"

"Keep it simple," Elizabeth advises. She says, "I am not a great cook. I'm a lazy one. I picked it up gradually, at home.

"I spend the least possible time cooking. In fact, I'm really not a cook. However, you might say I'm an inventor. So I did adapt another cookie recipe which had twice the amount of 'sweetening,' substituted certain ingredients, tried the results on the family, and came up with the Rhode Island Jonny Cookie (Deluxe). Another cookie followed which people liked, the Heritage Variety Jonny Cookie, but I never entered it in a contest. Both these cookies were popular at Bicentennial tours and fairs in Rhode Island.

"The reason for making this cookie was two-fold: To give my children a more wholesome sweet, and to spread the 'Good, naturally!' word.

"My advice to would-be cooks is to step right in, start with something simple, and something you like. That's what I did, and it was a great experience."

MY FAVORITE KRINGLE

4 cups flour
1 cup butter
1 pkg. yeast
3 T. sugar
1 cup milk scalded (cool to
    120 degrees)

1 tsp. salt
3 egg yolks (save whites for
    filling)

Measure flour, sugar, salt into bowl; blend well. Cut in butter, as for piecrust. Add egg yolks and yeast to cooled milk; beat slightly. Add to the flour mixture. Cover bowl and chill at least 2 and no more than 48 hours in refrigerator. Prepare fillings before shaping kringles.

Divide dough into 4 parts. Take out one and refrigerate the rest. Beat the egg whites.

Roll dough into an 8x20-inch rectangle. Spread 3-inch center strip with prepared filling, then with beaten egg white. Fold over one side of dough and then the other with a 1½-inch lap to cover fillings. Pinch dough to close the fold. Pick up kringle carefully and arrange it upside down, seam under, on baking sheet in oval, horseshoe, or stick shape. Prick in several places with fork. Pat flat.

Shape the other three kringles like the first. Let rise in warm place 30–35 minutes. Bake in hot oven, 400 degrees, for 15–25 minutes or until golden brown. While hot, using hot pad, pat flat to let out trapped air. Spread with sugar icing while hot.

If desired sugar top. Brush top with egg-white glaze by mixing 1 unbeaten egg white and 2 tablespoons water. Brush over kringle, sprinkle with white sugar. Do this right after placing on pan, *before baking*.

PECAN FILLING

6 T. butter   ¾ cup brown sugar

Cream until fluffy. Spread on rolled out dough. Spread beaten egg white over above. Sprinkle with ⅔ cup chopped nuts. Fills 2 kringles.

APPLE FILLING

½ cup brown sugar
1 cup finely chopped raw apple

Sprinkle sugar, then apples.

ALMOND FILLING

1 8-oz. can almond filling
1 cup sugar
½ cup butter
¼ cup milk

Cream butter and sugar until fluffy. Beat in almond and milk until smooth. Fills 4 kringles.

PRUNE FILLING

    1½ cups pitted stewed prunes   ¼ cup sugar
    3 T. lemon juice

Blend before spreading mixture.

DATE FILLING

    1 cup dates   ½ cup nuts (optional)
    ½ cup sugar   1 tsp. lemon juice
    ½ cup water   ⅛ tsp. salt

Cook dates, sugar, salt until soft. Add nuts and lemon juice. Cool before spreading on dough. Fills 4 kringles.

CHERRY, BLUEBERRY, OR PINEAPPLE FILLING

    1 12-oz. can prepared pie filling

Spread on dough. If you don't like the cherries so big blend in blender first. Fills 2 kringles.

PLAIN ICING

    1½ cups powdered sugar   ¼ tsp. vanilla
    2 T. milk

Mix together. Dab on; don't spread too much. Fills 2 kringles.

JAM FILLINGS

Jams may be used, but don't put on too thick. Have a tendency to ooze through and burn.

Pecan- and almond-filled kringles keep the longest without getting soggy. These freeze the best.

NAPOLEON KRINGLE OR PUFF PASTRY

    1 cup butter   ½ cup cultured sour cream
    1½ cups flour

Cut butter into flour with pastry blender. Stir in sour cream. Divide dough into 2 parts. Wrap each and refrigerate 8 hours or overnight. Roll pastry on well-floured cloth-covered board. Roll dough into 12x10-inch rectangle. Place on ungreased baking sheet. Spread to fill the sheet. Cut down the center lengthwise. Brush tops with sugar glaze, mixing 3 tablespoons sugar and 1 tablespoon water.
    Bake 15–18 minutes. Cool. Fill with cream filling. Frost with plain icing.

CREAM FILLING

2 cups milk	1 tsp. vanilla
3 T. cornstarch	½ cup sugar
3 eggs, separated	¼ tsp. salt

Beat egg yolks, add to milk. Heat till steaming but *not boiling.* Mix sugar, salt, and cornstarch thoroughly. Add to steaming milk and stir constantly until thickened. Beat egg whites until stiff. Stir in the hot mixture slowly. Add vanilla. Cool thoroughly.

After kringle is filled be *sure to refrigerate until time of serving.*

An avid recipe collector, Gladys works in a big, bustling, cheery farm kitchen. She cooks supper for eight to ten plus hired help. The kitchen really hums at Christmas time when she and her four daughters are baking Christmas cookies.

She told us her techniques for entering the fairs: "I freeze most of my entries. Some are the same for all the fairs, so then I get three entries out of a batch: start baking in April or May. Every time I make an entry, it fills in for dessert. My family enjoys eating the extras. When trying to develop a better recipe I look up all the recipes I have and then average them."

Gladys says that over the years there were always traveling casualties—fair entries that were the worse for wear from the trip to the fair along with her six kids!

Gladys and her husband both show at the fairs: "exhibiting dairy, eggs, vegetables, flowers, canning, baking, chickens." She entered the state fair when her children were exhibiting cattle and could take her entries; but she always shows at the two county fairs. "It's a lot of fun," she says. "We load up the pick-up with our exhibits, a wagon for the little ones, and some kids in the back to watch the stuff."

Two of Gladys's children were "fair babies"; Ruthann, now fourteen, was born the first day of the Racine County Fair. "We took some things there the day before so I told our older girls to take the baking entries I had thawing on the dining room table. Our Riley Peter, now ten, was born about nine days before the Racine County Fair, so we took him in the buggy as we put our things in place."

HANNAH HANSON
MINOT, NORTH DAKOTA

BLUE RIBBON, BAKING POWDER
BISCUITS, PREMIUM RIBBONS
FROM NORTH DAKOTA
WHEAT COMMISSION

HANNAH'S BAKING POWDER BISCUITS

2 cups flour
4 tsp. baking powder
¼ cup shortening

½ tsp. salt
¾ cup milk

Sift flour before measuring. Measure flour, salt, and baking powder, place in large flour sifter, and sift into a 3–4-quart bowl. Add shortening and cut flour and shortening as for pie pastry with 2 knives, dough blender, or a fork until mixture looks like coarse meal.

Measure milk and add to ingredients in bowl. Use fork to mix with very light strokes. Handle as little as possible—overmixing causes biscuits to be tough.

Sprinkle a small amount of flour on bread board, turn out dough, and knead about 30 seconds or just until it will hold together.

Pat dough into flat sheet about ½ inch thick. Cut with cookie cutter into rounds, place on cookie sheet, and bake in 425-degree oven for 15 minutes or until golden brown.

 Hannah Hanson has been cooking more than 50 years. She learned from her mother on the farm.

Although she cooks in a small kitchen, with little counter space, she comes up with blue-ribbon winners like these Baking Powder Biscuits and Bran Muffins.

JENNIFER HINER

Elliston, Montana

FIRST PRIZE, JUNIOR DIVISION
ALASKA STATE FAIR

GRANDMA'S STRAWBERRY COFFEE CAKE

2 cups sugar	1 cup milk
¾ cup butter	½ tsp. vanilla
3 eggs	½ cup sliced fresh strawberries
3 cups flour	½ cup strawberry jam/optional
2 tsp. baking powder	

Cream sugar and butter till creamy. Add eggs one at a time, beating well after each. Sift dry ingredients and add alternately with milk. Beat well, add flavoring, and gently fold in berries and jam. Pour into 9x12-inch well-greased pan and bake at 350 degrees for 45 minutes.

NOTE: Strawberry Coffee Cake can be sprinkled with powdered sugar, and two or three fresh strawberries placed in the center.

 Jenny started her cooking career making mud pies. She was only three, and her mother decided "the real thing was better to eat than the mud." Now Jenny is seven years old and one of our youngest blue-ribbon cooks.

She was born in Palmer, Alaska and learned to cook on the family homestead. She first entered the fair at age five, and when she was six a coffee cake she made from her great-grandmother's recipe won first prize. As you can imagine, her family is very proud of Jenny.

PAULINE'S APRICOT NUT BREAD

½ cup dried apricots
1 cup water
1 egg, well beaten
1 cup sugar
2 T. butter (melted)
2 cups sifted flour
1 T. baking powder

¼ tsp. soda
¾ tsp. salt
½ cup orange juice (strained)
¼ cup water
1 cup sliced Brazil nuts or
  almonds

Soak apricots in water for 30 minutes. Drain and dice.
Preheat oven to 350 degrees.
Beat egg until light; add sugar and blend well. Add butter. Sift flour with baking powder, soda, and salt and add alternately with orange juice and water. Add nuts and apricots and blend well.
Bake in greased 8½x4½-inch loaf pan for 1¼ to 1½ hours.

Yield: 1 loaf

NOTE: When I make sandwiches of this I use cream cheese with apricot jam.

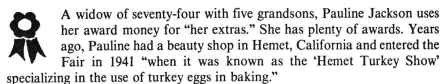

A widow of seventy-four with five grandsons, Pauline Jackson uses her award money for "her extras." She has plenty of awards. Years ago, Pauline had a beauty shop in Hemet, California and entered the Fair in 1941 "when it was known as the 'Hemet Turkey Show' specializing in the use of turkey eggs in baking."
She has won the baking sweepstakes at the California State Fair five times and she won the Baking Sweepstakes at the National Date Festival with this recipe.

ZELDA KERSHNER
RENICK, WEST VIRGINIA

FIRST PRIZE, CORNBREAD
WEST VIRGINIA STATE FAIR

OLD-FASHIONED CORN BREAD

1 cup yellow corn meal	1 stick oleo
¾ cup all-purpose flour	1 tsp. soda
2 T. sugar	3 tsp. baking powder
1 tsp. salt	2 cups buttermilk

In a 9x9-inch pan (or near this size) melt oleo. Mix well all dry ingredients in 1½-quart mixing bowl before adding the buttermilk. Add buttermilk gradually stirring well after each addition. Add immediately to melted oleo, stir until mixed in pan. Bake at 400 degrees about 15–20 minutes, or until golden brown.

Yield: serves 6–8

NOTE: I use water-ground corn meal. If the meal is very fine I add a little more (2 teaspoons) flour.

"I learned to cook as an experimental youngest under the supervision of my mother," says Zelda Kershner. She has been cooking more than 40 years and she cooks for from "one to twenty."

Now a widow, Zelda recalls, "As a bride I made a pudding using flavoring from a sample kit belonging to my husband. He inquired what flavoring I had used—when I showed him the bottle it had *liniment* in it rather than vanilla."

NUT BREAD

———————————————————•———————————————————

3 cups flour	1 beaten egg
1 cup sugar	1½ cups milk
4 tsp. baking powder	¼ cup cooking oil
1 tsp. salt	¾ cup chopped walnuts

In small bowl stir thoroughly the flour, sugar, baking powder, and salt. Use a large bowl to combine egg, milk, and oil; add dry ingredients, beating well (low speed). Stir in nuts. Turn into greased loaf pan. Bake at 350 degrees about 70 minutes. Remove from pan immediately. Cool on rack.

"Last year it was so hot during the fair that the frosting melted off my white cake, but it still got second prize!" Cindi tells us. She and her mother, Sharon McSwiggin, are consistent prizewinners at the Illinois State Fair. We have both winners and their recipes included in our book.

Try her mother's recipe, Spice Cake (page 247).

COFFEE CAKE

1 T. solid shortening	2 medium eggs
½ tsp. salt	1 cup light brown sugar
½ cup sugar (white)	1 tsp. cinnamon
1 cup hot milk	½ cup crushed pecans
2 pkgs. dry yeast	3 cups all-purpose white flour
½ cup warm water (lukewarm)	(more if needed)

GLAZE

½ cup honey (clover)   1 T. butter

Heat together and boil one minute. Brush onto top and sides of coffee cake as soon as you take it out of pan.

In a large mixing bowl, drop in shortening, salt, sugar. Scald the milk and pour over mixture, stir until shortening is melted. Cool until just warm.

Stir yeast cake into lukewarm water and pour into first mixture. Add eggs, beat well. Add flour by the cup, beating for 1 minute with wooden spoon for each cup.

Leave in bowl, set away from drafts, in warm room and let rise for 1 hour or until doubled in bulk.

Turn out on floured board and knead until smooth and elastic; this takes maybe 5 minutes. Don't be afraid to punch, hit, bang! The more you knead the better!

Cut off dough the size of unshelled walnuts and dip in 2 tablespoons of melted butter, then roll each in the brown sugar and cinnamon (mixed).

Put them side by side in a 9-inch tube pan. When one layer is complete, sprinkle with the crushed nut meats, add the next layer zig-zag fashion, and repeat until all the dough is used.

Let rise again for 10 minutes.

Bake at 375 degrees until golden brown, maybe 30 minutes. Turn out and brush at once with glaze. Break apart with 2 forks.

Yield: serves 8–12

"Once I made a beautiful maple chiffon cake for the fair," Mae Manning recalls. "I put it on a board on the back seat of the car and started for the fair. Two dogs came on the road in front of me. I slammed on my brakes and the cake slid off—on the floor top down." Like a true champion, Mae went home and started over. She got a blue ribbon for the second cake, too.

Mae cooks in a cheerful, bright, country-style kitchen. She started cooking when she was eight and never had a lesson. She has won 14 ribbons at the Champlain Valley Exposition.

She advises cooks everywhere "to always use the best ingredients. Never use too much flour in bread baking, a little stick is best for high, light bread and rolls and good eating."

KARLA MARTIN
APPLETON CITY, MISSOURI

FIRST PRIZE, GRAND CHAMPION,
CAKES, JUNIOR DIVISION
4-H DIVISION
MISSOURI STATE FAIR

SWEDISH TEA RING

1 cup lukewarm milk
½ cup sugar
1 tsp. salt
2 pkgs. dry yeast
2 eggs
½ cup soft shortening

4½–5 cups flour
2 T. butter
½ cup sugar
2 tsp. cinnamon
Nuts and cherries to decorate

Mix together milk, sugar, and salt. Sprinkle in the yeast. Stir in eggs and shortening. Mix in the flour, first with spoon, then with hands. Knead, then let rise until twice as big. Knead and roll into a 9x18-inch oblong. Spread with softened butter and sprinkle with sugar and cinnamon. Roll up tightly as for cinnamon rolls. Place sealed edge down in ring on greased cookie sheet. Join ends of ring and seal. Use scissors to cut ⅔ of the way through the ring at 1-inch intervals. Turn all sections in the same direction. Let rise. Bake 30 minutes at 375 degrees. Frost while warm. Decorate with nuts and cherries.

 Grand Champion Junior Cook Karla Martin is fifteen, and has been cooking for eight years. See page 248 for sister Karol's Buttermilk Cake!

MAXINE MOCK
POMEROY, WASHINGTON

GRAND PRIZE
GARFIELD COUNTY FAIR

TWO-TONE BREAD

5¼–5½ cups all-purpose flour	⅓ cup shortening
2 pkgs. dry yeast	1 T. salt
3 cups milk	3 T. dark molasses
⅓ cup sugar	2¼ cups whole wheat flour

In large mixer bowl combine 3 cups of the all-purpose flour and the yeast. In saucepan heat together milk, sugar, shortening, and salt just till warm (115–120 degrees), stirring constantly to melt shortening. Add to dry mixture in mixer bowl. Beat at low speed with electric mixer for ½-minute, scraping sides of bowl constantly. Beat 3 minutes at high speed. Divide dough in half. To one half, stir in enough remaining all-purpose flour to make a moderately stiff dough. Turn out on lightly floured board and knead till smooth and elastic (5 to 8 minutes).

Shape into ball. Place in well-greased bowl, turning once; set aside. To remaining dough, stir in molasses and whole wheat flour. Turn onto lightly floured surface. Knead till smooth and elastic (5 to 8 minutes), kneading in enough additional all-purpose flour (about 3 tablespoons) to make a moderately stiff dough. Shape into a ball. Place dough in well-greased bowl, turning to grease surface.

Let both doughs rise in warm place till doubled (1 to 1¼ hours). Punch doughs down, cover, and let rest 10 minutes. Roll out half the light dough and half the dark each to a 12x8-inch rectangle. Place dark dough on the light: roll up tightly into loaf, beginning at short side. Repeat with 2 remaining doughs. Place in 2 greased 8½x4½x2½-inch loaf pans. Cover. Let rise till doubled (45 to 60 minutes). Bake at 375 degrees for 30 to 35 minutes. Remove and cool.

Yield: 2 loaves

"Everyone seems to love homemade bread," says Maxine, "so when I bake, I always give one loaf away." She married young, at seventeen, and has five children, three of whom are married, and six grandchildren.

"We live in wheat country," she says, "so I feel my recipes are appropriate for this part of the U.S.A." No matter where you live, we think you'll like this bread recipe.

CAROLE S. MORELOCK
GREENWOOD, INDIANA

BUTTERCRUNCH NUT BREAD

2 T. sesame seeds
2 T. sugar
¼ tsp. cinnamon
¼ tsp. nutmeg
2 cups sifted all-purpose flour
1 tsp. baking powder
½ tsp. soda
1 tsp. salt

2 eggs
1 cup firmly packed brown
  sugar
3 T. melted butter
1 cup buttermilk
⅔ cup chopped nuts (hickory
  nuts or walnuts)

Combine sesame seeds, sugar, cinnamon, and nutmeg and set aside. Sift flour again with baking powder, soda, and salt. In large bowl beat eggs slightly, then add brown sugar and melted butter; mix together, then add the flour mixture alternately with the buttermilk. Stir just till blended, then stir in nuts. Pour into a greased 9x5-inch loaf pan. Sprinkle the top with sesame-seed–sugar mixture. Bake at 350 degrees for one hour. Cool slightly, then remove from pan and cool on rack.

Yield: 1 loaf

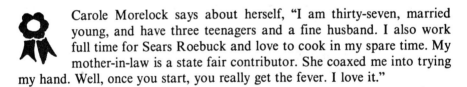

Carole Morelock says about herself, "I am thirty-seven, married young, and have three teenagers and a fine husband. I also work full time for Sears Roebuck and love to cook in my spare time. My mother-in-law is a state fair contributor. She coaxed me into trying my hand. Well, once you start, you really get the fever. I love it."

Try Carole's Honey Oatmeal Bread (page 138).

SUSAN MURLEY
LOUISVILLE, KENTUCKY

PUMPKIN BREAD

1⅔ cups unsifted flour	1½ cups sugar
¼ tsp. baking powder	½ cup salad oil
1 tsp. baking soda	½ cup water
¾ tsp. salt	1 cup pumpkin
½ tsp. cinnamon	2 large eggs
½ tsp. nutmeg	1 cup chopped walnuts
½ tsp. ground cloves	1 cup chopped dates

In large bowl combine dry ingredients. Add oil, water, pumpkin, and unbeaten eggs. Beat at medium speed for 2 minutes. Stir in dates and nuts. Bake in loaf pan for 1½ hours at 350 degrees (or in two smaller loaf pans for 60 minutes or four mini loaf pans for 40 minutes).

"I'm the oldest of thirteen children," says Susan, "and, thanks to my mother, I got a lot of on-the-job training in every phase of homemaking."

She said that just last month, "a custard pie that I had been serving for years decided to come out of the oven upside down. I have yet to figure out how the crust ended up on top of the custard. We called that one, 'Custard Upside Down Pie.'"

Try Susan's Caramels (page 377).

TYE NEEL
REDMOND, OREGON

PUMPKIN MUFFINS

2 cups biscuit mix
½ cup sugar
1½ tsp. pumpkin pie spice
¾ cup milk

½ cup canned pumpkin
1 slightly beaten egg
2 T. cooking oil

Thoroughly combine biscuit mix, sugar, and spice.

Combine milk, pumpkin, egg, and oil and stir into dry ingredients until blended. Fill greased muffin cups ⅔ full.

Bake in hot oven (400 degrees) about 20 minutes.

Yield: 1 dozen

Thirteen-year-old Tye Neel learned to cook "at home, from my Mom." He says he cooks for "six normally, but more on holidays." He has been cooking for five years.

Tye also gave us a blue-ribbon cake recipe from his grandmother, Lorraine Wing (See German Sweet Chocolate Cake, page 267).

TONYA PARKER
WASILLA, ALASKA

FIRST PRIZE
ALASKA STATE FAIR

ZUCCHINI BREAD

3 eggs
¾ cup oil
1½ cups sugar
1 tsp. orange bits
½ tsp. orange extract
¼ tsp. vanilla
2 cups unpeeled grated
    zucchini

2½ cups flour
¾ tsp. salt
1 tsp. soda
2 tsp. baking powder
½ cup chopped pecans

Mix all ingredients together in a bowl (or by mixer). Bake in greased bread pan at 350 degrees for one hour.

Yield: 1 large loaf

Tonya Parker says she learned to cook "at home. I'm still learning because I'm only ten years old." Once "I put one cup salt in popcorn balls instead of sugar," but we've all made lots of mistakes like that. She has one word to describe her recipe. "Delicious!"

GREGORY PATENT
MISSOULA, MONTANA

FINALIST
NATIONAL PINEAPPLE COOKING
CLASSIC—BREAD
TRIP TO HAWAII

ITALIAN FESTIVAL HERB CRESCENTS

1 1-lb., 4-oz. can crushed
    pineapple
1 cup finely chopped onions
1 cup shredded carrots
2 T. oil
1 4½-oz. can deviled ham
¾ tsp. garlic salt
¾ tsp. paprika
5 cups unsifted all-purpose
    flour
2 envelopes active dry yeast

2 T. sugar
2 tsp. salt
6 T. margarine
1 tsp. dried basil
1 tsp. dried oregano
1 tsp. dried sage
½ tsp. garlic powder
1 cup water
1 cup milk
⅓ cup grated Parmesan cheese

Drain pineapple well. Cook onions and carrots with oil, stirring occasionally, until tender but not browned. Add pineapple, ham, garlic, salt, and paprika. Cook over moderate heat, stirring occasionally, for 5 minutes. Set aside to cool. Combine 2 cups flour, yeast, sugar, and salt; set aside. Melt 3 tablespoons margarine. Stir in basil, oregano, sage, garlic powder, water, and milk. Heat to lukewarm (110 degrees). Add to flour mixture, stirring to moisten. Beat at medium speed on mixer 2 minutes. Stir in 1 cup flour. Beat at high speed 2 minutes. Remove from mixer and gradually stir in remaining 2 cups flour to make a stiff dough. Turn out onto floured surface and knead until smooth and elastic, about 5 to 10 minutes. Cover and let dough rest 15 minutes. Divide dough into thirds. Roll one third on floured surface to a 12-inch circle. Spread with ⅓ cooled filling, making a thin layer. Cut circle into 8 wedges. Roll each starting from wide end. Place rolls point side down 2 inches apart on greased baking sheets, curling ends to form crescents.

Repeat with remaining dough and filling. Cover and let rise in warm place 30 minutes. Rolls should rise slightly, but not double in size. Melt remaining margarine. Brush over crescents and sprinkle with cheese. Bake in center of moderately hot oven (375 degrees) 20 to 25 minutes, or until rolls are golden brown and spring back when touched lightly. Remove to racks and cool slightly. Serve warm or at room temperature.

Yield: 24 crescents

NOTE: Risen rolls may wait at room temperature while first pan is baking.

Do not serve butter or margarine or anything else with these rolls. It will only disguise their flavor. And be sure *not* to eat these hot.

To intensify pineapple flavor I now use crushed pineapple in syrup and save the syrup. After carrots and onions have cooked "until tender but not browned" I add the syrup, increase the heat, and cook, stirring, until syrup has been absorbed by the vegetables. Then I reduce heat to moderate and complete the filling as recipe directs. (I developed this procedure after the cook-off.)

I increase sugar in the dough to 3 tablespoons, also helping to enhance pineapple taste.

You can cut each circle of dough into 12 wedges instead of 8, making 3 dozen smaller dinner rolls.

The amount of melted margarine brushed over the rolls may be increased if desired. I usually use 4 to 5 tablespoons, so that I don't run out.

I find it most convenient to shape the rolls on 2 large (14x17-inch) cookie sheets. Both sheets can be baked at the same time if you adjust two oven racks to divide oven into thirds. Bake about 10–12 minutes, then reverse sheets top to bottom and front to back to bake an additional 10 minutes or until rolls are done. The rotation of the pans insures even browning and cooking.

Baked and cooled rolls may be frozen. To reheat, place frozen rolls uncovered on cookie sheet in 325-degree oven for 10 to 15 minutes.

No matter how tempted you are by the aroma, wait 10–15 minutes after baking before plunging in.

Greg Patent has a unique blend of interests; zoology, cooking and running—and he is high powered in all three. He earned three degrees including his Ph.D. in zoology. He has taken top honors in many cooking contests and to top it all off he has his own half hour television show, "Big Sky Cooking," now in its second year on Western Montana Television.

In spite of Greg's scientific work he has found time to enter cooking contests. As a teen-ager he won second prize in the Pillsbury Bake-Off. He has taken prizes in the Campbell Soup Contest, the National Chicken Cooking Contests, the Bon Appetit-Christian Brothers Sherry Contest. He is especially welcome in *The First Prize Cookbook* not only because he is a winner in some of the toughest cooking competitions in the country but especially because of his basic concern with nutrition and health.

GLORIA PECK
BETHANY, OKLAHOMA

SECOND PRIZE
OKLAHOMA STATE FAIR

FRESH BANANA MUFFINS
(May Use Peaches or Apples)

1 egg
¼ cup melted shortening
½ tsp. salt
1 tsp. lemon juice
2 cups unsifted flour
1 cup mashed bananas

1 cup milk
⅔ cup sugar
¼ tsp. cinnamon
¼ tsp. vanilla
3 tsp. baking powder

Stir together milk, shortening, sugar, salt, cinnamon, lemon juice and vanilla. Add beaten egg. Sift flour and baking powder and stir into milk mixture just until blended.

Fold in fruit and fill greased muffin cups one-half full. Bake at 425 degrees approximately 20 minutes.

NOTE: Glaze if desired while still warm with 1 cup confectioners sugar, 2 tablespoons milk, and 1 teaspoon vanilla.

CLAIRE PELLETIER
NORTH CONWAY, NEW HAMPSHIRE

GERMAN COFFEE CAKE

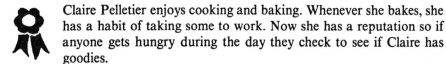

2 cups flour	1 cup sugar
1 tsp. baking soda	2 eggs
1 tsp. baking powder	¼ lb. butter (soft)
½ pt. sour cream	1 tsp. vanilla

TOPPING

½ cup sugar	½ cup nuts
1½ T. cinnamon	

Combine all dry ingredients. Beat in sour cream, eggs, butter, then vanilla until smooth at medium speed. In a greased and floured tube pan pour half the cake batter. Sprinkle with half the topping, then press topping lightly into batter with fork. Pour rest of batter, then topping, and again press topping lightly into batter with fork.

Bake at 375 degrees for 35 minutes.

Claire Pelletier enjoys cooking and baking. Whenever she bakes, she has a habit of taking some to work. Now she has a reputation so if anyone gets hungry during the day they check to see if Claire has goodies.

Other than cooking she told us her hobbies are, "macramé, needlepoint, crocheting, cross stitch, and racquet ball." The last one surprised you, didn't it?

Try Claire's Sheet Gingerbread (page 336).

MARY PROUTY
BRYANT, SOUTH DAKOTA

FIRST PRIZE
SOUTH DAKOTA STATE FAIR

APRICOT BREAD

1 cup dried apricots	2 cups flour
1 cup sugar	2 tsp. baking powder
2 T. soft butter or margarine	½ tsp. soda
1 egg	1 tsp. salt
¼ cup water	½ cup chopped nuts
½ cup orange juice	

Cover apricots with warm water and soak 30 minutes. Drain, and cut with scissors.

Cream sugar and butter or margarine. Add egg, water, and juice.

Sift together dry ingredients and add. Blend in nuts and apricots, and pour in greased 9x5x2-inch pan. Let stand 20 minutes. Bake 55–60 minutes, or till toothpick comes clean, in 350-degree oven.

Try Mary's Chocolate Pinwheels too (page 338).

JACKIE SANDBLOM
BOULDER, COLORADO

FIRST PRIZE
NATIONAL OATS
"BIG-LITTLE CONTEST"

BANANA BLUEBERRY BREAD

½ cup fresh or frozen blue-
    berries
1½ cups all-purpose flour
⅔ cup sugar
2 tsp. baking powder
½ tsp. salt

1 cup mashed bananas
½ cup oats
2 eggs, beaten
⅓ cup vegetable oil or melted
    shortening

Sprinkle blueberries with 2 teaspoons flour; set aside. Sift together remaining flour, sugar, baking powder, and salt. Stir in oats. Combine eggs, shortening, and bananas. Add to dry ingredients, stirring until just combined. Fold in blueberries. Pour batter into greased and floured 9x5x3-inch loaf pan. Bake at 350 degrees for 55–60 minutes, or until done. Let cool 10 minutes. Remove from pan and cool completely. Wrap bread in foil and store 24 hours in refrigerator before serving.

STRAWBERRY YOGURT BREAD

½ cup butter or margarine
½ cup sugar
½ tsp. vanilla
⅛ tsp. lemon extract
2 eggs
1½ cups all-purpose flour

½ tsp. salt
½ tsp. cream of tartar
¼ tsp. baking soda
⅔ cup strawberry preserves
¼ cup strawberry yogurt
½ cup broken walnuts

Cream butter, sugar, vanilla, and lemon extract until fluffy. Add eggs one at a time, beating well after each addition. Sift together dry ingredients. Combine preserves and yogurt; add to creamed mixture alternately with dry ingredients. Stir in walnuts.

Pour batter into a greased 9x5x3-inch pan. Bake at 350 degrees 55–60 minutes, or until done. Let cool in pan 10 minutes. Remove bread from pan and cool completely. Wrap bread in foil and store in refrigerator for 24 hours before serving.

"In the beginning I learned to cook with the standard trial-and-error method, and I learned as much from my mistakes as from my successes. Recently, however, I have been fortunate to attend two cooking schools: an American session of Cordon Bleu of Paris and an Italian cooking school in Florence, Italy."

Try Jackie's Banana Salad (page 112).

NONYEAST BREADS, SPECIALTY BREADS, AND COFFEE CAKES 199

MORAVIAN COFFEE CAKE

1 heaping tsp. solid shortening, creamed together
   with
1 cup granulated sugar

1 cup milk
2½ cups flour
2 T. baking powder
Pats of butter

Mix well. Grease 2 8-inch pans. Divide batter. Cover with brown sugar and cinnamon. [Take pats of butter and push down through batter to bottom of pan.] Bake 20–25 minutes at 350 degrees.

Learning in "4-H and with my Mother" Gloria Shober cooks for four people every day in her modern kitchen.
   Gloria describes her Moravian Coffee Cake as a "very simple and delicious coffee cake."

You may want to try Gloria's Walnut Penuche (page 380).

MURIEL SMITH
LITCHFIELD, MAINE

FIRST PRIZE, BREAD
LITCHFIELD FAIR

ZUCCHINI BREAD

3 eggs, beaten	2 tsp. baking powder
2 cups sugar	1 T. cinnamon
1 cup oil	1 tsp. salt
1 tsp. vanilla	½ tsp. soda
3 cups flour	2 cups grated zucchini

Mix well. Pour into 2 greased and floured loaf pans. Bake for 1 hour at 350 degrees.

"When I was first married," Muriel told us, "I made a blueberry pie, only I put one and a half cups of flour instead of sugar. It came out about four inches thick and light purple. My husband ate every bit so he wouldn't hurt my feelings."

She learned to cook at home and through Girl Scouts, and advises others, "Do not hurry, and enjoy yourself."

ANNA STONE
CIRCLEVILLE, OHIO

HONEY SWIRL COFFEE CAKE

1 cup milk	1 cup lukewarm water
½ cup shortening	2 eggs
½ cup sugar	6 cups sifted flour
2 tsp. salt	Honey Nut Filling
2 pkgs. dry yeast	(recipe follows)

Scald milk. Stir in shortening, sugar, and salt. Cool to lukewarm.

Sprinkle yeast on lukewarm water; stir to dissolve. Add yeast, eggs, and 2 cups of flour to milk mixture. Beat with electric mixer at medium speed about 2 minutes, scraping bowl occasionally.

Gradually add enough remaining flour to make a soft dough. Turn onto floured surface and let rest 10 minutes.

Knead dough until smooth and satiny, about 5 minutes. Place dough in lightly greased bowl; turn over to grease top. Cover and let rise in warm place until doubled, about 1½ hours. Punch down dough. Let rise again until doubled, about 45 minutes.

Divide dough in half. Roll each into 18x2-inch rectangle. Spread each with half of Honey Nut Filling to within 1 inch of edges. Roll up like jelly roll from long side. Seal edges. Curl each loosely into coil on 2 greased baking sheets. Let rise until doubled, about 45 minutes.

Bake in 350-degree oven 40 minutes or until golden brown. Remove from baking sheets; cool on racks. Frost with confectioners sugar icing.

HONEY NUT FILLING

Beat together 2 eggs, ½ cup honey, and ¼ cup melted butter or oleo. Stir in 3 cups very finely chopped walnuts, 2 teaspoons cinnamon, and 1 teaspoon vanilla. Mix well.

CONFECTIONERS SUGAR ICING

1½ cups powdered sugar
6–8 tsp. water or hot coffee

Put sugar in bowl. Stir in enough liquid, 1 teaspoon at a time, to make a thin glaze.

NOTE: On coffee cake I turn the baking sheet upside down, and place coffee cake on it. It will brown more evenly near bottom without the sides.

Also you will want to make Anna's Fresh Blackberry Pie (page 299).

LOTTE TAYLOR
JUNCTION CITY, KANSAS

CINNAMON ROLLS

In large mixer bowl combine 2 cups of flour and 1 package dry yeast. Heat 1 cup milk, ¼ cup sugar, ¼ cup shortening, and 1 teaspoon salt till warm (115–120 degrees), stirring to melt shortening. Add to dry mixture. Add 2 eggs. Beat on low speed with electric mixer for ½ minute, scraping bowl. Beat 3 minutes at high speed. By hand, stir in 1½ to 2 cups flour to make a moderately stiff dough. Knead on lightly floured surface till smooth (8 to 10 minutes). Shape into a ball. Place in greased bowl, turning once. Cover and let rise till doubled (45 to 60 minutes). Punch down; divide in half. Let rest 10 minutes.

FILLING

¼ cup butter or oleo, melted
½ cup sugar
2 tsp. ground cinnamon

Roll each half of dough into a 12x8-inch rectangle. Brush each with half the melted butter. Combine sugar and cinnamon and sprinkle over dough. Roll up each piece, starting with long side; seal seams. Slice each into 12 rolls. Place rolls, cut side down, in 2 greased 9x1½-inch round baking pans. Cover and let rise till doubled, about 35 minutes. Bake at 375 degrees for 12 to 20 minutes. Drizzle icing over warm rolls.

Yield: 24 rolls

ICING

1 cup sifted confectioners sugar
½ tsp. vanilla
Enough milk to make drizzling consistency, about 1 T.

"I was born in Germany, and I come from a family with five children, so I helped my mother cook plus home economics in school. I have four children and have hired men in the summer as I am a farm wife. Also I am county chairman for breads, food, and nutrition, and have been for 15 years—this has taught me a lot—and still learning."

Lotte's recipe for German Apple Slices is on page 395.

SUE THELEN
ELKHORN, WISCONSIN

RHUBARB BREAD

1½ cups brown sugar
1 egg
⅔ cup liquid shortening
1 cup sour or buttermilk
1 tsp. salt

2½ cups flour
1 tsp. baking soda
1 tsp. vanilla
1½ cups rhubarb, diced
½ cup chopped nuts

Combine sugar and shortening; stir in egg and sour or buttermilk. Add vanilla and sifted dry ingredients. Stir in rhubarb and nuts. Pour into 2 well-greased loaf pans. Bake at 325 degrees about 40 minutes; do not overbake. Remove from pans after 2–3 minutes; cool on rack. This bread keeps very well in the freezer. You can use frozen rhubarb.

Sue Thelen began cooking "in 4-H at age ten." Now, "at age twenty-one, I love it even more!" She advises new cooks to avoid getting discouraged. "If you make a mistake, just consider it a lesson in cooking; keep trying new recipes, and don't be afraid of a challenge. Even if it doesn't turn out—practice makes perfect!"

Married for just two years, Sue cooks for her husband and herself in her "typical Wisconsin farm kitchen." She has plenty of cupboards (lucky girl) and "no shortage of counter space," all decorated with her antique plate collection.

WILLIAM TULLY
Louisville, Kentucky

FIRST PRIZE
KENTUCKY STATE FAIR

COFFEE CAKE

2 cups sifted flour
2 cups sugar
3 tsp. baking powder
1 tsp. salt
¼ tsp. nutmeg
¼ tsp. cinnamon

⅓ cup soft butter
1 egg
1 cup milk
¼ tsp. vanilla
½ cup chopped walnuts

Heat oven to 350 degrees. Grease 9x9x1¾-inch square pan.
Blend dry ingredients. Add butter, eggs, vanilla, nuts, and milk. Beat hard 2 minutes. Pour into pan. Cover with Crunchy Topping. Bake 35–40 minutes. Cool slightly, dribble with thin icing, and sprinkle with more nuts and a few milk chocolate chips.

CRUNCHY TOPPING

3 T. soft butter
½ cup sugar
3 T. flour
1 tsp. cinnamon

3 tsp. chocolate powdered
drink mix
½ cup chopped nuts

Mix with fork.

THIN ICING

Sift a little confectioners sugar into bowl. Moisten with cream or milk to spreading consistency. Add flavoring. Dribble over slightly warm cake.

 William Tully says he learned to cook "at home as a small child when I became bored with nothing to do." He has been cooking for 35 years "off and on" and he cooks in a "medium-sized apartment kitchen."

Try Bill's Batter Bread–Cheese-Bacon Bread (page 156).

NONYEAST BREADS, SPECIALTY BREADS, AND COFFEE CAKES 205

KAY WARE
DENAIR, CALIFORNIA

DATE NUT BREAD

2 cups dates
2 cups boiling water
2 T. shortening
4 cups sifted flour
6 tsp. baking powder

1 tsp. salt
1½ cups sugar
2 eggs
2 cups chopped nuts

Combine dates, boiling water, and shortening. Cover and cool. Sift flour, baking powder, and salt together, set aside. Beat eggs and sugar together with mixer, add cooled dates alternately with dry ingredients. Add nuts. Pour into greased and floured loaf pans, let stand 20 minutes. Bake in slow oven (325 degrees) for 50 to 60 minutes. Turn onto cake rack and cool.

Yield: 2 1-pound loaves

"The first time I made bread I didn't let it rise before putting it in the oven, therefore I had some good, hard bricks." Now Kay gets beautiful high loaves, and blue ribbons, too. She learned to "cook and bake from my mother and aunt in Duluth, Minnesota," and she has been cooking for 37 years.

CHAPTER NINE

CAKES

CAKES

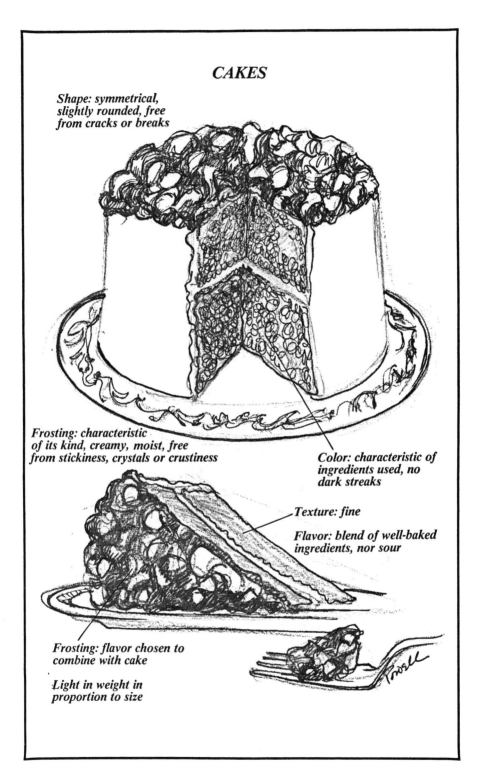

Shape: symmetrical, slightly rounded, free from cracks or breaks

Frosting: characteristic of its kind, creamy, moist, free from stickiness, crystals or crustiness

Color: characteristic of ingredients used, no dark streaks

Texture: fine

Flavor: blend of well-baked ingredients, nor sour

Frosting: flavor chosen to combine with cake

Light in weight in proportion to size

CHARLES O. ADAM
MIDWEST CITY, OKLAHOMA

FRUIT CAKE

1½ cups sugar	3 cups flour
1 cup shortening	1 lb. raisins
2 cups cold water	1 lb. dates
1 tsp. ground cloves	1½ lbs. pecan meat
2 tsp. cinnamon	8 ozs. candied pineapple
¼ tsp. salt	8 ozs. candied cherries
1 tsp. soda	25 small spice gumdrops

In a 4-quart saucepan boil for 5 minutes raisins, half of dates (whole), shortening, sugar, water, salt, and spices. Add cut-up pineapple and cherries after mixture has cooked 4 minutes, cook remaining minute, let cool. Add other half dates, pecan meats, gumdrops; mix well.

Add soda to flour and sift into batter, mixing well. Pour into 9-inch tube pan and bake in preheated (325-degree) oven for 2 hours.

Yield: 1 6–6½-pound cake

NOTE: After I put the batter in tube pan I garnish the top with pecan halves, cherries, and colored pineapple (I make designs).

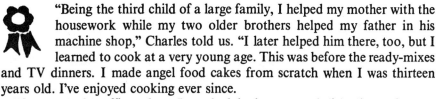

"Being the third child of a large family, I helped my mother with the housework while my two older brothers helped my father in his machine shop," Charles told us. "I later helped him there, too, but I learned to cook at a very young age. This was before the ready-mixes and TV dinners. I made angel food cakes from scratch when I was thirteen years old. I've enjoyed cooking ever since.

"One year the office where I worked had a covered-dish dinner for our Christmas Party. I took my Fruit Cake and, after eating it, different ones asked if I would bake them one. The next year at Christmas, I baked 36 cakes! I still bake cakes for several friends each year."

GERTIE MAE ALEXANDER

MOULTON, ALABAMA

FIRST PLACE, POUND CAKE
ALABAMA STATE FAIR

THE MILLION-DOLLAR POUND CAKE

4 cups cake flour	1 cup butter
3 cups sugar	1 cup margarine
6 eggs (large)	2 tsp. orange flavor
¾ cup milk	2 tsp. lemon flavor

Sift flour once and measure, then sift twice more. Cream butter to soften. Add sugar a cup at a time and cream well. Add eggs one at a time. Beat after adding each one. Add flour alternately with milk. Last added should be flour. Bake in 10-inch tube pan for 1 hour and 30 minutes at 325 degrees. Cool in pan 5 or 10 minutes. Turn out on cake rack.

Gertie Alexander has won top honors for four years straight at the Alabama State Fair with this recipe.

She has been cooking since she was eight years old, and she has raised seven children.

Gertie told us about one Christmas when she had to bake 44 cakes "for the public" in three days. Unexpectedly her son came home as a surprise. She was very tired but wanted to make his favorite cake. On her 45th cake in three days she forgot to put in the eggs.

ALYSSA ANN ARNETT
LOUISVILLE, KENTUCKY

PINA COLADA CAKE

1 stick margarine	1 tsp. rum extract
½ cup shortening	1 small can (3½ oz.) flake
2 cups sugar (granulated)	coconut
5 egg yolks	1 small can drained crushed
2 cups flour—all purpose	pineapple
1 tsp. soda	5 egg whites, stiffly beaten
1 cup buttermilk	

Cream margarine and shortening: add sugar and beat until smooth. Add egg yolks and beat well. Combine flour and soda and add to creamed mixture alternately with buttermilk. Stir in rum flavoring. Add coconut, pineapple, fold in beaten egg whites.

Pour batter into 3 greased and floured 8-inch cake pans. Bake at 350 degrees 25–35 minutes. Frost with Cream Cheese Frosting, leaving room in center for Pineapple Filling.

CREAM CHEESE FROSTING

1 8-oz. pkg. cream cheese	½ stick butter
1 lb. confectioners sugar	1 tsp. rum flavoring

Beat together until smooth. Frost cakes leaving room in center for pineapple filling.

PINEAPPLE FILLING

1 T. flour	1 small can crushed pineapple
¼ cup sugar	with juice

Combine in saucepan. Cook until thick, stirring constantly. Cool completely. Spread in center of cake. Cover remaining icing with more flaked coconut (frozen is best).

Here is half of the unbeatable mother-daughter combination Alyssa and Penny Arnett. Penny tells us about her daughter:

"Alyssa is only thirteen years old. She was eleven when she entered her first state fair. She was twelve when she entered her favorite cake in the "My Favorite Cake" division where she competed against women, not other juniors. This division is also one of the most popular at the fair. Also, it should be noted that her recipe is an original which she concocted through trial and error. She is presently taking Home Economics in Junior High and is an excellent pupil."

Alyssa says, "I cook for the family but mostly for my brothers."

SANDRA BINFORD

TURLOCK, CALIFORNIA

EASY WINE CAKE WITH SHERRY

1 pkg. yellow cake mix
1 4-oz. pkg. instant vanilla
    pudding mix
4 eggs

¾ cup oil
¾ cup cream sherry
1 tsp. pumpkin pie spice mix
Walnuts (optional)

Mix altogether the ingredients for 5 minutes at medium speed. Grease and dust bundt pan with flour, pour batter in. Bake at 350 degrees for 45 minutes or until done. Cool in pan for about 5 minutes. After cooling out of pan sprinkle with confectioners sugar.

 "I learned by my own mistakes, cookbooks, and a 'little more of this and a little more of that.' I'll try anything once," says Sandra, "and by a lot of laughs and corrections from good old Mom (a great Assyrian cook who really helped me a lot)."

Sandra has been cooking since she married 18 years ago—and she cooks for five every day.

MARLA CAMPBELL
WARREN, MICHIGAN

BUTTERMILK COCONUT CAKE

2 cups sugar
½ cup shortening
½ cup butter or margarine
5 eggs, separated (room temperature)
1 cup buttermilk (room temperature)

1 tsp. vanilla
2 cups flour
1 tsp. baking soda
1 tsp. salt
2 cups coconut

Cream sugar, shortening, and butter or margarine. Add the egg yolks and beat well. Add buttermilk and vanilla. Sift flour, soda, and salt together and add to first mixture. Beat well. Add coconut. Beat the egg whites stiff and fold into the batter. Pour into 3 greased and floured 8-inch round cake pans.

Bake at 350 degrees for 35 to 40 minutes or till done.

Frost with your favorite frosting. Spread between layers and top and sides of cake. Decorate top and sides with additional coconut.

You'll want to try Chocolate/Caramel Squares (page 359), another of Marla's prizewinners.

EUNICE L. CASEY
MINOT AFB, NORTH DAKOTA

FIRST PLACE
NORTH DAKOTA STATE FAIR

BLUE RIBBON CHOCOLATE CAKE
AND FROSTING

4 whole eggs	1½ tsp. baking soda
½ cup oil	1¾ cups packed brown sugar
1½ cups whole milk	⅔ cup instant chocolate
3 cups flour	1 cup chocolate syrup
½ tsp. salt	⅔ cup nuts, chopped fine
4 tsp. baking powder	

Mix eggs and milk, beat with electric mixer till foamy. Add oil and mix well. Then add flour, salt, baking powder, baking soda, brown sugar, and chocolates till smooth. During the last few seconds add nut meats. Pour into a well-greased and floured 10-inch pan. Bake in a 350-degree oven till tests done.

CHOCOLATE FROSTING

2 lbs. powdered sugar	1 tsp. vanilla
1½ cups shortening	1 cup chocolate syrup
½ cup milk	Walnut halves

Mix sugar, shortening, milk, and vanilla till smooth, then add syrup. Mix till totally combined. Decorate with walnuts.

 "When I was first married I made a from-scratch lemon meringue pie. My husband came home from work. Thinking it was a box filling, he took the blue food coloring and put it in the pie. The filling was green, the crust was blue, the meringue was brown on top, pale green on bottom. I was mad and made John eat it all."

Eunice learned to cook in Muncie, Indiana ("the Gas Company, Girl Scouts, and high school") and she got her first cookbook when she was nine.

"Since my husband is in the U.S. Air Force, we live in base housing. The kitchen is small with little counterspace."

ROSEMARY THOMPSON CAVANAUGH
LOUISVILLE, KENTUCKY

"I LOVE YOU" CHOCOLATE CAKE

2 cups no-sift flour
2 tsp. baking powder
½ tsp. baking soda
1 tsp. salt
3 cups brown sugar, packed
1⅓ cups sour cream
½ cup butter, soft

½ cup milk
½ cup honey
3 eggs
2 tsp. vanilla
4 oz. unsweetened chocolate, melted

Grease and flour 3 8-inch or 2 9-inch pans. Combine all dry ingredients.

Cream butter and add sour cream, eggs, and vanilla. Mix well. Alternate milk and honey with dry ingredients. When batter is smooth and well blended add chocolate. Mix well.

Do not fill pans over half full.

Bake at 300 degrees for 40–50 minutes. Cake is done when pick comes out clean.

"I LOVE YOU" CHOCOLATE FROSTING

1½ lbs. confectioners sugar
½ cup soft butter
4 oz. unsweetened chocolate, melted

1 tsp. vanilla
1 egg
¼ cup milk
Dash salt

Beat until creamy ⅓ of confectioners sugar and butter. Add chocolate, vanilla, and salt, blend. Beat in egg. Add remaining confectioners sugar alternately with milk, beating after each addition.

"This was the first time I had ever entered this type of competition. On the morning of the last day to enter cakes I began to bake. I wanted to insure as fresh a cake as possible. My three daughters, aged five, three and one at the time, seemed content and everything went smoothly. When the cake was almost ready to be removed from the oven there was a scream for help. By the time I had everything settled again my cake had burnt. So I just baked another one. As my cake cooled on the table I relaxed and prepared a batch of biscuits that I also had entered. Unfortunately, Erin, my one-year-old, decided to test the cake—she dug in with both hands. By this time I was in a panic. We all rushed to the store for new supplies. When this cake was baked I guarded it closely. I had to ice the cake while it was warm and truthfully was ready to call it quits but my mother and aunts insisted that I enter anyway. I arrived with my cake and biscuits only 20 minutes before entries were closed.

"When my husband, daughters, and I went to the fair later that week I didn't even want to see the cake exhibit. But when I saw #17 with the blue ribbon I couldn't believe it. We checked and it was mine. That afternoon everyone I knew received a call."

Rosemary also told us how she learned to cook: "My grandparents let me 'assist' them in the kitchen. They owned a restaurant so there was always a lot of cooking going on, and I suppose a lot of customers would have been shocked to know who was helping in the kitchen. On Monday afternoons when the restaurant was closed the family would prepare traditional Lebanese food, this was always a lot of fun. The restaurant is still operating and occasionally I play in the kitchen. There is still a lot of family cooking going on. Also I was a home ec major in college so there was a lot of cooking there—slightly more scientific, and not as much fun."

Rosemary cooks for five every day in her cheery, warm-toned kitchen.

MADELINE CLEERE
MOULTON, ALABAMA

FIRST PRIZE
MOULTON COUNTY FAIR

HOLIDAY POUND CAKE

2 cups butter or margarine
2 cups sugar
1 T. vanilla
2 T. bourbon
9 eggs

4¼ cups flour (plain)
½ cup chopped candied
    cherries
½ cup chopped nuts
1 tsp. salt

Cream butter until soft and fluffy. Add sugar gradually, beating well. Add vanilla and bourbon. Add eggs, one at a time, beating well after each egg is added.

Sprinkle cherries and nuts with ¼ cup flour. Sift remaining flour with salt and fold, ½ cup at a time, into the creamed mixture, mixing only until smooth. Fold in cherries and nuts with last addition of flour.

Bake in greased, floured 10-inch tube pan or in 2 loaf pans (9x5x3) at 325 degrees for 1 hour and 30 minutes. Bake loaf pans 1 hour, 15 minutes.

This is very good and freezes well. I used my mother's basic pound cake recipe to develop this.

Madeline Cleere developed the prizewinning Holiday Pound Cake recipe from her mother's basic recipe. She says she has had "good success" with her recipe.

Madeline cooks in a "big country kitchen with rocking chairs and a place to eat."

Her pound cake is "good warm or cold. It keeps for days and gets better every day."

MARY COOMES
LOUISVILLE, KENTUCKY

SOFT SPRINGERLE

4 eggs
1 lb. confectioners sugar
½ stick soft butter
1 T. honey

1 tsp. baking powder
¼ tsp. anise oil
1 lb. flour (3½–4 cups)

Beat eggs with electric mixer for 15 minutes, add powdered sugar and beat 15 minutes longer. Beat in the butter, honey, baking powder, anise oil, and half the flour. When smooth, remove from beater and stir in remainder of flour by hand. The dough should have the consistency of biscuit dough. Roll out on floured board a scant ½-inch thick. Mark with springerle mold or springerle rolling pin and cut apart with a sharp knife. Place on waxed paper and let set overnight to allow the designs to dry. Bake on a very lightly greased baking sheet at 300 degrees for about 12 minutes or until very light straw colored. Cool and store in a tightly covered container.

 "My kitchen is full of calories, love, and good smells," says Mary Coomes. She has won in her specialties of cakes, cookies, and decorated cakes. Although her prizes have included silver trays and porcelain bowls, the real award is in prestige.

Mary told us she cooks for four, "a wonderful man and two teenage daughters." She told us: "The very best advice I can offer to anyone who is interested in learning to cook, or trying to improve their cooking is to go to it and do not be upset if you do not achieve the desired result the very first time. Try the same recipe more than once, especially proven recipes, which are a must for beginners."

BETTY DRANSFIELD

UNION, WEST VIRGINIA

COCONUT-PECAN CREAM-CHEESE CAKE

1 cup shortening	1 tsp. vanilla
2 cups sugar	1 small can shredded coconut
5 egg yolks	1 cup chopped nuts
2 cups flour	5 egg whites, beaten stiffly
1 tsp. soda	1 cup buttermilk

Cream shortening and sugar; add egg yolks and beat until light and fluffy. Sift together flour and soda; add alternately with buttermilk and vanilla, beating smooth each time. Stir in nuts and coconut; fold in beaten egg whites. Pour into 3 greased layer pans; bake in preheated 350-degree oven for 25 minutes. Cool before adding frosting.

CREAM CHEESE ICING

¼ lb. margarine, melted
1 lb. confectioners sugar
1 8-oz. pkg. cream cheese (room temperature)
1 tsp. vanilla

Combine all ingredients; beat until light and fluffy. Spread between layers and on top of cake (and sides, if desired).

Betty Dransfield says the eye-appealing recipes in magazines made her decide to teach herself to cook in her first years of marriage.

She tells a cute story about the first time she made cookies: "This type, after baking, was to be coated in confectionery sugar. And coating each individual cookie took time. I decided to shorten this by placing confectionery sugar and cookies in a paper bag and shaking *well*. Upon opening the bag—all I had was crumbs."

MARTHA ESTRADA
BETHANY, OKLAHOMA

ITALIAN CREAM CAKE

2 cups sugar
2 sticks oleo
5 eggs
2 cups sifted flour
1 tsp. baking soda
½ tsp. salt

1 cup buttermilk
1 cup chopped nuts
2 cups flaked coconut
½ cup drained chopped
   maraschino cherries

Cream sugar and oleo. Separate eggs. Beat yolks and add to sugar mixture. Mix sifted flour, soda, and salt. Add alternately with buttermilk. Add nuts, cherries, and coconut. Beat egg whites until stiff and fold into cake mixture.

Bake in 2 9-inch or 3 8-inch cake pans, well greased and floured, 35–40 minutes at 350 degrees.

ITALIAN CREAM CAKE FROSTING

1 8-oz. pkg. cream cheese
1 [regular box] confectioners
   sugar
1 cup flaked coconut

1 stick oleo
1 cup chopped nuts
1 tsp. vanilla

Cream oleo, cream cheese, and powdered sugar thoroughly. Add remaining ingredients and spread on cake.

Martha has a very diplomatic mother. She told us about the first time she made frosting for a cake for her. "I used granulated sugar instead of powdered. Mother said it was good even though I could hear the grit of the sugar with each bite."

RUTH ETTEN
ELKHORN, WISCONSIN

FIRST PRIZE
WALWORTH COUNTY FAIR

LAZY DAISY CAKE

1 cup flour	1 cup sugar
1 tsp. baking powder	½ cup milk
¾ tsp. salt	1 T. butter
2 eggs	1 tsp. vanilla

Beat eggs, add sugar gradually, beat until fluffy. Sift flour, salt, and baking powder together. Add to egg mixture. Beat thoroughly. Heat milk and butter to boiling point. Add to batter. Add vanilla. Beat slightly. Pour into greased 8x8-inch cake pan. Bake in 350-degree oven 30 minutes. When done you can spread immediately with topping and place under broiler until browned.

TOPPING

5 T. brown sugar	½ cup coconut
3 T. cream	½ cup chopped pecans
3 T. butter	

Mix all ingredients and heat just enough so it is of the right consistency to spread. When cake is done spread immediately with topping and place under broiler until browned.

Ruth's Mexican Wedding Cakes (page 322) took the grand prize at the Walworth County Fair.

MARTHA FEHLMAN
POWELL, WYOMING

FIRST AWARD, CAKE
WYOMING STATE FAIR

ANGEL FOOD CAKE

Set oven at 425 degrees. Put empty angel food cake pans in oven while mixing the cake.

1½ cups fresh egg whites (room temperature)
1 tsp. cream of tartar (be sure it is fresh)
¼ tsp. salt

1 cup granulated sugar
1 cup powdered sugar, sifted
1 cup cake flour, sifted
1 tsp. vanilla or almond extract

Beat egg whites until frothy. Add cream of tartar and salt. Beat until they hold peaks that stand up. I use an electric mixer and lift up the beaters now and then. Using a whisk, fold in the cup of granulated sugar, pulling the whisk up to allow more air in batter. Add 2 tablespoons at a time. Sift powdered sugar and cake flour together 5 times. Fold into egg whites, 2 tablespoons at a time, allowing about 20 strokes until all gone. Add flavoring, pour into hot pan, and set in the middle of the oven and bake exactly 25 minutes. Remove from oven and turn on rack to cool upside down.

Martha Fehlman has been cooking for 60 years, since she "was a girl on the ranch." In 1977 she even published her own cookbook, *Martha's Wyoming Cookbook.*

FLORENCE A. M. FOX
GREENWOOD, INDIANA

RED DEVIL'S-FOOD CAKE (Moist)
and CHOCOLATE FROSTING

2 cups sugar	1 tsp. vanilla
3 eggs	2 tsp. soda
¾ cup shortening	2½ cups flour
1 cup buttermilk	⅔ cup powdered cocoa
1 cup boiling water	Pinch of salt

Prepare oven for baking at 375 degrees.

Cream shortening well. Add eggs and beat until light and fluffy.

Sift dry ingredients together and add alternately with the buttermilk. Add vanilla.

Dissolve soda into the boiling water and stir it into your cake batter thoroughly.

Pour cake batter into 3 greased and floured cake pans and bake 25–30 minutes until done. Turn out on wire racks to cool before frosting.

NOTE: I always test it by a straw or touch lightly with finger and it will spring back and cake will shrink loose around sides of pan.

CHOCOLATE FROSTING

2 cups sugar	¼ cup half-and-half
½ cup cocoa	1 tsp. vanilla
½ cup margarine	

Combine all ingredients except vanilla and mix well. Place on medium heat until dissolved. Bring to a full rolling boil and cook until mixture forms a soft ball in *cold* water. Add vanilla and beat until creamy consistency to spread. Frost each layer except top one. Then frost sides and top layer last.

"I cater to recipes made from scratch, as they say, even though your prepared box mixtures are all right. I've tried some, but prefer those made from scratch."

These are the words of prizewinning cook Florence Fox, who is also a retired teacher. She enters many categories at the fair, including cookies, whole wheat bread, and candies.

CHOCOLATE CAKE

¾ cup butter or margarine
2¼ cups sugar
1½ tsp. vanilla
3 eggs
3 cups sifted cake flour

1½ tsp. baking soda
¾ tsp. salt
1½ cups ice water
3 1-oz. sqs. unsweetened
chocolate, melted

Cream together butter and sugar in mixing bowl until light and fluffy. Beat in vanilla. Add eggs, 1 at a time, beating well after each addition. Blend in chocolate. Sift together cake flour, baking soda, and salt. Add dry ingredients alternately with water to creamed mixture, beating well. Pour batter into 3 greased and waxed-paper-lined 8-inch cake pans.

Bake in 350-degree oven 30–35 minutes or until cake tests done. Cool in pans on rack 10 minutes. Remove from pans. Cool. Frost.

Yield: serves 12

"Very busy at fair time," is Bonnie Gesler's description of her kitchen. A cook for 19 years, Bonnie enters many categories in the fair. Once she locked her fudge and divinity in the trunk of her Volkswagen and when she got to the fair, she couldn't get the trunk open. She had to have her entries in before noon. After she'd driven all over the city, finally a "kind gentleman" helped out, and the trunk was open at 11:45. She rushed back to the fairground and delivered her entries, just in time. "Both my fudge and divinity won blue ribbons. What a day!"

STRAWBERRY-RHUBARB CHEESECAKE

CRUST

1 cup sifted all-purpose flour	½ cup butter or margarine
¼ cup sugar	1 slightly beaten egg yolk
1 tsp. grated lemon peel	¼ tsp. vanilla

FILLING

5 8-oz. pkgs. cream cheese	¼ tsp. salt
¼ tsp. vanilla	4 or 5 eggs (1 cup)
¾ tsp. grated lemon peel	2 egg yolks
¾ tsp. grated orange peel	¼ cup whipping cream
1¾ cups sugar	(unwhipped) (heavy type)
3 T. all-purpose flour	

CRUST

Combine first three ingredients. Cut in butter until crumbly. Add egg yolk and vanilla; mix well. Pat ⅓ of dough on bottom of 9-inch springform pan (sides removed). Work with fingers so dough is well distributed over bottom. Bake at 400 degrees about 5–8 minutes (burns easily) or until golden; cool. Pat remaining dough on sides of pan to about height of 1¾ inches (where filling will reach). Make sure the dough is patted to uniform thickness.

(Chill dough if it becomes sticky, then pat in wax paper. Try to work in cool kitchen.)

FILLING

Let cream cheese stand at room temperature to soften (1½–3 or so hours, or lumps will occur in cheesecake even after baking). Beat until *creamy;* add vanilla, lemon and orange peels. Mix sugar, flour, and salt well; gradually blend into cheese. Add eggs and egg yolks one at a time, beating after each, just to blend. Gently stir in cream.

Turn into crust-lined pan. Bake at 450 degrees for 12 minutes; reduce heat to 300 degrees; bake 1 hour longer or until knife inserted off center comes out clean (usually mine bakes for about 20 or so minutes longer). I use a thin-bladed sharp knife so as to avoid making large cuts in cake which can cause the cake to split). Remove from oven; cool one-half hour; loosen sides of cheesecake from pan with spatula. Cool one-half hour more; remove sides of pan. Cool 2 hours longer. Meanwhile, make topping.

TOPPING

I sometimes just spread some of my homemade strawberry-rhubarb jam on top of the cake. *Or,* crush 1 cup fresh strawberries; add ½ cup precooked (softened) fresh rhubarb and ¾ cup water. Cook 2 minutes; sieve. In saucepan, combine 2 tablespoons cornstarch and ½ cup sugar; gradually stir in hot berry mixture. Bring to boil, stirring constantly. Cook and stir until thick and clear. (Add a few drops red food coloring, if needed.) Cool to room temperature. Place 1 cup whole fresh strawberries on cooled cheesecake. Pour berry-rhubarb glaze over strawberries. Chill at least 2 hours.

If in a hurry, pour cherry pie filling over for topping.

Yield: serves 12

 Donna Gilbertson describes herself as a "self-taught cook—a perfectionist who uses a timer without fail." The kitchen of her 200-year-old house is without a cupboard save for one old-fashioned one built over 100 years ago. Her baking equipment is kept in a pantry "out back."

She always has to remember to put her eggs in a secure place because the kitchen floor is at an angle. "I have lost many an egg rolling off the table," she says.

"I had a crazy experience with Christmas cookies and my 'modern Glenwood' (circa 1803) wood stove. I promised the children's teachers Christmas cookies for their parties. However, we blew some fuses (the antique kind that one has to buy special—it occurred after store hours) and to make a long story short (my electric stove was functioning at half power, very frustrating!) I resorted to the big black-and-chrome wood stove. Quite an experience. I give my ancestors a lot of credit for being able to cope with and produce such perfect baked goods during their reign. Out of every tray of butter cookies (cut and rolled type) six would be perfect, three uncooked and three burned to a crisp! I went through a lot of cookie dough that day."

Donna says about her Strawberry Rhubarb Cheesecake, "I guarantee compliments—many 'cheese cake connoisseurs' have tested the recipe!"

MERCEDES GLOGOWSKI
DEARBORN HEIGHTS, MICHIGAN

FIRST PREMIUM, ROLLS, BREAD,
CRUMBCAKE, STREUSEL
COFFEE CAKE
MICHIGAN STATE FAIR

RICH CRUMBCAKE

1¾ cups plus 2 T. sifted flour	1½ cups sugar
3 tsp. baking powder	3 eggs
¾ tsp. salt	¾ cup milk
⅓ cup butter	½ tsp. vanilla extract

CRUMB TOPPING

⅓ cup brown sugar	½ tsp. cinnamon
¼ cup flour	3 T. butter

Preheat oven to 350 degrees and butter a 9-inch angel cake, or tube, pan. Sift together flour, baking powder, and salt. Work butter until creamy: then add sugar gradually. (This will be a granular mixture, rather than creamy.)

Separate eggs, and beat yolks slightly. Add to sugar mixture, and continue beating until no drops of yolk are apparent. Add flour mixture alternately with milk, beginning and ending with flour. Beat whites until they form peaks; then fold gently into batter. Stir in vanilla. Pour into prepared pan, and bake 50 minutes, or until cake tester inserted in center comes out clean. Sprinkle Crumb Topping evenly over cake and return to oven 10 minutes.

 Mercedes has won many blue ribbons. She says, "Much of my success in cooking is due to the fact that I like to cook. If I had problems making anything I did it over until I was successful. My first attempt at stuffed cabbages, the recipe did not specify to cook the rice. The rice did not absorb enough liquid during the cooking—making it feel like you were eating grit. My new husband, not to hurt my feelings, kept eating until I said I couldn't eat those terrible stuffed cabbages."

She learned to cook by "reading cookbooks and articles on cooking. Later, when I married, my mother-in-law told me how to cook certain ethnic foods."

CAKES   227

WHITE VELVET CAKE

⅔ cup solid shortening
2 T. boiling water
1 tsp. almond flavoring
½ tsp. salt
½ cup unsweetened pineapple
    juice
4 tsp. baking powder
1 tsp. vanilla flavoring
½ tsp. glycerin
1 cup cold water
3½ cups cake flour
4 egg whites

Cream shortening and sugar, add boiling water, and beat until creamy with electric beater. Add flavorings and glycerin. Sift salt and flour 4 times and add alternately with the water and juice to the creamed mixture; start with the flour and end with the liquids. Sprinkle baking powder over batter. Add beaten egg whites and fold together gently.

Bake in 2 9x9-inch loaf pans in 350-degree oven for approximately 25 minutes or until toothpick comes out clean.

CAKE VARIATIONS

After the batter has been beaten 3 minutes, add any of the following:

For Coconut Layer Cake, omit almond flavoring and sprinkle 1 teaspoon coconut flavoring between layers and on top of frosting. Add coconut flavoring to frosting too.

For Cherry Nut Cake, add ⅔ cup chopped nuts and ½ cup chopped red candied cherries.

For Nut Cake, add ⅔ cup chopped nuts to batter and sprinkle nuts on top.

For Pineapple Cake, add ⅓ cup well-drained crushed pineapple. Omit icing and vanilla flavoring and add 1 teaspoon lemon flavoring.

FROSTING

1 egg white (unbeaten)
½ cup shortening
1 tsp. almond flavoring
4 cups confectioners sugar
¼ tsp. salt

Beat all together with electric beater. Usually a little milk or cream has to be added to make it right consistency to spread. I use milk.

A three-year sweepstakes winner in cakes at the Des Moines State Fair, Mrs. Groen learned to cook "with good hints from my mother" when she joined 4-H. She has been a 30-year prizewinner at the Clay County Fair. Once, though, she used pancake flour instead of cake flour for an angel food cake. "Even the dogs and cats wouldn't eat it!" Her Banana Chiffon Cake has been her entry many times at many fairs and she has gotten a blue ribbon every time except one.

"The White Velvet Cake, I can really say is a blue-ribbon cake. It's an old recipe and I used it ever since I learned to bake [50 years ago]. I truthfully can say I have *never* had a flop with it and I have won many, many blue ribbons with it."

VERNEAL HAMILTON
RECTOR, ARKANSAS

FIRST PRIZE
GREENE COUNTY FAIR

CHEESE CAKE

1 pkg. lemon gelatin
1 cup hot water
3 T. lemon juice
1 8-oz. pkg. cream cheese
1 cup sugar
1 tsp. vanilla

1 tall can chilled evaporated
  milk
½ lb. graham crackers
½ cup oleo, melted
¼ cup cracker crumbs

Crush graham crackers, add melted oleo. Line a 9x13-inch pan with the crumbs. Dissolve gelatin in hot water, add lemon juice, and cool. Cream the cheese, add sugar and vanilla, mix. Whip the milk, add cream cheese mixture to the gelatin, then fold in milk. Pour mixture into pan and sprinkle top with graham cracker crumbs. For variation, add a can of well-drained pineapple to mixture. Chill before serving.

Verneal's recipe for Arkansas Millionaire Candy is on page 369.

MARY ANN HILDRETH
FAIRBORN, OHIO

HONEY CHOCOLATE CAKE

3 sq. unsweetened chocolate, melted
⅔ cup honey
1¾ cups sifted cake flour
1 tsp. soda
¾ tsp. salt

½ cup butter
½ cup sugar
1 tsp. vanilla
2 eggs
⅔ cup water

Blend chocolate and honey; cool to lukewarm. Sift flour once, measure, add soda and salt; sift together 3 times. Cream butter thoroughly, add sugar gradually, and cream together until light and fluffy. Add chocolate-honey mixture and vanilla. Blend. Add eggs 1 at a time, beating thoroughly after each addition. Add flour alternately with water, a small amount at a time, beating after each addition until smooth. Bake in 2 greased 8-inch layer pans in moderate oven (350 degrees) 30 to 35 minutes. Cool. Spread with Honey Chocolate Frosting.

HONEY CHOCOLATE FROSTING

1¾ cups powdered sugar
¾ cup cocoa
¼ tsp. salt
3 T. butter

3 T. vegetable shortening
1 T. honey
1 egg white
2 T. milk

Sift dry ingredients together into mixing bowl. Add remaining ingredients except milk. Mix until smooth.

Add milk and mix at low speed on mixer until light. Spread on cake.

"Once I put cough syrup in a cake," Mary Ann Hildreth confesses. "I thought it was vanilla." In 40 years of cooking, one little mistake is not much—besides, it sounds like a delicious cold remedy! Mary Ann says her kitchen is "my heaven."

Esther B. Holm
Kensal, North Dakota

FIRST PLACE, SPONGE CAKE (UNFROSTED)
MINOT STATE FAIR

SPONGE CAKE

3 cups cake flour	1 tsp. vanilla
2½ tsp. baking powder	½ tsp. lemon juice
½ tsp. salt	1 cup cold water
10–12 egg yolks (1 cup)	

Sift dry ingredients together 3 times. Beat egg yolks in mixer until light and fluffy. Add vanilla, lemon juice and cold water gradually. Bake 1 hour at 350 degrees. Use large angel food pan. Invert pan, cool. Loosen with a spatula and remove from pan.

"My specialties are canning 350 quarts of fruits, meats, jellies, and jam each year and baking pies, cakes, buns, and bread for several hungry men each day. We operate a large farm and also have a dairy herd. We sell cream and eggs locally.

"My advice to those learning to cook is, 'If at first you don't succeed try, try again!' Don't save all your smiles for the parlor, use some in the kitchen. Invite your neighbors in for a cup of coffee and a caramel roll plus a friendly chat."

ELAINE HOLMES
EUREKA, CALIFORNIA

FIRST PRIZE
HUMBOLDT COUNTY FAIR

CHEESECAKE

2 eggs	2 T. sugar
½ cup sugar	¼ cup butter
12 oz. cream cheese, softened	1 cup sour cream
½ tsp. vanilla	2 T. sugar
1 tsp. lemon juice	½ tsp. vanilla
1½ cups graham cracker crumbs	

Beat eggs until light with whisk. Add sugar gradually, beating after each addition. Add cream cheese, vanilla, and lemon juice, beat thoroughly.

Combine cracker crumbs, sugar, and butter with fork; press onto bottom, up sides of 9-inch pie pan.

Pour in cheese mixture, spread evenly. Bake 20 minutes at 375 degrees. Cool 1 hour.

Combine sour cream, sugar, vanilla; spread evenly over cooled cake. Bake 10 minutes at 400 degrees. Sprinkle top with nutmeg, cool, chill.

Lucky Elaine told us, "My husband used to work for Wearever Aluminum, so I have a complete set of cookware and cutlery. The cookware all hangs above the stove, along with lids, for easy access."

Although Elaine learned to cook after marriage, by the "trial-and-error method," she has been cooking for ten years and has developed a number of prizewinning recipes.

RENDA HOUSTON
DOTHAN, ALABAMA

PEANUTTY CREAM CHEESE CAKE

1 stick oleo
½ cup peanut oil
2 cups sugar
1 cup buttermilk
1 [small] can coconut
1 cup crunchy peanut butter

5 egg yolks
2 cups cake flour
1 tsp. soda
1 tsp. vanilla
5 egg whites (beaten stiff)

Cream oleo and peanut oil, add sugar, beat well. Add egg yolks and beat. Sift flour and soda twice, add to mixture, then add buttermilk. Add crunchy peanut butter, stir in vanilla and coconut. Fold in stiffly beaten egg whites. Bake at 350 degrees until done (3 thick or 4 thin layers).

FROSTING

1 8-oz. pkg. cream cheese
½ cup oleo
½ cup chopped roasted peanuts

1 tsp. vanilla
1 box confectioners sugar

Beat cream cheese and oleo, add confectioners sugar and vanilla. Put the chopped peanuts on top of cake.

Renda told us that one time "while baking a Red Velvet Cake, I suddenly realized that I had no red cake coloring. I substituted green and my family would not eat it. I knew it was psychological, as it tasted the same." Renda began cooking when she was about five—she was taught by her grandmother.

This champion cook has a very helpful hint—"Always sift flour twice for correct measurements."

CONFETTI ANGEL FOOD CAKE

1 cup cake flour
¾ cup sugar
12 egg whites
1½ tsp. cream of tartar
¼ tsp. salt

1½ tsp. vanilla
½ tsp. almond extract
¾ cup plus 2 T. sugar
2¾ oz. round confetti candies

Sift flour and ¾ cup sugar together, set aside. In large mixing bowl beat egg whites and cream of tartar, vanilla, almond extract, and salt at medium speed till soft peaks form. Gradually add remaining sugar. Continue beating till stiff peaks form. Fold in the flour-and-sugar mixture about a quarter at a time. Next fold in the candies. Turn into an ungreased 10-inch tube pan. Bake in a 375-degree oven for 35 to 40 minutes. Invert pan and completely cool cake before removing from the pan. To help get cake out of pan, run a spatula around the sides of the pan to loosen it.

Sandi cooks for four, "two daughters, a husband, and me." She has been cooking since she was nine.

Sandi told us a story on herself that illustrates how well organized she is: "One Sunday, I was cooking dinner for my in-laws, who were coming over. Everything was going smooth, the lasagna was done, the green salad was made, the garlic bread was ready to go in the oven as soon as the blueberry pie came out. As I was taking the pie out of the oven, I bumped the counter, and soon the pie was all over my counter and the floor. With my in-laws due any minute, I just stood there and cried for a few minutes. Soon I had the pie mess all cleaned up, but it was too late to make another pie, so my husband went to the store and bought a frozen pie. It was still in the oven when my in-laws arrived, everyone got a good laugh out of the mishap."

STELLA JEZEWSKI
DETROIT, MICHIGAN

POPPY SEED CAKE

½ cup poppy seeds
2 cups sugar
4 tsp. baking powder
1 tsp. salt
1½ cups oil

4 eggs
1 can evaporated milk
1 tsp. vanilla
4 cups flour (all-purpose)

Beat eggs, milk, vanilla and sugar until creamy. Sift dry ingredients and add to cream mixture. Beat till smooth, add poppy seeds.

Bake at 350 degrees, 1 hour, in well-greased and -floured pan. Doesn't need frosting. The top of cake will crack up, and that is sure pretty. This is a big cake. It will keep 2 weeks in a cool place. Best 2 or 3 days after baking.

"If something goes wrong don't give up," advises Stella. "Try again, it may not be your fault." She has been cooking for 35 years and has won in many categories.

Try Stella's Red Tomato Marmalade (page 419).

SHREDA DYE JONES
NORTH TAZEWELL, VIRGINIA

DECORATED CAKE

3¾ cups all-purpose flour	3 cups sugar
1 tsp. baking powder	6 eggs (room temperature)
½ tsp. salt	1 cup sweet milk (room
⅛ tsp. nutmeg	temperature)
1 cup solid shortening	1 tsp. butter flavoring
1 cup butter (real butter	1 tsp. lemon flavoring
is best)	

Stir together flour, baking powder, salt, and nutmeg. Set aside.

Cream butter, shortening, and sugar. Add eggs 1 at a time, mixing well after each. Add flour to creamed sugar mixture, then milk. Mix at low speed until blended.

Bake in a 13x9x2-inch pan, with any mix left over baked in a small loaf pan. Bake for 1 hour at 325 degrees, then test with toothpick in center of cake. If not done bake 10 to 15 minutes longer.

FROSTING DECORATORS

2 T. egg whites or powdered	1 lb. confectioners sugar
egg whites	(sifted)
⅔ cup solid shortening	½ tsp. vanilla flavoring
2 T. milk (as needed to soften)	1 tsp. butter flavoring

In large mixing bowl combine sifted sugar, shortening, and 1 tablespoon milk. Mix at low speed and add milk just till icing will mix together well. Add butter flavoring, blend well, then add vanilla flavoring and egg whites. Mix and add small amounts of milk as needed until icing is spreadable.

My prizewinning cake was iced in white frosting with yellow trim (shells) around the top and bottom borders and along the four corners. The loaf cake was cut to make a small rectangle which was covered with a yellow icing quilt draped at 2 corners and a satin yellow ribbon edge. This cake bed contained two round balls under the quilt to resemble a sleeping baby or small child whose head was on a mound icing pillow. The ends of the bed were made of icing to resemble a four-poster bed of brown color, and a green-and-yellow icing rug with fringes of green was under the bed on one side. All around the bed and on the rug were the child's toys, all hand formed of icing—a yellow-and-blue duck on wheels, a truck, a rocking horse of white with red spots on green rockers, a white dog with brown eyes and tail, a brown and white teddy bear, a baseball glove and ball and bat. The caption for my cake was: "Dream Tomorrow's Big Dreams, Little Man."

Shreda Dye Jones, one of our few cooks who learned from her father, cooks in a "very compact" kitchen.

Once she and her mother made a beautiful custard pie—"really a picture of a pie—just turned out beautifully." Then a cousin tasted it and couldn't stand it—not even one bite—for the cooks had used salt instead of sugar.

About her prizewinning decorated cake Shreda Dye Jones says, "I enjoyed making and baking this cake, and was pleased with the end product and my blue ribbon and the money." However, she warns that it is a costly cake to make.

DIUOMA KIBBE

SOMERS, CONNECTICUT

FIRST PRIZE
FOUR TOWN FAIR
SOMERS, CONNECTICUT

HOLIDAY GIFT CAKE

1 8-oz. pkg. cream cheese (room temperature)	1½ tsp. baking powder
1½ cups sugar	¾ 8-oz. jar well-drained maraschino cherries (half
1 cup butter	red and half green,
1¼ tsp. vanilla	chopped)
4 eggs	½ cup chopped walnut meats
2¼ cups sifted cake flour	

Thoroughly blend softened cream cheese, butter, sugar, and vanilla. Add eggs, 1 at a time, mixing well after each addition.

Gradually add 2 cups flour sifted with baking powder. Combine remaining flour with cherries and nuts and fold into batter.

Grease a 10-inch angel cake pan. Pour batter into pan. Bake in a preheated oven at 325 degrees for 1 hour and 20 minutes. Test for doneness with a toothpick, cook longer if necessary. Cool for 5 minutes, remove from the pan. When cool frost with Fluffy Frosting.

FLUFFY FROSTING

3 cups sifted confectioners sugar	¼ cup butter
½ cup solid shortening	4 T. juice from red maraschino cherries

Mix all ingredients and beat hard until mixture is fluffy. Frost top, sides, and hole of cake. Decorate top with red cherries and nut meats.

 "My mother made bread every day but Sunday on the farm," says Diuoma. "I learned to cook from her when I was little. She used to cook daily from the time I was fifteen till I was thirty-one for eight people."

Still cooking in a "farm kitchen," Diuoma has come up with some prize-winning recipes.

SARITA KAY KOOPMAN

SHERIDAN, INDIANA

SWEEPSTAKES OVER ALL,
LAYER CAKES—GERMAN
CHOCOLATE CAKE, CHAMPION
OVER ALL, LARD CAKES—
CHOCOLATE LARD CAKE
INDIANA STATE FAIR
INDIANAPOLIS, INDIANA

LARD DEVIL'S-FOOD CAKE AND CHOCOLATE ICING

2 cups sifted cake flour	2 tsp. baking powder
⅔ cup lard	1 tsp. baking soda
2 sq. baking chocolate	1 tsp. vanilla
(melted)	1 cup milk
1¼ cup sugar	2 eggs
1 tsp. salt	

Line bottom of 2 8-inch layer cake pans with waxed paper. Cream 1 cup of flour and lard and beat thoroughly. Stir in melted chocolate. Add remaining dry ingredients, vanilla, and ¾ cup milk. Beat vigorously until smooth and fluffy. Add remaining milk in 2 portions, beating until thoroughly mixed. Add eggs 1 at a time, beating well after each addition.

Bake at 375 degrees, 25 to 30 minutes. Ice with favorite icing. I used hand mixer to mix the cake. The secret is to mix your lard and flour well, about 15 minutes.

CHOCOLATE ICING

¾ cup cocoa	1 tsp. vanilla
4 cups powdered sugar	½ cup evaporated milk
½ cup butter (soft)	

Sift cocoa and sugar, cream butter and half cocoa mixture. Blend in vanilla and ½ oz. milk, add remaining cocoa mixture. Add remaining milk to desired consistency.

 Sarita Koopman learned to cook "mostly from my mother (a farmer's wife). I experimented on my own, I watched both of my grandmothers very closely when I was little and kept my eyes and ears open for anything new. My sister-in-law taught me to decorate cakes."

She told us about her first experience cake decorating. "The cake was completely finished (a sixteen-hour job). My mother moved the cake and stuck her thumb in a rose and the corner. My mother, sister-in-law, and I all sat down and cried. Then we proceeded to fix up the cake, and it received First Place!"

FLORENCE MAY KREIDER

QUARRYVILLE, PENNSYLVANIA

FIRST PRIZE

SALANEO COMMUNITY FAIR
LANCASTER COUNTY, PENNSYLVANIA

PENNSYLVANIA DUTCH CHOCOLATE CAKE AND EASY CARAMEL FROSTING

3 cups yellow sugar
¾ cup shortening
3 eggs
1 cup buttermilk
2½ cups flour

¾ cup cocoa
⅛ tsp. salt
¾ cup boiling water
2 tsp. soda

Mix first 3 ingredients until light and fluffy. Add sifted dry ingredients alternately with buttermilk. Add boiling water to which soda has been added. Bake at 375 degrees 35–40 minutes.

This recipe can be used for layer cakes, loaf cakes, or cupcakes. Bake cupcakes approximately 18 minutes.

EASY CARAMEL FROSTING

Melt ½ cup butter and add 1 cup brown sugar. Cook over low heat for 2 minutes. Add ¼ cup milk and cook, stirring, until mixture comes to a boil. Remove from heat and cool slightly. Add 1½ to 2 cups sifted 10X sugar and beat.

Yield: covers a 9-inch layer cake

"We live in the heart of the Pennsylvania Dutch country, where cooking is at its best. Traditions are handed down from one generation to another. Amish, Mennonite and Brethren and many others have many delicious recipes. Cookbooks and good restaurants are in abundance in our area. Come and see."

Doesn't she make Pennsylvania sound wonderful?

Florence works in a beautiful, sunny colonial kitchen. She told us about the time her husband's aunts and uncles were guests for noon supper. "About 3 o'clock I realized there were four dishes of filling still in the oven. Very well done."

KRISTY LAUDERDALE
ELKHORN, WISCONSIN

JELLY ROLL

4 eggs (beaten until light and thick)
1 cup sugar
1 cup flour

1 tsp. vanilla
2 tsp. baking powder
½ tsp. salt
½ tsp. lemon

Bake at 350 degrees for 15 minutes. Take out of oven and lay on a damp cloth for 5 minutes. Cut outside crust off, then spread with jelly and roll. After it is rolled sprinkle the top with powdered sugar.

"My grandmother always enjoyed cooking," says Kristy. "She and I would bake for the family. I then picked up on all of her secret recipes and ingredients, and now I bake for my family."

Although her kitchen is small, Kristy says "there is an abundance of happiness within." Once, the night before a fair, she dropped a chocolate layer cake. At 10:30 another cake had to be baked, cooled, and frosted. "It was very late when we went to bed," she says. "However, we won a first-prize ribbon, so our effort was rewarded."

Advice? "Cooking takes a special loving touch; a person should enjoy cooking and always have fun."

MARIE LAWSEN
FORTUNA, CALIFORNIA

PRUNE CAKE

2¼ cups sifted all-purpose flour	½ cup shortening
2 tsp. baking powder	½ cup milk
¼ tsp. soda	½ cup prune juice
1 tsp. salt	2 eggs
½ tsp. cinnamon	1 tsp. vanilla
¼ tsp. nutmeg	

Sift dry ingredients together, then add shortening, milk, and prune juice and beat 1½ minutes. Add eggs and vanilla and beat 1½ minutes. Bake in 2 layer pans at 375 degrees for 20 to 25 minutes.

FROSTING

2 egg whites	2 tsp. lemon juice
1 cup brown sugar	¼ cup well-drained chopped
¼ cup light syrup	prunes
¼ tsp. salt	

Beat egg whites, sugar, and syrup, then add salt, lemon juice, and prunes.

 Marie was born in Denmark, and her early experiences there were important in her cooking education. She has been cooking for 50 years. Now she cooks for two, but she used to cook for 16 every day.

COCONUT LAYER CAKE

¼ cup milk	3½ cups self-rising flour
1 cup shortening	3 tsp. baking powder
2 cups sugar	½ tsp. salt
1 tsp. vanilla	1 cup milk
½ tsp. almond flavoring	8 egg whites (unbeaten)

Cream well milk, shortening, sugar, vanilla, and almond flavoring in mixer. Sift baking powder, flour, and salt 3 times. Add dry ingredients alternately with milk, then add egg whites unbeaten. Pour in 3 well-greased pans and bake in 350-degree oven for 30 minutes.

FILLING

2½ cups milk	1 tsp. vanilla
2 cups coconut	2 cups sugar

Boil milk and coconut about 5 minutes. Remove from heat and add vanilla. Spread between layers and on top. Let cake cool before icing.

ICING

1 cup sugar	5 T. water
2 egg whites	1 tsp. cream of tartar
2 T. white corn syrup	

Using mixer, beat and cook for 7 minutes in double boiler. Spread on sides and top of cooled cake. Sprinkle top and sides with coconut.

"I started cooking in 1920 when I was ten years old for my mother, father and six brothers and sisters." Ida Bell used to cook for nine—now for two.

FAMOUS MARBLE CAKE

3 cups sifted cake flour	1 tsp. vanilla
3 tsp. baking powder	4 large eggs
½ tsp. salt	1 cup milk
1 cup butter	1 4-oz. pkg. sweet bakers'
2 cups sugar	chocolate

Line a 10-inch tube pan with waxed paper and sift together in a medium mixing bowl the flour, salt, and baking powder.

In a large mixing bowl cream butter, sugar, and vanilla for 10 minutes with an electric mixer, longer if by hand. Add eggs 1 at a time, beating well after each addition.

Gently beat in flour mixture in 4 additions alternately with the milk, until smooth after each addition.

Turn half the batter into prepared pan.

In a small saucepan, melt chocolate over low heat, then cool. Fold into remaining batter. Spoon over plain batter, being careful not to spread it thickly around tube. During baking the chocolate batter, being heavier than the plain, will sink to the bottom, creating a marble effect.

Bake in a preheated 350-degree oven until cake tester inserted in center comes out clean, about 1 hour and 15 minutes.

With a small spatula, loosen cake from sides of pan and around tube. Turn out on wire rack. Cool, store in tightly covered box.

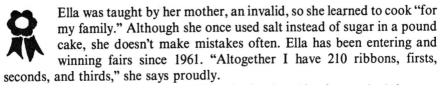

Ella was taught by her mother, an invalid, so she learned to cook "for my family." Although she once used salt instead of sugar in a pound cake, she doesn't make mistakes often. Ella has been entering and winning fairs since 1961. "Altogether I have 210 ribbons, firsts, seconds, and thirds," she says proudly.

About this recipe, Ella told us: "The fascinating thing is you don't have to intertwine the chocolate batter with the plain batter to marble it."

JANET K. LYONS

LEWISBURG, WEST VIRGINIA

SECOND PRIZE
WEST VIRGINIA STATE FAIR

GERMAN CHOCOLATE CAKE

4 oz. German chocolate
1 cup sweet butter
4 egg yolks (extra large)
2 cups sugar
2¼ cups flour (do not sift)
1 cup buttermilk (do not
 substitute)

4 egg whites, stiffly beaten
 (extra large)
½ cup hot water
1 tsp. baking soda
½ tsp. salt
1 tsp. vanilla

Melt chocolate in water over double boiler. Cream butter and sugar till fluffy. Add egg yolks 1 at a time, beat well. Stir in vanilla, soda, salt. Beat till smooth. Alternately add flour and buttermilk. Beat till smooth. Fold in stiff egg whites. Pour into 2 9-inch cake pans, greased and floured. Bake at 350 degrees 30–40 minutes.

After baking, remove from pans to cooling rack immediately. Cool.

FILLING

1 cup evaporated milk
 (undiluted)
1 cup sugar
½ cup sweet butter
1 tsp. vanilla

3 egg yolks, slightly beaten
¼ tsp. salt
2 cups flaked coconut
2 cups pecans (hand broken)

Combine milk, sugar, egg yolks, butter, vanilla, and salt. Cook over medium low heat, stirring continuously till thickened. Add coconut and nuts. Cool in refrigerator. Spread on cooled cake, *tops* only.

NOTE: I use my own vanilla, but regular vanilla extract can be substituted.

 Janet Lyons told us about the time she left the flour out of a cookie recipe. Needless to say, "I had one big cookie all over the cookie sheet." Usually all the ingredients are there in Janet's cooking, for she is a prizewinner.

SHARON McSWIGGIN
SPRINGFIELD, ILLINOIS

SPICE CAKE
(100% Honey)

1¾ cups sifted flour	¼ tsp. ginger
½ tsp. salt	¼ tsp. mace
1 tsp. baking soda	½ tsp. nutmeg
½ tsp. baking powder	½ cup soft shortening
1 tsp. cinnamon	1¼ cups honey
½ tsp. allspice	1 cup buttermilk
¼ tsp. cloves	

Preheat oven to 350 degrees. Grease and flour 12x8-inch pan. Sift together flour, salt, soda, baking powder, and spices. Cream together honey and shortening. Add flour mixture alternately with buttermilk. Scrape bowl, mixing until well blended. Pour batter evenly into pan. Bake 45 to 50 minutes.

This can also be baked in a bundt pan, which makes a prettier cake. Bake at 350 degrees for 40 minutes.

"When baking for competition one must be *very* organized and never lose one's sense of humor! Even when things don't turn out and must be remade," says Sharon McSwiggin. "With two of us [her daughter Cindi is included in Specialty Bread chapter] baking for the fair each year, it is an engineering feat in itself to get everything made on time. It is like a three-ring circus around here that weekend because I generally have from eighteen to twenty entries and Cindi has about six or eight more!"

She told us about the 1976 Illinois State Fair. "My ankle swelled up the day before I had to do all the baking. I thought I had just twisted it. I went ahead and managed to get everything made and taken out to the fairgrounds on time (in spite of the ankle and a *two-week-old baby*). I had the ankle X-rayed the next day and found out I had done all of this with a broken bone. In spite of everything I managed to bring home eight ribbons that year."

KAROL MARTIN
APPLETON CITY, MISSOURI

MILE-HIGH BUTTERMILK CAKE

4 cups sifted cake flour
½ tsp. baking powder
1 tsp. baking soda
½ tsp. salt
1 cup butter

3 cups sugar
1 T. vanilla
2 cups buttermilk
6 egg whites

Sift together cake flour, baking powder, baking soda, and salt. Cream together butter and sugar until light and fluffy. Beat in vanilla. Add dry ingredients alternately with buttermilk, beating well after each addition. Add egg whites; beat at medium speed 2 minutes. Pour batter into 3 waxed-paper-lined 9-inch round cake pans.

Bake in 350-degree oven 20 minutes; reduce heat to 325 and bake 25 more minutes or until cakes test done. Cool in pans on racks 10 minutes. Remove from pans; cool on racks.

Yield: 12 servings

 One of two Grand Champion sisters, thirteen-year-old Karol won the prized purple rosette in the Junior Division of the Missouri State Fair. Her sister Karla is also a prizewinner (see her Swedish Tea Ring (page 188).
Karol learned to cook from her mother, too.

ELIZABETH MEITNER
FERNDALE, CALIFORNIA

FIRST PRIZE, UNFROSTED CAKE
CALIFORNIA STATE FAIR

APPLESAUCE CAKE

4 cups all-purpose flour
2 cups sugar
4 tsp. soda
½ tsp. each cinnamon, nutmeg,
   cloves, and allspice

1 tsp. vanilla
2 T. cornstarch
3 cups applesauce
1 cup cooking oil

Sift together all dry ingredients; add applesauce, oil, and vanilla in large mixing bowl until blended. Bake in a greased and floured 9x13x3-inch pan at 350 degrees for 1 hour.

Elizabeth Meitner taught herself to cook, and has been cooking for 25 years.
    Once she baked a birthday cake for her daughter and left it to cool on the counter. When she returned the cat was eating it.

Try Elizabeth's Strawberry Jam (page 425).

PEANUT BUTTER FUDGE CAKE

2 cups sugar
2 cups plain flour

1 tsp. soda

BRING TO A BOIL:

2 sticks margarine
4 T. cocoa
1 cup water

½ cup buttermilk
2 beaten eggs
1 tsp. vanilla

Pour boiled mixture over sugar, flour, and soda and mix well with spoon. Pour into a 9x13-inch well-greased and -floured sheet pan. Bake for 25 minutes at 350 degrees. Let cool in pan.

PEANUT BUTTER MIXTURE

1½ cups creamy peanut butter   1½ T. peanut oil

Mix well together and spread over cool cake.

FUDGE FROSTING

1 stick margarine
4 T. cocoa
6 T. buttermilk

1 lb. powdered sugar
1 tsp. vanilla

Bring margarine, cocoa, and buttermilk to a boil. Pour boiled mixture over powdered sugar, add vanilla, and mix well with a spoon. Spread over the peanut butter mixture. Cut into squares.

Linda cooks for five every day in her nice, big kitchen. Linda's mother taught her to cook, and she recommends experimentation to others. She experiments and, although she once fried up some fish with the scales still on them, those experiments can pay off. Linda won $300 as well as an all-expenses-paid trip to New York and Washington with this recipe.

PATRICIA PETERSON
BOISE, IDAHO

CARROT CAKE

3 cups grated carrots
1¼ cups salad oil
1¾ cups sugar
2 cups whole wheat flour
2 tsp. soda

½ tsp. salt
1 tsp. cinnamon
1 tsp. vanilla
1 cup chopped nuts
4 eggs, unbeaten

Grate carrots, put into mixing bowl, add eggs, oil, and sugar. Beat until well blended. Add rest of ingredients and mix well. Bake about 40 minutes, in any size pan.

Frosting: brown sugar, peanut butter, cream cheese, or just eat it plain.

NOTE: See page 141 for Patricia's method of grinding her own wheat and her bread recipe.

CATHERINE LARKIN PEXTON
DOUGLAS, WYOMING

APPLESAUCE CAKE

½ cup butter or margarine
1 cup cold unsweetened
   applesauce
1 tsp. soda
½ tsp. cloves
½ cup chopped nuts

1 cup sugar
2 cups flour (sift before
   measuring)
1 tsp. cinnamon
1 cup raisins (either whole or
   cut-up)

Cream butter or margarine. Add sugar gradually and beat thoroughly. Add applesauce and stir well. Add flour, sifted with soda and spices, beating thoroughly. Fold in raisins and nuts. Bake in greased and floured 8x8-inch cake pan 40 minutes in moderate oven (350 degrees) or until done.

Cake can be iced with a butter icing or cream cheese frosting; served plain; or topped with ice cream or whipped cream.

NOTE: Commercially canned applesauce does not make as moist a cake as does home canned. When making this cake for competition, I bake it in a 9¼x5¼x2¾-inch loaf pan, as this entry is classified as "Loaf Cake, Applesauce (Iced)."

How many of us can say, "At branding time I cook for forty"? Catherine Pexton does—and she also baked the cakes for her own wedding! "I started cooking when I was nine by baking a cake. By the time I was eleven, I was cooking complete meals and using a pressure cooker to can vegetables. As my mother worked, I was expected to have meals ready to serve at noon and in the evening during summer months, plus helping to can."

Cooking is just part of a very active life. Mrs. Pexton serves on so many community boards and committees (including being appointed by the governor to the Wyoming Council for the Humanities) that if we told you all of them we wouldn't have room for her recipes.

Catherine also has prizewinning Cucumber Rings (page 432).

BARBARA PUCKETT
BONNIEVILLE, KENTUCKY

SPICE CAKE

2¼ cups sifted all-purpose
    flour
1¾ cups light brown sugar,
    packed
3 tsp. baking powder

½ tsp. salt
1½ tsp. cinnamon
½ cup margarine
1 cup milk
2 eggs

Preheat oven to 350 degrees. On waxed paper, sift flour, sugar, cinnamon, and baking powder. Put margarine in bowl and beat till fluffy and soft. Add flour mixture alternately with milk until well mixed. Add eggs and beat well. Turn into 2 8-inch greased and floured pans. Bake 25 to 30 minutes at 350 degrees. Cool. Frost with Caramel Frosting.

CARAMEL FROSTING

¾ cup butter
1½ cups light brown sugar,
    packed
½ cup milk

About 3 cups confectioners
    sugar
1½ tsp. vanilla

Melt butter in small saucepan over low heat. Remove from heat. Add brown sugar, stirring until smooth. Over low heat, bring to boil. Stir constantly; boil 1 minute. Remove from heat. Add milk. Return to low heat just to boiling. Remove from heat and let cool until bottom of pan feels lukewarm. Add powdered sugar and beat till of spreading consistency.

NELLIE E. RADMACHER

LOUISVILLE, KENTUCKY

JAM CAKE

5 eggs, beaten
2 cups sugar
3 cups flour
1 cup shortening
1 cup buttermilk
1 tsp. soda
¼ tsp. salt

½ tsp. cinnamon
1½ tsp. cloves
1½ tsp. allspice
1 cup raisins
1 cup nuts
1 cup strawberry jam

Cream butter, gradually add sugar and well-beaten eggs. Sift flour, add spices and salt. Dissolve soda in buttermilk, add alternately with flour mixture to butter-sugar-egg mixture. Beat after each addition. Lightly flour nuts and fruit and add. Add jam and stir. Bake in 2 9-inch cake pans at 325 degrees for 40 minutes or until done. Ice with caramel icing.

See Nellie's Bread and Butter Pickles (page 434).

PHYLLIS RAML
GOODWIN, SOUTH DAKOTA

FIRST PRIZE, CAKE
SOUTH DAKOTA STATE
FAIR

PUMPKIN PUDDING CAKE

1¼ cups flour
1 cup pumpkin
½ cup sugar
½ cup brown sugar
½ cup buttermilk
½ tsp. cinnamon

1½ tsp. baking powder
½ tsp. allspice
¼ tsp. salt
1 egg
½ tsp. baking soda

Preheat oven to 350 degrees. Into large bowl, measure all ingredients. With mixer at low speed, beat ingredients until batter is smooth. Pour batter into greased 9x9-inch pan. Bake 50 minutes.

Double recipe makes 9x13-inch pan.

Raisins and/or nuts may be added after mixing.

 "I grew up on the farm," said Phyllis, "and my mother helped in the fields so I had to do the cooking." She cooks for five "unless its harvest time," and when her six children and their spouses are home "there are fifteen at a meal."

Phyllis has won with baking and canning entries at both the county and state level.

See Phyllis's Short Cut Chili Sauce (page 435).

BROWN SUGAR ANGEL FOOD CAKE

1¼ cups sifted cake flour
2 cups firmly packed brown
    sugar
1½ cups egg whites (10–12)

1½ tsp. cream of tartar
1 tsp. salt
2 tsp. flavoring (1 tsp. vanilla
    and 1 tsp. burnt sugar)

Combine cake flour and 1 cup of brown sugar, mixing well. Beat egg whites, cream of tartar, and salt until foamy.

Gradually add 1 cup of brown sugar, beating until stiff, glossy peaks form. Add flavoring and blend well.

Add flour mixture, gradually folding in carefully. Spoon into ungreased 10-inch tube pan. Bake in 350-degree oven 40–45 minutes. Invert pan until cool.

QUICK CREAMED FROSTING

½ cup honey
½ cup butter
1 tsp. vanilla
2 egg whites

1 cup sifted confectioners
    sugar
1 sq. unsweetened chocolate,
    melted

Cream honey and butter. Stir in vanilla. Beat egg whites until they form soft peaks. Add sifted confectioners sugar gradually, beating after each addition. Fold egg-white mixture gradually into honey mixture. Add melted chocolate to ⅓ of frosting. Use the chocolate part between the layers. Spread the white frosting on top and sides of cake.

 "I have been cooking as long as I can remember. My first husband was an avid hunter and I have cooked almost every kind of wild game native to this area. I'll never forget the time I served roast quail and was horrified when my husband began to carve, to learn I had not removed the crop. There it was, filled with grain!"

Hazel learned to cook from "my mother and grandmother, who were both excellent cooks—home ec in high school, and the university extension service." She has been cooking about 55 years. She told us how she started competing at the fair.

"I began entering canned and baked goods (along with sewing and livestock, etc.) in the local county fair in Northwest Missouri. In the 1960s I started taking things to the Missouri State Fair. I took so many things out there that my husband said he felt perfectly 'at home' on the fairgrounds. I won many ribbons and a few dollars. One year I won second on my white angel food cake and the judges told me the only reason I did not get first was that I had turned my cake upside down when the instructions plainly stated 'right side up.' Anyway, the next year my husband and son insisted I enter again, promising to help me with my other household duties. I baked about a half-dozen cakes, but none ever seemed just right. I put all of them in the freezer and needless to say we had angel food cake quite a few meals. They did taste good, but were not too pretty!

"Collecting recipes is something I cannot resist and you can be sure after all of these years I have plenty!"

PAT ROTH
Ephrata, Pennsylvania

FIRST PRIZE
EPHRATA FARMERS' DAYS FAIR

APPLE BUTTER CAKE

½ cup shortening	½ tsp. baking soda
1 cup sugar	½ tsp. salt
3 eggs	½ tsp. cinnamon
1 cup apple butter	¼ tsp. nutmeg
2½ cups sifted cake flour	1 cup sour milk
3 tsp. baking powder	½ cup apple butter

Cream shortening and sugar. Beat in eggs (1 at a time). Beat till light and fluffy. Stir in 1 cup apple butter. Sift together flour, baking soda and powder, salt, cinnamon, and nutmeg. Add dry ingredients to creamed mixture alternately with sour milk.

Grease and flour 2 9-inch pans. Bake at 350 degrees for 30 to 35 minutes. Spread bottom of cooled cake with half the remaining apple butter. Top with 1 cup Fluffy Frosting, spreading evenly to cover apple butter. Frost sides and top of cake with remaining frosting. Swirl remaining apple butter onto frosted top to give a marbled effect.

FLUFFY FROSTING

2 egg whites	⅓ cup cold water
1½ cups sugar (granulated)	Pinch of salt
¼ tsp. cream of tartar	1 tsp. vanilla

Place egg whites, sugar, cream of tartar, water, and salt in top of double boiler (not over heat). Beat 1 minute with electric beater. Place over boiling water and cook, beating constantly till frosting forms still peaks—about 7 minutes. Remove pan from boiling water and add vanilla and beat till spreading consistency (about 2 minutes).

 Pat has won a lot of prizes for her cakes, including first prizes in the white, yellow, and spice cake divisions. Her heritage is Pennsylvania Dutch ("my mother, grandmother, and great-grandmother were very good cooks"); and this recipe reflects this regional interest.

RICK ROY
MAHOMET, ILLINOIS

ITALIAN COCONUT CREAM CAKE

2 cups granulated sugar
5 eggs (separated)
½ cup butter
½ cup solid shortening
2 cups flour

1 tsp. soda
1 cup buttermilk
2 cups coconut
1 tsp. vanilla
½ cup chopped pecans

Cream together sugar, egg yolks, butter, and shortening.
Add flour, soda, buttermilk, coconut, vanilla, and pecans. Mix well.
Beat egg whites until stiff and fold into the above mixture.
Pour batter into 3 8-inch cake pans that have been greased and floured.
Bake in a 350-degree oven until done—about 30 to 35 minutes. Remove from pans and cool completely. Frost cake and decorate to your taste.

NOTE: This is a very rich, moist, and heavy cake.

ICING

8 oz. cream cheese
6 T. butter
2 cups sifted confectioners
    sugar
1 tsp. vanilla

Cream cheese, butter, and vanilla, then add confectioners sugar. Mix until smooth.

Rick Roy is a grain farmer, and he loves to cook. He calls it his hobby. He's so good he's not cooking for competition any more, he is judging at Illinois County fairs.
    Rick learned to cook in a boys' 4-H baking club in the sixth grade, and he gives credit to the ladies of his "rural country church" for recipes and cooking hints.
    Even champions make mistakes. Once Rick made a beautiful apple pie for a county fair—and discovered halfway through baking that he had sprinkled the top with salt instead of sugar.

BETTY J. RUCKS

ELKHORN, WISCONSIN

FRIED CAKES

1½ cups sugar	1½ tsp. nutmeg
6 T. melted shortening	½ tsp. salt
3 eggs	1 tsp. soda
2 cups buttermilk	3 tsp. baking powder
1 tsp. vanilla	5 cups flour

Mix by hand in large mixing bowl. Cream sugar and shortening well, add eggs and mix well. Add vanilla. Sift all dry ingredients and add, alternating with the buttermilk. Roll out on floured board and cut and fry in 375-degree hot oil. Place on paper towel. Can be frozen when thoroughly cooled.

Yield: 3 dozen

 Betty is creative in many areas—canning, sewing, crocheting, painting, and photography as well as cooking. She starts working on her entries in January and is "busy working on them the night before." She starts her baking six weeks before the fair.

Betty passed on to us a few of her methods that you might want to try: "When trying a new recipe I mark the results by the family—satisfied, if not I discard it. I bake a lot of things on the same day and put in the freezer; this way I always have something on hand to use on short notice. Baked things freeze very well."

Although Betty has been married for 39 years she remembers an event from the first year when she made a blueberry pie for her husband. "I used one can of blueberries and too big a pie tin. So I had two layers of crust with a streak of blueberries. My husband brings this up often when company is here, and when I make something with blueberries."

Try Betty's Dinner Rolls (page 145).

BLACK WALNUT CAKE

1½ cups light brown sugar
1 cup sugar (granulated)
¾ cup solid shortening
3 eggs
3 cups sifted flour
1½ tsp. soda

¾ tsp. nutmeg
1½ tsp. cinnamon
¾ tsp. salt
1½ cups buttermilk
1 cup broken black walnuts

Grease and dust with flour 2 9-inch cake pans.

Cream sugar and shortening until well blended. Sift flour, measure, and sift again with all dry ingredients. Set aside. Add eggs to creamed shortening and sugar. Beat well 2 minutes at medium speed. Add dry ingredients, alternating with buttermilk at 3 different intervals. Beat until smooth. Add black walnuts. Bake at 325 degrees for 40 minutes.

FROSTING

2 T. water
4½ T. granulated sugar
2⅓ cups 10X sugar
1 egg

⅔ cup solid shortening
1 tsp. vanilla
½ cup black walnut crumbs

Boil water and granulated sugar together until sugar dissolves. Mix 10X sugar and egg and blend with syrup and shortening. Add vanilla. Beat until creamy. After cake is frosted sprinkle with black walnut crumbs.

Esther learned to cook "some from my mother, but mostly by experience after we were married 25 years ago." She tells a story on herself that we won't admit ever happened to us:

"When I was first married I was trying to split a recipe in half. After many figures on paper and becoming very frustrated, my husband made his appearance, wondering what was wrong. He told me it was very simple—½ of ⅔ is ⅓. I never forgot that. (Nor did he)."

GEMMA SCIABICA
MODESTO, CALIFORNIA

ALMOND SPONGE WINE CAKE

1 cup ground almonds
1½ cups flour
1 tsp. baking powder
½ tsp. cinnamon
7 eggs
¼ tsp. nutmeg
1½ cups sugar

⅔ cup sweet wine (light white, although port or muscatel could be substituted)
Grated rind of 2 oranges
2 T. olive oil

In large bowl of electric mixer beat egg whites until they hold peaks. Beat in half of sugar—set aside. In smaller bowl, beat yolks, add rest of sugar, wine, oil, and dry ingredients. Mix well and pour slowly over beaten egg whites, folding together gently and thoroughly.

Pour into ungreased 10-inch tube pan (with removable bottom).

Bake in a 325-degree oven until the top springs back when touched lightly (about 1 hour). Invert pan until completely cooled. Remove cake from pan and spread top and sides with a thin layer of apricot jam. Press sliced almonds on top of cake into jam.

Try Gemma's Stuffed Beef Balls (page 48).

LIGHT FRUIT CAKE

1 cup shortening
1 cup sugar
5 eggs
1 tsp. rum flavoring
1½ cups sifted enriched flour
1½ tsp. baking powder
1 tsp. salt
½ cup unsweetened pineapple juice
¼ lb. candied citron, chopped fine (½ cup)
¼ lb. candied orange peel, chopped fine (½ cup)
¼ lb. candied lemon peel, chopped fine (½ cup)
½ cup chopped candied cherries
1¼ cups chopped candied pineapple
½ cup chopped dates
½ cup chopped dried apricots
½ cup chopped dried figs
½ lb. (1½ cups) white raisins
½ cup sifted enriched flour
2 cups moist shredded coconut
2 cups slivered blanched almonds

Stir the shortening to soften. Gradually add sugar, and cream together until light and fluffy.

Add eggs, 1 at a time, beating well after each addition. Stir in flavoring.

Sift together 1½ cups flour, baking powder, and salt. Add the flour mixture to the creamed mixture alternately with the pineapple juice, beating well after each addition.

Dredge the fruits with ½ cup flour. Add the floured fruits, coconut, and nuts to the batter; stir only till well mixed.

Line two 8½x4½x2½-inch loaf pans with paper, allowing ½ inch to extend above all sides of pan. Or use a tube pan, teflon coated. Pour into pans. Bake in very slow oven (275 degrees) 2½ hours, or till cakes are done. (Have a pan of water on bottom shelf of oven while baking.)

If desired, glaze cooled cakes by brushing lightly with hot corn syrup. Decorate with candied cherries, other candied fruits, and blanched almonds.

This cake may be baked in graduated sizes of round layer pans for a groom's cake (fill pans ¾ full of batter).

Yield: about 5 pounds of cake

NOTE: 1¾ pounds candied fruit mix may be used in place of candied citron, fruit peels, cherries, and pineapple.

"I live in a mobile home; I haven't room to do much, so I do all of my heavy cooking for my entries in the Kentucky State Fair at my mother's. They eat my mistakes."

TROPICAL CHIFFON CAKE

2¼ cups sifted cake flour
3 tsp. baking powder
1½ cups sugar
1 tsp. salt
½ cup oil
¾ cup (8) egg yolks

1 tsp. grated orange peel
 (fresh)
¾ cup orange juice (squeezed
 from fresh oranges)
1 cup (8) egg whites
½ tsp. cream of tartar

Sift dry ingredients together in large bowl. Make a well in the center and add in order: oil, egg yolks, orange peel, and orange juice. Beat until satin smooth. In large bowl beat egg whites with cream of tartar till very stiff peaks form. Pour batter in thin stream over beaten egg whites. Fold in gently with spatula. Bake in ungreased 10-inch tube pan in slow oven (325 degrees) about 55 minutes or until done. Invert on pop bottle—cool.

FLUFFY WHITE FROSTING

Combine 1 cup granulated sugar, ⅓ cup water, ½ teaspoon cream of tartar, and a dash of salt in saucepan. Bring to boil, stirring till sugar dissolves. Very slowly add sugar syrup to 2 unbeaten egg whites, beating constantly with electric mixer till stiff peaks form, about 7 minutes. Beat in 1 teaspoon vanilla (or almond) extract.

Like so many of our prize winners, Syreda Tye learned when "I had to do the cooking while my mother worked." Although her kitchen is a little smaller than she would like, it is very convenient. She told us that once she put the icing ingredients right in the cake mix—surprisingly, it turned out to be "very good." She follows her cake recipe with a frosting recipe "if desired."

LYDIA VAN VLECK
KANKAKEE, ILLINOIS

FIRST PRIZE
KANKAKEE COUNTY FAIR

POPCORN CAKE

Have about 5 quarts of popcorn popped in large pan or bowl. Do not salt. Butter an angel food cake pan. In a large cast aluminum kettle bring to a boil 1 cup sugar; 1 cup white corn syrup; 1 tablespoon vinegar, and ¼ cup of water. After cooking about 15 minutes drop about ½ teaspoon in a cup of very cold water till it has cooked enough to make it tingle against the cup.

Take off fire, blend in ¼ teaspoon soda; 2 tablespoons of butter or oleo; 1 teaspoon vanilla.

Pour over the popped corn and stir until all corn is covered.

Quarter about 1 cup of red and green maraschino cherries and fold in popcorn mixture.

Press popcorn in angel food cake pan, let set until cold. Then take out of cake pan and put on a cake plate. See that the maraschino cherries are showing on top and sides of cake. If necessary more cherries can be pressed on top and sides of cake.

 Lydia Van Vleck remembers being six years old and wanting to bake cookies. Although her mother wasn't home, her father agreed. She was too little to get the lid off the sugar jar. She made the cookies anyway and now says, "They looked like cookies but they didn't taste like cookies."

Lydia tells us her blue-ribbon Popcorn Cake is pretty for Christmas holidays.

SOUR CREAM CHOCOLATE CAKE

2 cups flour
2 cups sugar
1 cup water
¾ cup sour cream
¼ cup shortening
1¼ tsp. soda

1 tsp. salt
1 tsp. vanilla
½ tsp. baking powder
2 eggs
4 oz. melted unsweetened
  chocolate (cooled)

Heat oven to 350 degrees.

Mix ½ minute on low speed, scraping bowl constantly. Beat 3 minutes on high speed, scraping bowl occasionally. Pour into pans. Bake in oblong pan 40 to 45 minutes, layer pan 30 to 35 minutes. Cool and frost. I always bake this cake in 2 9-inch layer pans.

SOUR CREAM CHOCOLATE FROSTING

⅓ cup butter or margarine
  softened
3 oz. melted unsweetened
  chocolate (cooled)

3 cups confectioners sugar
½ cup sour cream
2 tsp. vanilla

Mix butter and cooled chocolate thoroughly. Blend in sugar. Stir in sour cream and vanilla. Beat until frosting is smooth and spreading consistency.

"I learned to cook when I was eleven years old," says Juanita Walker, who won first prize in the dairy entries at the Kentucky State Fair. She enjoys decorating cakes as well as baking them and does her work in a small but well-planned kitchen.

LORRAINE WING
REDMOND, OREGON

GERMAN SWEET CHOCOLATE CAKE

1 pkg. German sweet
   chocolate
½ cup boiling water
1 cup butter or margarine
¾ cup brown sugar
¾ cup white sugar
4 egg yolks, unbeaten

1 tsp. vanilla
2½ cups cake flour
1 tsp. baking soda
½ tsp. salt
1 cup buttermilk
4 egg whites, stiffly beaten

Melt chocolate in boiling water. Cool.

Cream butter and sugar until light and fluffy. Add egg yolks 1 at a time, beating after each. Add vanilla and chocolate, mix until blended. Sift flour with soda and salt. Add sifted dry ingredients with buttermilk, a little of each, beating after each addition until batter is smooth. Fold in stiffly beaten egg whites. (For beginners: you *never* hit pans to get out air bubbles when folding in egg whites. O.K.) Pour into 4 8-inch pans, greased and floured generously. Bake at 350 degrees for 20 minutes. Two 11-inch pans bake 35–40 minutes.

Yield: a beautiful 4-layer cake

COCONUT-PECAN FROSTING AND FILLING
FOR GERMAN CHOCOLATE CAKE

1 can evaporated milk
½ cup brown sugar
½ cup white sugar
3 egg yolks

¼ lb. butter or margarine
1 tsp. vanilla
1 cup chopped pecans
1⅓ cups coconut

Combine milk, sugar, egg yolks, butter, and vanilla in a saucepan. Cook over medium heat, stirring constantly until mixture thickens (about 12 minutes).

Remove from heat, add coconut and pecans. Cool a little then place in refrigerator until quite chilled and ready to spread (even an hour or more). This covers four layers nicely. It is rich. I place a maraschino cherry in the middle and it is sooo good.

Lorraine Wing advises, "Do all things with love and patience. Mom always said a good cook tastes."

Prizewinning cook, Lorraine is one-half of the only grandmother/grandson winners featured in our book. We discovered this outstanding Oregon cook when her grandson, Tye Neel, submitted Lorraine's prizewinning recipe along with his own (Pumpkin Muffins, page 192).

CHAPTER TEN

PIES

PIES: CHERRY

Crust golden brown, contrast with fruit, flaky and light

Filling holds together

Fruit evenly distributed

Texture smooth, fruit not mushy or lost in filling

KAREN APIADO
SALEM, OREGON

STATESMAN JOURNAL "BEST APPLE PIE"
FIRST PRIZE
OREGON STATE FAIR

KAREN'S APPLE PIE

---

6 cups pared, cored apple slices (preferably Gravenstein)	¾ tsp. cinnamon
	¼ tsp. nutmeg
	⅛ tsp. salt
1 cup sugar	1 T. butter
2 T. flour	

Sift together sugar, flour, spices, and salt. Pour sugar mixture over apples in a container with a lid. Shake in container to thoroughly coat apples.

Arrange apples in pastry-lined 9-inch pie pan. Dot with butter. Lay top crust over apples and flute edges. Cover edge of pie crust with 1½-inch-wide aluminum foil strip to prevent excessive browning. Bake at 425 degrees for 45 minutes.

NEVER-FAIL PIE CRUST

3 cups flour	1¼ cups shortening
¾ tsp. salt	1 beaten egg
½ tsp. baking powder	1 T. vinegar
1 T. sugar	5 T. water

Sift flour, salt, baking powder, and sugar together. Cut shortening into dry ingredients.

Mix together egg, vinegar and water. Add 8 tablespoons of liquid mixture to dry ingredients. Mix lightly with fork. Roll between two pieces of plastic wrap. Can be stored in refrigerator or freezer without changing final product.

"I always have better success in baking," says top prizewinner Karen Apiado, "if I measure all ingredients accurately. When rolling out pie crust, always roll between two pieces of plastic wrap for easier handling and to eliminate use of extra flour, which tends to make a crust tough."

Karen is following her mother's example as a winner at the Oregon State Fair baked goods competition. She entered a peach and an apple pie. Both won a blue ribbon, and her apple pie was so good it won the newspaper's special award for the best apple pie.

If you think Mom and apple pie go together how about Karen's mother, Betty Smith, who won ten ribbons for her pies this year? Both mother and daughter feel their Never-Fail Pie Crust is the secret to their pies.

LEE CHURCH
LOUISVILLE, KENTUCKY

PEANUT BUTTER PIE

⅓ cup smooth peanut butter
¾ cup powdered sugar
½ cup granulated sugar
⅓ cup all-purpose flour
⅛ tsp. salt

2 cups scalded milk
3 slightly beaten egg yolks
2 T. butter or margarine
1 tsp. vanilla

Mix peanut butter and powdered sugar together with a pastry blender until it reaches the consistency of corn meal. Set aside. Stir together the granulated sugar, flour, salt, and scalded milk. Cook, stirring, until thick. Add a little of the hot mixture to the egg yolks, stir, and then add yolks to hot mixture. Cook over low heat, stirring, about 3 minutes. Then remove from heat and stir in butter or margarine and vanilla.

MERINGUE

3 egg whites at room
   temperature
½ cup sugar

1 tsp. cornstarch
¼ tsp. cream of tartar

To make meringue, beat egg whites until stiff, then add remaining ingredients and beat until the meringue almost looks like marshmallow whip.

Sprinkle bottom of browned pie crust with the peanut butter mixture, reserving about 1½ to 2 tablespoons to sprinkle over meringue. Pour on custard mixture. Top with meringue and sprinkle with reserved peanut butter mixture. Bake at 350 to 375 degrees until meringue is golden brown.

NEVER-FAIL PIE CRUST

3 cups flour
1 tsp. salt
1¼ cups shortening

1 beaten egg
6 T. cold water
1 tsp. vinegar

Sift flour with salt. Cut in the shortening with a pastry blender until crumbly. Mix in the egg, water, and vinegar. Chill, or roll out immediately and fit into pie pans. Prick bottoms and sides with fork. Bake at 375 degrees until golden brown.

Yield: 4 9-inch crusts

Lee Church's first attempt was a winner. Her prize Peanut Butter Pie took the blue the first time she entered it. However, she has baked for years and "don't even remember where I got the recipe."

Members of her church and friends, as well as her husband and three sons, encouraged her to enter her pie.

RACHEL S. COLE
COLUMBIA, SOUTH CAROLINA

LEMON MERINGUE PIE

1½ cups sugar
7 T. cornstarch
¼ tsp. salt
2 cups boiling water
3 large eggs (separate for meringue)

⅓ cup lemon juice (make from real lemons)
2 tsp. grated lemon rind (make from real lemons)
1 baked pie shell

Blend sugar, cornstarch, and salt. Stir in the boiling water and cook until thick and clear (about 20 to 25 minutes).

Stir in the beaten egg yolks (blend the egg yolks with the pudding a little at a time so as not to make lumps). Return to heat and cook for about 3 minutes, possibly 5. *Stir constantly while cooking.*

When pudding is cooked to satisfaction, remove from heat and add lemon juice and lemon rind and blend well into pudding.

Important: Do not cook after the juice and rind have been added. You may add a small piece of oleo to pudding if desired (about a teaspoonful).

Cool. Pour pudding into baked shell and top with meringue.

MERINGUE

Have eggs at room temperature
Beat eggs until stiff
While beating add 2 tablespoons of sugar per egg white (this would be about 6 tablespoons of sugar)

½ teaspoon vanilla (*colorless, if you can find it*)

Bake at 325 degrees for 10 to 15 minutes or until golden brown.

NOTE: Beater blades and container for egg whites must be *free of grease.* Any grease collection will cause meringue to fall.

½ stick butter	3 eggs
1 cup *light* brown sugar	1¼ cups broken nuts (not cut)
1 cup white corn syrup	1 tsp. vanilla
¼ tsp. salt	1 unbaked pie shell

Cream butter; add sugar and syrup. Beat eggs until foamy and add. Add broken nuts and vanilla.

Pour into pie shell and bake at 350 degrees for about 50 minutes (until golden brown).

NOTE: I have had success at baking at 325 degrees. This could vary with oven.

CHOCOLATE PIE
(From Scratch)

1½ cups sugar	4 egg yolks
3 T. cocoa (no substitute)	2 cups milk
3 T. flour (plain or self-rising)	1 tsp. vanilla
1 piece butter about size of egg	1 baked pie shell

Mix dry ingredients.

Beat egg yolks with very *small* amount of water (enough to make pastelike) and stir into dry ingredients.

Heat milk and stir the above mixture into milk so as not lumpy. Cook until thick (about 20 to 25 minutes). *Stir constantly while cooking.* Pour into a baked pie shell and top with meringue, bake at 325 degrees 10 to 15 minutes or until brown. Can be served without the meringue topping if desired.

When Rachel Cole went to claim her first-place-winning pecan pie last year she noticed that an extra slice had been taken out of it. "Only one slice was necessary for judging," she tells us.

Her pies have been consistent winners for her at the South Carolina State Fairs year after year. "I feel that taste comes first but unless this taste is paralleled with attractively arranged food, interest could be lost; maybe first prizes also," Rachel states.

COTTAGE CHEESE CHIFFON PIE

CRUST

1½ cups fine zwieback crumbs   ½ cup (1 stick) butter, melted

Combine crumbs and butter. Reserve ¼ cup and pat the remaining mixture onto bottom and sides of pie plate. Chill.

FILLING

1 envelope unflavored
  gelatine
⅔ cup sugar
½ tsp. salt
2 eggs, separated
1½ cups creamed small curd
  cottage cheese, sieved

1 tsp. lemon peel
3 T. lemon juice
⅓ cup sugar
½ cup whipping cream,
  whipped

Combine gelatine, ⅔ cup sugar, and salt in saucepan. Blend in milk and slightly beaten egg yolks. Cook and stir over medium heat until slightly thickened. Remove from heat and add cottage cheese, lemon peel, and lemon juice.

Beat egg whites until soft peaks form; gradually add remaining sugar and beat to stiff peaks. Fold into cottage cheese mixture. Fold in whipping cream and chill, until mixture mounds. Pile in crust. Top with reserved crumbs. Chill until firm, about 4 or 5 hours.

Lelia grew up in a big family, ten girls and one boy, on a 60-acre farm near Boaz, Wisconsin. Her mother was a fine cook and each daughter in turn learned from her: "As the older ones left home, we got our time to cook!" Six of the eleven children became teachers, and at eighteen Lelia began to teach in a one-room school near Boaz.

She taught 20 to 30 children in all grades from first to eighth, built the fire and tended the wood stove, washed the chimneys of the kerosene lamps and kept them lighted, and after school carried the wood and scrubbed the floor. She laughs about it now. "We had to be our own janitors—at eighteen you didn't think anything about it. I enjoyed it."

One November she got married, and finished the school term before she and her bridegroom went off to farm for 19 years in Richland County. After farming, they operated the general store in Gillingham for 16 years. When they sold the store eight years ago, they retired to a new home they built nearby, where Lelia cooks in a pretty maple kitchen that looks out over the fields.

Last year she entered her first cooking contest, a dairy bake-off, and placed first in the county. Then she entered the *State Journal* Cookbook Contest, and won her second Grand Prize. These are the only contests she's entered to date.

Try Lelia's Onion Cheese Bread (page 7) and Home Comfort Doughnuts (page 175).

ANNE DAWSEY
DOTHAN, ALABAMA

GRAND PRIZE
NATIONAL PEANUT FESTIVAL
DOTHAN, ALABAMA

NUTTY LEMON MINI-PIES

24 mini pie shells
3 oz. and 8 oz. cream cheese
⅓ cup lemon juice
1 can evaporated milk
1 can lemon pie filling

8 oz. peanut butter
4 T. milk
1 cup powdered sugar
1 tsp. vanilla
½ cup roasted peanuts

Mix 3 ounces cream cheese, powdered sugar, milk, and peanut butter. Spread layer in pie shells. Mix 8 ounces cream cheese and milk until smooth. Add lemon juice and vanilla. Mix until thick, then add pie filling. Mix well. Spread on peanut butter layer. Top with roasted peanuts.

Anne won $275 for this recipe in the National Peanut Festival competition. She gives credit to her mother for teaching her to cook, and she cooks for four every day.

Although Anne once made the mistake we have come to think of as "the universal cooking mistake"—leaving out the baking powder—she doesn't trip up very often, because she is a really good cook.

NANCY ENGEL
PALMER, ALASKA

CARROT CUSTARD PIE

2 cups carrots, cooked and mashed	1 tsp. cinnamon
1 cup evaporated milk	¼ tsp. ginger
⅓ cup orange juice	¼ tsp. nutmeg
¼ cup yogurt or sour cream	¾ tsp. salt
2 slightly beaten eggs	1–2 tsp. grated orange rind
¾ cup packed brown sugar	1 tsp. vanilla
⅓ cup honey	½ cup walnuts or pecans, chopped

Mix all ingredients except nuts, beat well. Pour into 9-inch pie crust (unbaked). Bake at 400 degrees 10 minutes. Sprinkle on the nuts. Reduce oven temperature to 325 degrees and bake an additional 45 minutes or until firm. Plain or vanilla-flavored yogurt may be used.

The forests of Alaska supplied the birch for her kitchen cabinets, "4-H, her mother, school and cookbooks" supplied her cooking education.

Nancy says, "My husband and boys (seven and four) are never short on praise, so it's a *pleasure* and *joy* cooking for them."

THERESA FRANCOEUR
WAREHAM, MASSACHUSETTS

FIRST PRIZE
MASSACHUSETTS CRANBERRY
FESTIVAL

CRANBERRY PINEAPPLE PIE

2 baked 8- or 9-inch pie shells
1 6-oz. can frozen cranberry
    juice concentrate
1 9-oz. container Cool Whip
1 14-oz. can sweetened
    condensed milk

1 cup cranberry-orange relish
1 8-oz. can juice-pak crushed
    pineapple, drained
⅔ cup chopped walnuts

In a large bowl, using wooden spoon, mix condensed milk and frozen cranberry juice concentrate. Fold in Cool Whip: stir in cranberry-orange relish, drained pineapple, and nuts. Spoon into pie shells; refrigerate 2 hours before serving.

NOTE: This pie can be frozen; leftover portions (if any) can be refrozen.

 "Not many hits and plenty of misses," Theresa Francoeur said about her early cooking days. Now she has been cooking for 31 years and is a champion. "Don't be afraid to experiment," she tells others, "be an 'I wonder if' cook.

"Once," she says, "two hours before entries were due, I decided I would enter the Coffee Cake category. In my haste I used twice as much margarine for the top and bottom crust. This made a rather cookielike cake and had to be drained on paper towels. There was no time to rebake, so I brought them anyway, since I'd promised I would. They took second place!"

She told us another story on herself. "I was making individual pizzas for New Year's Eve, and I forgot they were in the oven. When I took them out they looked like hockey pucks."

BIRDIE'S PINEAPPLE PIE

1 unbaked 8-inch pie shell	2 eggs
1 stick oleo	1 small (flat) can crushed
½ cups sugar	pineapple, drained slightly
2 T. flour	

Blend oleo in mixer until soft. Add sugar and mix until sugar is dispersed through oleo. Blend in the flour, then add the eggs and mix until all ingredients are blended. Add pineapple. Stir in by hand. Mixture will look curdled. Pour into pie shell and bake at 350 degrees about 45 minutes or until knife inserted slightly off center comes out clean.

ORANGE RAISIN PIE

1 6-oz. can frozen orange juice	¼ cup water
1½ cups water	1 T. butter
1½ cups raisins	1½ cups sifted flour
1½ cups sugar	½ tsp. salt
¼ cup cornstarch	½ cup shortening

Combine juice, water, and raisins. Cook over medium heat until raisins are plump. Combine sugar, cornstarch, and water, stir until smooth. Add to cooked raisins and cook, stirring constantly, until thickened. Cool.

Sift flour and salt together. Cut in shortening. Sprinkle with water, stirring slightly with fork. Add water until dough holds together. Form two-thirds of dough into a ball. Roll out and place loosely into pie pan; roll out remainder of crust and cut into half-inch strips. Spoon filling into crust and top with strips; flute edges. Bake at 450 degrees for 10 minutes, then at 350 for 20 minutes.

 "This year I'm already planning entries; the fair is 'in my blood'," says Hazel Godfrey. "It's a fun time, and a challenge. The friends one makes, the new and unusual items, are always fascinating, and the learning skills are invaluable. Every ribbon, or no ribbon, serves as constructive criticism for one's own personal goals and abilities."

Hazel was organizational leader for the 4-H clubs in her town; she attributes her drive and inspiration to compete in the fair to 4-H. She certainly is outstanding—in 1978 she entered 65 articles in the Oklahoma State Fair and received 51 ribbons. She learned to cook on her parents' farm. With a family of eight, she says, "Mother needed help." Hazel had polio as a child and "couldn't play too much," so she spent time in the kitchen.

Advice to others? "Cook easily served food for relaxed dinners. Color and textures play an important part in satisfying guests. Plan-ahead foods take stress off the hostess when completing the meal."

Also try Hazel's prizewinning Raised Doughnuts (page 130) and her Most Wonderful Toffee (page 367).

HELEN HANDELL
SAUNDERSTOWN, RHODE ISLAND

FIRST PRIZE
HONEY COOKERY CONTEST
RHODE ISLAND BEEKEEPERS
ASSOCIATION

NUTTY OATMEAL PIE

1 unbaked pie shell
½ cup vegetable oil
3 T. ice water
1¾ cups whole wheat flour
½ tsp. salt
¼ cup butter

1 cup honey
½ tsp. cinnamon
½ tsp. cloves
3 eggs
1 cup rolled oats
1 cup chopped nuts

Beat oil in ice water until foamy. Put whole wheat flour, and salt into pie plate. Stir in oil and water. Press into shape as you would a crumb crust. Pour in pie the butter and honey creamed together. Add cinnamon and cloves. Beat in eggs, one at a time. Stir in oats and nuts. Bake at 350 degrees about one hour (or less) or until knife inserted comes out clean.

Helen says, "We use natural foods—they taste better and are better for you." Although her family is small she enjoys entertaining young people and experimenting. Last winter she camped on the open desert in Arizona and cooked with a reflector over a wood fire.

BETTY HIATT
OAKDALE, CALIFORNIA

HOMEMADE MINCEMEAT

7 lbs. apples, grated
2 lbs. raisins, ground
   (preferably)
½ cup lemon juice
1 cup dark molasses
1 cup white corn syrup
3 cups brown sugar
2 tsp. allspice
2 tsp. cinnamon

½ tsp. salt
Grated rind of 2 lemons, or
   2 tsp. commercial kind
1 qt. fruit juice, apricot or
   whatever you have
   (can mix)
4 tsp. nutmeg
2 tsp. cloves
½ tsp. mace

Mix all together and boil 10 minutes or until desired consistency. Enough for 2 large pies. Freeze until you need it.

Try Betty's Homemade Beef Jerky (page 36), and Bar B Q Beef (page 36) and Blueberry Peach Jam (page 417).

Dawn C. Hill
Ethridge, Tennessee

PASTRY

Crust Size	6-inch Double	8-inch Double	9-inch Single	9-inch Double
INGREDIENTS				
sifted flour	1 cup	2 cups	1½ cups	2¼ cups
salt	½ tsp.	½ tsp.	½ tsp.	1 tsp.
shortening	⅓ cup	⅔ cup	½ cup	¾ cup
water	2 T.	4 T.	3 T.	4 T.

Mix flour and salt in bowl. Cut shortening into flour until pieces are about the size of peas. Blend ⅓ cup of shortening-flour mixture and the water. Add to remaining shortening-flour mixture and mix with fork until dough holds together. Shape into a round flat mass with no breaks at the edges. Roll dough about ⅛ inch thick. Let rest.

PECAN PIE

3 eggs
1 cup sugar
½ cup corn syrup
Pinch salt

1 tsp. vanilla
¼ cup margarine
1 cup pecans

Beat eggs slightly. Add sugar, syrup, salt, and vanilla. Mix well. Pour in melted margarine. Add nuts. Pour mixture in 9-inch pie shell. Bake at 400 degrees for 10 minutes, or 350 for 30–35 minutes.

CHESS PIE

1⅓ cups sugar
½ cup margarine
1 T. corn meal
⅓ cup milk

1 tsp. vanilla
1 tsp. vinegar
3 eggs

Melt margarine. Allow to cool. In a bowl measure sugar, meal, milk, vanilla, vinegar, and eggs. Stir mixture *only* after all ingredients have been added. Pour in margarine, mix well. Pour in pie shell. Bake at 350 degrees for 50 minutes.

Dawn said, "I'm 29 years old and started cooking in the fourth grade (4-H cooking contest), so that makes twenty years of cooking."

She cooks for five, "but drop-ins are not uncommon," and "because of my weakness for dishes, my kitchen is probably the best-equipped room in the house."

Her district prizewinners also happen to be very sought-after southern recipes—Pecan Pie and Chess Pie.

LORRAINE JACOBS
Nahunta, Georgia

ORANGE–PEANUT-BUTTER SURPRISE PIE

CRUST

1 cup crunchy peanut butter	3 T. granulated sugar
1 cup graham cracker crumbs	

Mix all together with hands. Press into a 10-inch pie plate. Bake 8 to 10 minutes at 325 degrees.

FILLING

1 8-oz. pkg. cream cheese (softened)
1 9-oz. carton Cool Whip
1 can condensed milk
1 6-oz. can frozen orange juice concentrate (thawed)
1 6½-oz. can mandarin orange slices, drained and cut up
¼ cup ground roasted peanuts

Mix all together and pour into crust. Garnish with an extra can of orange slices around outside of pie. In center of pie spread ½ cup Cool Whip, forming a circle. Sprinkle peanuts on top of Cool Whip. To make it even prettier take 1 fresh orange, cut 1 slice about ¼-inch thick out of center. Cut into 3 sections. Instead of sprinkled peanuts on top of Cool Whip make a flower out of orange slice. Cut a stem and 2 leaves from orange peel. Put half of a maraschino cherry in center of orange slice, put stem and leaves on, and then sprinkle on peanuts if you wish.

Lorraine grew up on a small farm in "a very small community in South Georgia." Her mother began teaching her how to cook when she was ten years old, "as she did with my other five sisters." They started "making biscuits and corn bread," and then on to other things.

Now Lorraine lives on a 392-acre farm, with a great big kitchen, fully equipped with three ovens and all the conveniences. She loves all aspects of cooking—"I love cookbooks like people love novels"—and has started a catering business. She has cooked for 230 people in one sewing factory and 75 in another, for Christmas dinner.

Lorraine says that you have to eat your cooking mistakes. However, "Don't give up, try again—learn to taste things to get them just right. My husband is my cake taster. When he says the batter is just right, it really is."

This prizewinner speaks for a lot of cooks when she says, "When you love food and people, you will be a great cook. Try to make the best better every day."

See also Lorraine's Stuffed Celery (page 9), and Fanci-Chicken Salad (page 104).

DONNA L. JANSEN
BOULDER, COLORADO

FINALIST
SAVORY SEASON CONTEST

STRAWBERRY ICE CREAM PIE

16 marshmallows
2 T. crushed strawberries
2 egg whites
¼ cup sugar
¼ tsp. salt

⅔ qt. vanilla ice cream
1 baked pastry shell
1 cup fresh strawberries,
    sliced
8–10 hulled strawberries

Heat marshmallows with crushed strawberries slowly, folding over and over until marshmallows are half melted. Remove from heat and continue folding until mixture is smooth and fluffy.

Beat egg whites until they hold a peak; add sugar slowly, beating constantly. Add salt. Blend lightly with marshmallow mixture.

Place ice cream in pastry shell, cover with sliced strawberries, and top with marshmallow meringue, swirled attractively. Brown quickly in broiler or very hot oven (450 degrees) ½ minute or until tips of meringue swirls are browned.

Remove from oven, tuck strawberries into the swirls, and serve immediately.

NOTE: For variety, use peaches or raspberries, heating marshmallows with hot water instead of crushed strawberries. Or omit berries and use chocolate ice cream.

 Donna once baked a cake to take on a camping trip and left home without the cake and with the oven still on. "We returned home fast after being on the road 20 minutes."

Donna's Cocoa Zucchini Brownies are on page 326.

DeAnn Johnson
Minot, North Dakota

STRAWBERRY ANGEL PIE

1 3-oz. pkg. strawberry-
flavored gelatine
1¼ cups boiling water
1 cup fresh strawberries or
1 10-oz. pkg. frozen sliced
strawberries

1 cup of whipped topping
1 Meringue Shell

Dissolve gelatine in boiling water. Chill until gelatine mixture is partially set. Whip the cream till soft peaks form; fold cream and strawberries into gelatine mixture. Chill until mixture mounds slightly when spooned. Pile into Meringue Shell. Chill 4 to 6 hours or overnight. Top with additional whipped cream and strawberries.

MERINGUE SHELL

3 egg whites
1 tsp. vanilla
¼ tsp. cream of tartar

Pinch of salt
1 cup sugar

Have egg whites at room temperature. Add vanilla, cream of tartar, and salt. Beat till soft peaks form. Gradually add sugar, beating until stiff peaks form and sugar is dissolved (meringue will be glossy). Cover baking sheet with plain ungreased brown paper. Using 9-inch round cake pan as a guide, draw circle on paper. Spread meringue over drawn circle. Shape into shell with the back of a spoon, making bottom ½ inch thick and sides about 1¾ inch high. Bake at 275 degrees for 1 hour. Turn off heat and let dry in oven (door closed) at least 2 hours.

NOTE: I usually make this recipe into 3 individual pies. Instead of a 9-inch circle I make a 2½-to-3-inch circle.

DeAnn helps with the family cooking. She learned to cook from her mother, and has been an active competitor in 4-H.

She used this recipe in the County Favorite Food Fair and won Grand Champion. It also won a blue ribbon at the North Dakota State Fair. She describes it as a "light, delicious pie to serve anyone."

DOROTHY KOEBEL
DONALD, OREGON

FIRST PLACE, PIES
OREGON STATE FAIR
CLACKAMAS COUNTY FAIR

LEMON MERINGUE PIE

CRUST

Blend 1 cup plus 2 tablespoons flour with ½ teaspoon salt. Add 6 tablespoons shortening. Cut into flour mixture with pastry blender until the size of small peas. Add 3 tablespoons of very cold water, stir with fork to blend. Shape into a ball. Roll between two sheets of waxed paper that has been dusted lightly with flour. Put crust in 9-inch pie pan, flute edge, and pinch *very close* all over pie shell with table fork. Bake at 450 degrees about 10 minutes, or until lightly browned. Cool

FILLING

Mix ¼ cup cornstarch, ½ cup sugar, and ¼ teaspoon salt in double boiler top. Slowly stir in 1½ cups water. Cook over boiling water, stirring constantly, until thick enough to mound slightly when dropped from spoon. Cover and cook 10 minutes, stirring occasionally. Beat 3 egg yolks and ½ cup sugar slightly. Blend a little hot mixture into egg yolks, then stir all into remaining hot mixture. Cook 2 minutes, stirring constantly. Remove from boiling water. Gently stir in 2 tablespoons butter, 1½ teaspoons grated lemon rind, and ½ cup lemon juice. Cool to room temperature. Turn into baked pastry shell.

MERINGUE

Mix 1 tablespoon cornstarch and 2 tablespoons sugar with ½ cup water. Cook until clear, set aside. Add a bit of salt to 3 egg whites, beat until foamy and standing in peaks. Add cornstarch mixture, beat until creamy. Add 6 table-spoons sugar one at a time, beat until creamy. Put on top of pie, making sure it is sealed against fluted edge. Bake at 325 degrees 30 minutes. Cool on rack, at room temperature.

"The first thing I baked by myself, age eleven, in a wood stove," was the funniest thing Dorothy has ever done cooking. "My family had gone to town shopping. I thought I would surprise them and bake a cake. I decided on a chocolate cake from the Watkins cookbook, our only cookbook at the time. The recipe called for half a cup of coffee. I put in a half cup of ground coffee. Thought it looked a little strange but baked it anyway.

"When it was baked and cooled I followed the delicious recipe for icing the cake. It called for confectioners sugar. I didn't know what that was, as we always referred to it as powdered sugar. So I used granulated sugar. Kept adding and adding sugar and ended up with syrup. Finally realizing I blew it I fed the whole mess to the chickens, cleaned up, and never did tell my family. Good thing chickens don't talk, huh!"

CHARLENE LAWSON
CARVER, MASSACHUSETTS

FIRST PRIZE, BEST OF SHOW
MASSACHUSETTS CRANBERRY
FESTIVAL

CRANBERRY ORANGE CUSTARD PIE

3 eggs, separated
¼ cup soft margarine
¼ cup flour
2½ cups cranberries, cut up
⅓ cup chopped nuts

1¼ cups sugar
3 T. frozen orange juice
  concentrate, thawed
¼ tsp. salt
Pastry for a 9-inch pie shell

Line pie pan with pastry and make a high fluted rim. Beat egg whites until stiff. Add ¼ cup of the sugar gradually, beat very well. Set aside. Add margarine and orange juice concentrate to egg yolks; beat thoroughly. Add remaining 1 cup sugar, flour, and salt; beat well. Add cranberries to mixture, stir well. Gently fold in beaten egg whites. Pour into pastry-lined pan, sprinkle with nuts. Bake on bottom rack at 375 degrees for 15 minutes; reduce heat to 325, bake 45 to 50 minutes more.

An amusing story from Charlene Lawson concerns a friend of hers. "I gave her some cranberries to cook with. Later when I talked to her, she said she really appreciated the cranberries, but it sure was a lot of work to get all those little seeds out!"

ALVINA LUTTIG MERRY

YUBA, WISCONSIN

BLUE RIBBON

RICHLAND COUNTY DAIRY BAKE-OFF

STRAWBERRY CHEESE PIE

CRUST

1½ cups fine graham cracker
    crumbs
⅓ cup butter or margarine,
    melted

3 T. sugar

Combine crumbs, butter and sugar. Mix well with pastry blender. Press over bottom and sides of 9-inch pan. Heat in 350-degree oven for 3 minutes. Chill well.

FILLING

1 8-oz. pkg. cream cheese,
    room temperature
½ cup lemon juice

1 14-oz. can sweetened
    condensed milk
Dash of salt

Prepare filling while crust is chilling. Beat cream cheese until smooth and fluffy. Add condensed milk gradually and beat until smooth. Stir in lemon juice and salt. Pour into crust. Chill until firm.

TOPPING

1 pint fresh strawberries,
    hulled, washed, and
    drained
2 T. cornstarch

½ cup sugar
½ cup water
Red food coloring

Cut 1 cup strawberries in half, arrange on top of filling. Mash remaining strawberries, combine sugar and cornstarch in pan, mix well. Stir in water and mashed strawberries. Cook, stirring constantly, until clear and thickened. Add red food coloring as desired. Pour over strawberries. Chill well. Serve plain or topped with whipped cream.

Yield: 6–8 servings

"Use standard measuring cups and spoons," advises Alvina Merry, prizewinning cook. "Have ingredients at room temperature, and use the right baking temperature."

She began winning prizes when she "made cookies and a cake and took them to our fair and received first on both of them—so I kept right on doing good."

As a girl, she cooked; once, she baked a chocolate cake and forgot to put in the soda. "Mother made us eat it anyway. It was a good lesson because it never happened again."

See also Alvina's Lime Party-Salad (page 108).

GRAND CHAMPION APPLE PIE

8 cups tart apples (if lack tartness, sprinkle with 1 T. lemon juice)	1 tsp. cinnamon
	2 T. butter
	2 T. flour
1 cup sugar	Dash each nutmeg and salt

Core, peel, and slice apples into large mixing bowl. In small bowl, combine sugar, flour, cinnamon, nutmeg, and salt. Add to apple slices (sliced thin) and mix well. Cover bowl and set in refrigerator while making pie crust. Line 9-inch pie pan with pastry; fill with apple mixture. Dot with butter. Cover with lattice top crust, trim and seal edge. Sprinkle top with sugar.

Cover lightly with plastic wrap and set overnight in refrigerator.

Fold strip of foil around rim of crust. Bake in 400-degree oven 55 to 60 minutes.

GOLDEN EGG PASTRY

2 cups flour	1 egg, slightly beaten
⅔ cup plus 2 T. lard (room temperature)	1 tsp. salt
	3 T. cold water

Stir flour and salt together in mixing bowl. Cut in lard thoroughly. Beat egg slightly; beat in water and pour into flour mixture. Mix with fork until flour is moistened. Gather in 2 balls. Roll out 2 inches larger than pan. Cut in circle. Line 9-inch pie pan with pastry. Add fruit and butter. Roll out second pastry ball and cut for lattice top. Lay strips across top and seal edges.

This recipe makes 1 2-crust pie or 2 pie shells. (To bake pie shell—poke bottom and sides with fork—bake 475 degrees.)

During her senior year in high school, a friend taught Pat Patton how to make a pie, "and I've been working on improving that skill ever since."

This Grand Champion pie baker told us, "My family consists of my husband and two-year-old son. They have few dislikes so I try new recipes for them." She adds, "I have only been entering exhibits in the State Fair the last four or five years, but it has really given me a confidence in my baking that I did not have before and consequently has helped me improve this skill."

PATRICIA PETERSON

BOISE, IDAHO

PIE CRUST

1½ cups whole wheat flour
1 cup white flour
½ cup lard
½ cup shortening

¼ cup water
1 egg, beaten
1 T. vinegar
1 tsp. salt

Combine flours, lard, and shortening, using a pastry blender.

Mix water, beaten egg and vinegar and salt. Add to flour mixture. Stir with a fork just until all the flour is dampened. Form into a ball (gently). Divide and roll out on a well-floured sheet. Bake at 400 degrees for 15 to 20 minutes.

This dough is soft so I can make a ball and flatten it in flour and then turn it over so that it is coated on both sides with flour.

Yield: 2 double pie crusts

This is Pat's unusual pie crust she uses for her prizewinning pies.

Patricia's scrumptious Carrot Cake recipe appears on page 251 and her Whole Wheat Bread is on page 141.

WENDY LEE REAVES
CERES, CALIFORNIA

ENGLISH WALNUT PIE

¼ cup oleo
¾ cup sugar
 2 eggs (unbeaten)
¾ cup dark corn syrup

¼ tsp. salt
1 tsp. vanilla
1 cup chopped walnuts

Use pastry blender or fork to cream oleo. Add sugar gradually, cream until fluffy. Add remaining ingredients and blend well with a wooden spoon. Pour into unbaked 9-inch pie shell and bake on lower rack of 350-degree oven for 45–55 minutes.

Wendy has been baking for five years. Once "while putting together a boysenberry cobbler," she said, "I decided to use not so much of the juice. It turned out, most of the sugar was in the juice. It was like eating a lemon!"

Wendy said she learned to cook with "a little help and a lot of practice at home."

PUMPKIN PIE

1 unbaked pie shell
1½ cups cooked or canned
    pumpkin
1 cup brown sugar, firmly
    packed
¾ tsp. salt

1 tsp. cinnamon
½ tsp. ginger
½ tsp. nutmeg
4 eggs, slightly beaten
1½ cups undiluted evaporated
    milk

Combine pumpkin, brown sugar, salt, and spices. Stir in eggs and milk. Pour into pie shell. Set pecan halves on border around edge of filling if desired. Bake pie 15 minutes at 425 degrees, then reduce heat to 350 and bake 40 minutes longer or until knife inserted in center comes out clean. Serve with whipped cream.

Mrs. Shannon has been cooking for "close to 60 or 65 years." She learned from her mother, who cooked for a large family. She cooks for three each day, and has won prizes on her pies, cookies and biscuits.

APPLE PIE

PIE CRUSTS

2 cups flour
¾ cup solid shortening
¼ tsp. salt

Approximately ½ cup cold water

Mix all ingredients in large bowl with fingers until crumbly. Add cold water, a little at a time, until mixture holds together in a ball and is easily workable.

Flour counter and turn out half the dough onto flour. Roll out about 4 inches larger than 9-inch pie plate. Press in, fill crust, add top crust.

FILLING

6 cups Cortland or MacIntosh apples (pared and sliced thin—approx. ¼-inch)
2 tsp. cinnamon
½ tsp. nutmeg

2 T. oleo
¼ tsp. salt
1 cup sugar (granulated)
1 tsp. flour

Into bottom crust put 3 cups apples, 1 tablespoon oleo (dots), ½ teaspoon flour (sprinkled on), and half of prepared mixture of sugar, nutmeg, cinnamon, and salt. Add remaining apples, ½ teaspoon flour (sprinkled on), 1 tablespoon oleo (dotted on), and remaining sugar mixture. Place crust on top and pick with fork several times to expel air while cooking.

Bake at 350 degrees for approximately 50–60 minutes.

Sandra learned to cook "from school, a sweet aunt, a dear mother—and mistakes." Working in her bright, neat kitchen, she cooks for five daily. She also told us a little story on herself:

"One day I was preparing Jello (it was about 20 below zero outside) and the phone rang. I guess I talked too long, because while I was on the phone my six-year-old son came in and left the door open. The cold air set the gelatin, and when I got off the phone the spoon was stuck."

She has a helpful hint: "For a beautiful brown crust, brush a little milk on top of the crust before baking the pie."

BILLIE LOU SOLLE

FRANKLIN, PENNSYLVANIA

CHERRY PIE

I take 1 quart of home-canned sweet cherries. Pour juice in pan with 1 cup of sugar and ¼ cup of cornstarch. Cook until thick, stirring to keep from burning. When thick put pitted cherries in and a dash of almond extract and a few drops of red food coloring. Put filling in crust-lined pan, dust with cinnamon lightly, and dot generously with butter. Put top crust on which has slits and spread crust with thick cream. Put in 450-degree oven for 15 minutes, turn to 350 degrees and bake until well browned, about 30 minutes. Take from oven and sprinkle top with sugar. Let cool before cutting.

NOTE: We raise our own pork and I render lard and use it for all my baking. For pie crust I use 2 heaping cups of flour, ¾ cup of lard, a scant teaspoon of salt, and enough ice water to form dough in ball. Mix and handle dough as little as possible.

"To be a good cook you have to stay at home and prepare a meal; you cannot throw something in a pan a half-hour before dinner," says Billie Lou. "Good food requires love and time—you must cook because you love to, not because you have to. I have my own fresh milk, cream, butter, eggs, and honey, which makes a big difference. I am making maple syrup now, I tap trees we have here at the farm—just enough for our own use."

Billie Lou also has a 40-ewe flock, and raises lambs for market and to sell wool. She does spinning "and lots of knitting."

She says, "I never thought of myself as a prizewinning cook, even though I have won ribbons on pies, cookies, rolls, candy, canned chicken, canned beans, beets, sweet cherries, pickles, blueberries, currant jelly, strawberry preserves, rose geranium jelly, and mint jelly.

"Some years ago when our Venango County 4-H Fair started I had two boys of age to join. I have always been interested in 4-H and I believe it is great for our young people. I can all my own fruits, jelly, and vegetables and do all my own baking from scratch. I've always entered exhibits at the fair because I believe the more people enter the bigger and better fair it makes for our young people. I have a large box of ribbons I value very much. I have never entered anywhere else. I got a blue ribbon for my Cherry Pie."

ANNA STONE
CIRCLEVILLE, OHIO

FRESH BLACKBERRY PIE

1½ cups sugar
⅓ cup flour
½ tsp. cinnamon

4 cups fresh berries
1½ T. oleo

Heat oven to 425 degrees. Mix sugar, flour, and cinnamon. Mix lightly through berries. Pour into pastry-lined pyrex pan. Dot with oleo. Cover with top crust which has slits cut in it. Seal and flute. Cover edge with 1½-inch strip of foil to prevent excessive browning. Bake 35 to 45 minutes or until crust is nicely browned and juice begins to bubble from slits.

PASTRY

1 cup sifted flour
½ tsp. salt

⅓ cup lard
3 T. cold water

Combine flour and salt. Cut in lard with pastry cutter until the mixture is the size of peas.

Sprinkle on cold water, 1 tablespoon at a time, tossing with a fork. Add water each time to driest part of mixture. Dough should be just moist enough to hold together when pressed firmly. Shape dough into ball. Roll out between waxed paper.

Anna Stone likes trying new recipes. She said she also has learned from "reading articles by James Beard and cookbooks."

Anna told us about a mistake she made while making pie crusts for the fair last summer. "A storm came up. I had part of the shortening measured—left it to pick berries before the rain hit them. When I came back I forgot to put in the rest of the shortening. What a tough crust!"

See also Anna's Honey Swirl Coffee Cake (page 202).

Mrs. A. G. Sykes
Williamsburg, West Virginia

BROWN SUGAR PIE

½ cup margarine or butter
3 cups brown sugar
3 eggs

3 T. flour
1 cup milk
1 tsp. vanilla

Mix margarine and sugar, stir in eggs. Add flour, stir in milk and vanilla. Pour into unbaked pie shell. Bake at 350 degrees until filling is firm, approximately 35 minutes. Watch closely—it's easy to burn.

Mrs. Sykes has won over a thousand dollars in baking prizes. She learned to cook from her sisters, as "my mother died when I was nine and my father when I was ten."

Even good cooks like Mrs. Sykes have made mistakes: "Once I baked salt-rising bread. It didn't rise and was so hard the dog wouldn't eat it—but now it's one of my specialties."

JOYCE WENTHOLD
OKLAHOMA CITY, OKLAHOMA

FIRST PRIZE, SPECTACULAR DESSERTS
OKLAHOMA STATE FAIR

CHOCOLATE PEANUT DELIGHT

CRUST

> 1 cup flour
> ⅔ cup chopped roasted peanuts
> ½ cup butter

Dump flour, peanuts, and butter in 9x13-inch pan (or 2 pie pans) and mix together with fingers; press into pan. Bake in preheated 350-degree oven for 20 minutes; cool.

SECOND LAYER

> ⅔ cup peanut butter
> 1 8-oz. pkg. cream cheese
> 1 cup powdered sugar
> 2 cups prepared whipped topping

Cream together peanut butter and cream cheese. Add powdered sugar and whipped topping. Spread over pie crust.

 Joyce has been entering food contests at the Oklahoma State Fair for six years and always comes away with prizes. She has been cooking "as long as I can remember," and she cooks every day for her family of four.

Her advice to other cooks is: "Treat your family like company and company like family."

One Christmas she forgot to put the sugar in her cranberry-orange nut bread. She had mixed and half baked six loaves before discovering the mistake. She said, "the birds enjoyed it, but it sure was expensive bird food."

See Joyce's Super Salad Sandwich (page 114).

GENNELL WIELAND

WEATHERFORD, OKLAHOMA

COCONUT CREAM PIE

3 cups milk, heated
3 T. cornstarch
2 T. flour
1¼ cups sugar
Pinch salt

4 egg yolks
3 T. butter
2 T. vanilla
¼ cup coconut

Add mixed dry ingredients to milk and cook until thick. Remove from fire and add egg yolks, butter, and vanilla. Mix well.

Fill crust and top with cool whip when filling is cold.

NOTE: Bake crust beforehand and let cool.

See also Gennell's Strawberry Ice Cream recipe (page 396).

MARY SUE WILLIAMS
PUEBLO, COLORADO

FIRST PRIZE, PEACH PIE
COLORADO STATE FAIR

FRESH PEACH PIE

PASTRY FOR 2-CRUST 9-INCH PIE

2 cups sifted flour	⅔ cup plus 2 T. solid shortening
1 tsp. salt	¼ cup water

Mix salt, flour together. Then with pastry blender cut in shortening till particles are the size of giant peas. Sprinkle with water, a tablespoon at a time, mixing lightly with fork until flour is moistened.

Gather dough together, press firmly into a ball, then divide dough in half. Roll out about ⅛-inch thick. Be careful not to add extra flour—that makes the pastry tough.

Roll out about 1 inch larger than the pie pan, being careful not to stretch the pastry. This will cause it to shrink during baking. Prepare filling, place in lined pie pan, trim off overhanging edges.

Roll out other part of dough for top crust large enough to extend 1 inch beyond edge of pie pan. Place pastry evenly on top of filling. Make slits near center of pie to allow steam to escape. Leave ½-inch rim of pastry beyond rim of pan, then fold the top pastry under. Seal by pressing with fingers. Form fluted edge all around.

FILLING

⅞–1 cup sugar depending on the tartness of the peaches	¼ tsp. nutmeg
	1 T. butter
	6–8 peaches (depends on the
4 T. flour	size)
¼ tsp. cinnamon (if desired)	

Remove skin from peaches and cut in thin slices. Sprinkle with half the sugar. Let stand 10 to 15 minutes. Line 9-inch pie pan with pastry.

Mix together remainder of sugar, flour, nutmeg, cinnamon and blend lightly through peaches. Pour into pie pan. Dot with bits of butter. If fruit is dry sprinkle 2 tablespoons of water over the fruit.

Cover with slitted top crust. Bake in 425-degree oven until crust is nicely browned and juice begins to bubble through slits, about 35 to 45 minutes.

"I always look for new and different ways of cooking," says Mary Sue Williams. "My kitchen is my pride and joy. I live in my kitchen." Mary Sue has been cooking "since I was a girl about 60 years ago." She cooks for a family of seven and "always had hired help."

"One funny lesson," she says succinctly. "Quick car-stop scrambles pies on way to fair."

Mary Sue won the first "Queen of the Kitchen" title, the much coveted Colorado State Fair award given only to the top cook. In order to even enter and be considered for the title, you must enter 12 categories and place in ten!

CHAPTER ELEVEN

COOKIES

COOKIES

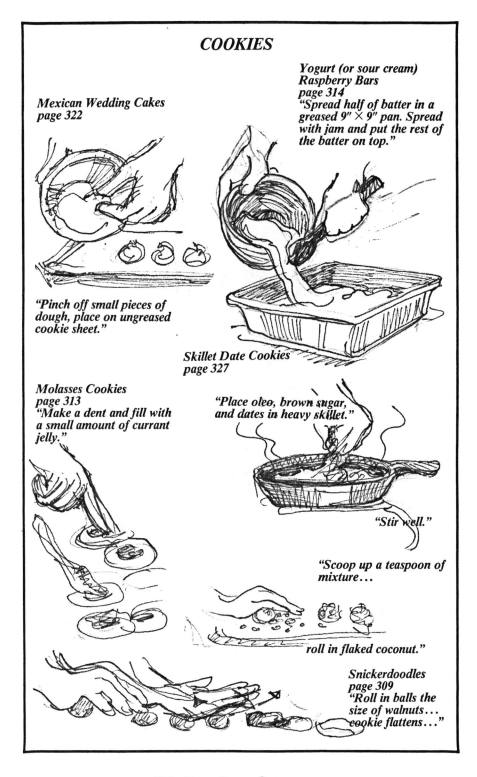

Yogurt (or sour cream) Raspberry Bars
page 314
"Spread half of batter in a greased 9" × 9" pan. Spread with jam and put the rest of the batter on top."

Mexican Wedding Cakes
page 322

"Pinch off small pieces of dough, place on ungreased cookie sheet."

Skillet Date Cookies
page 327

Molasses Cookies
page 313
"Make a dent and fill with a small amount of currant jelly."

"Place oleo, brown sugar, and dates in heavy skillet."

"Stir well."

"Scoop up a teaspoon of mixture...

roll in flaked coconut."

Snickerdoodles
page 309
"Roll in balls the size of walnuts... cookie flattens..."

DORIS BARB
ELDORADO, KANSAS

BUTTERSCOTCH OATMEAL CHIPS

1 cup shortening	1½ cups all-purpose flour
¾ cup granulated sugar	1 tsp. soda
¾ cup brown sugar	2 cups quick-cooking
2 eggs (beaten)	oatmeal
1 tsp. vanilla	1 large pkg. butterscotch
1 T. hot water	chips

Cream the shortening and sugars. Add the eggs, vanilla, and water. Sift together the flour and soda and add to the creamed mixture. Blend in the oatmeal and the butterscotch chips. (Before adding the chips I run them through a nut-chopper.)

Bake on very lightly greased cookie sheet at 350 degrees for 10 minutes.

Yield: at least 7 dozen medium-sized cookies

Doris Barb won 20 blue ribbons last year at the Kansas State Fair. She told us, "I am by profession a teacher and am now retired. My best therapy after a day in the classroom was some activity in the kitchen. It was actually through an older sister that I started exhibiting at the state level. I had exhibited some in the county so decided to prepare a few items and go along with her to keep her company. As I met with success I prepared more entries and returned each year." (Doris's sister, Josephine Smith, is also an outstanding prizewinner. See page 150.)

Doris is a champion example of the adage, "If at first you don't succeed..." (instead of "Oh well, that's how the cookie crumbles"). She told us: "Since retiring I have made two attempts at winning a first on the Governor's Cookie Jar award. Thinking a third time might be the charm I decided to try very hard to take the winner and it did prove to be the first place entry. This is an open class offered to all women of Kansas. For winning the top award, I received the beautiful purple rosette that was the sweepstakes ribbon, $14.00 cash, a new *Better Homes and Gardens Cookbook,* a ten-dollar coupon book, and the honor of presenting my jar to Governor Carlin at the fair arena. The judges count 25 percent for the jar itself and 75 percent for the contents. There were 13 varieties of cookies in the jar."

Doris learned to cook "through my mother's encouragement. She was a very good cook and when I was quite young I enjoyed watching and helping her. In her later years she liked to remark about how proud she was of her three daughters being good cooks. So—it seems I have been cooking most of my life.

My husband is deceased now but he appreciated and enjoyed the results of my interest in cooking. He gave me support and inspiration in my culinary ambitions. I enjoy cooking for myself now but many of my special preparations go to family and friends or into the freezer. I do have guests in quite often."

Her advice to young cooks is, "Have the courage to try—if you lose, just remember someone else did a better job, but by trial and error we learn and can reach success."

Doris's Bran Bread recipe is on page 164. Her sister, Mrs. Smith, is another prizewinner, whose Tropical Fruit Cookies are on page 341.

DENISE BARRETT
PALMER, ALASKA

FIRST PRIZE, COOKIES
ALASKA STATE FAIR

SNICKERDOODLES

1 cup soft shortening (part
   butter)
1½ cups sugar
2 eggs

2¾ cups sifted flour
2 tsp. cream of tartar
1 tsp. soda
¼ tsp. salt

Heat oven to 400 degrees. Mix shortening, sugar, and eggs thoroughly. Sift remaining ingredients together and stir in. Roll into balls the size of walnuts. Roll in mixture of 2 tablespoons sugar and 2 teaspoons cinnamon. Place 2 inches apart on ungreased baking sheet. Bake 8 to 10 minutes or until lightly browned but still soft. (These cookies puff at first, then flatten out.)

Yield: 5 dozen cookies

 Twelve-year-old Denise Barrett has been cooking for three years. She learned to cook from her mom, she says, and she works in a "well-used, modern, convenient kitchen."

GAYLORD BERGMEIER
DeWITT, NEBRASKA

PEANUT BUTTER COOKIES

½ cup butter or margarine
½ cup white sugar
½ cup brown sugar, firmly
    packed
1 egg, well beaten

½ tsp. vanilla
½ cup peanut butter
1½ cups flour
1 tsp. soda
Pinch of salt

Cream butter, peanut butter, and sugars together. Add eggs and vanilla. Sift the flour, soda, and salt together and blend with first mixture. Chill dough. Roll into balls the size of walnuts. Place on greased cookie sheet. Flatten with fork dipped in flour. Bake at 375 degrees for 12 to 15 minutes.

Gaylord Bergmeier learned to cook "from scratch and decorating for the March of Dimes Cake Bake-Off." He decorated the cakes, judged them, and auctioned them too for the March of Dimes.

JULIANN F. BLOOM
RONKS, PENNSYLVANIA

FIRST PRIZE, PRESSED COOKIES
SOUTHERN LANCASTER COUNTY
COMMUNITY FAIR

PRESSED COOKIES

1 cup shortening	⅛ tsp. salt
¾ cup sugar	¼ tsp. baking powder
2¼ cups sifted flour	1 tsp. almond extract

Cream shortening and add sugar. Cream. Add eggs and beat. Add dry ingredients and flavoring. Mix well. Put batter in cookie press and form on ungreased cookie sheet. Bake 10 minutes at 375 degrees.

ROYAL FANS

2 cups sifted flour	½ cup brown sugar
¾ cup shortening	2 T. water (more if needed)

Blend flour and sugar. Cut in shortening as for pastry. Add water until dough is consistency of pie crust. Roll out ⅛-inch thick and cut in circles. Cut circles in half and score lightly with knife. Bake at 375 degrees for 8–10 minutes.

 Cooking in her modern, complete Pennsylvania kitchen Mrs. Bloom is a prizewinner in the Pressed Cookies class. She cooks for six people and she learned "at home and in 4-H club."

CATHY BRIDGE
WATERVILLE, NEW YORK

SUGAR COOKIES

1 cup sugar
1 egg
½ cup shortening
½ cup sour milk
1 tsp. baking powder

½ tsp. baking soda
2½ cups flour
1 tsp. vanilla
Pinch of salt

Cream together sugar, egg, and shortening in mixing bowl. Combine flour, baking soda, and powder in sifter. Slowly add a little of each mixture until well blended. Spoon on greased cookie sheet. Bake at 350 degrees for 8–10 minutes or until done.

EDNA MAY BUEHLER
LOUISVILLE, KENTUCKY

FIRST PRIZE, CULINARY
SENIOR CITIZENS
KENTUCKY STATE FAIR

MOLASSES COOKIES

¾ cup sweet margarine or butter	2½ cups flour (unsifted)
1 cup granulated sugar	½ tsp. ground cloves
¼ cup light molasses	½ tsp. ginger
1 egg	1 tsp. cinnamon
2 tsp. baking soda	½ tsp. salt

Melt margarine over low heat and cool. Add sugar, molasses, and egg; beat well. Sift together flour, soda, cloves, ginger, cinnamon, and salt 3 times to mix well. Add to first mixture. Cover and chill in refrigerator overnight. Form in 1-inch balls, roll in granulated sugar, and place on greased cookie sheets 2 inches apart. With finger make a dent and fill with small amount of currant jelly. Bake in moderately hot oven (375 degrees) for 8–10 minutes.

"For the past four years I worked as a cook in a Christian private school, from 1931–41 I worked as a waitress, sometimes making salads, syrups for the soda fountain, or at the sandwich counter. I've always loved to work around food."

Edna May told us a funny story about baking: "When I was married about two weeks, my fourteen-year-old brother-in-law asked me if I'd bake a birthday cake for my father-in-law. I told him I would. Well, I proceeded to gather all the ingredients and everything I needed when I realized I was out of baking powder. I sent him down to the corner store to get a can of Calumet baking powder. When he returned he had a can of double-acting baking powder I had never heard of. Well, I used it and mixed the cake, put it in the oven to bake. Well, you never saw anything like it. The cake was going up and down like it was alive and breathing. We both laughed until we were sick. When the cake was done and I put it on cake racks to cool it went down like an elevator, non-stop from top floor to the basement.

"I had three layers and I wanted to throw them out but he said no. My father-in-law came home and told me to ice it. He'd eat it if it killed him. I cut the layers in half and iced them. The cake stood about two inches high when I finished. After forty years when we all get together the breathing cake is brought up and we still get a good laugh."

KATHY COONS
LOUISVILLE, KENTUCKY

YOGURT (OR SOUR CREAM) RASPBERRY BARS

½ cup butter
½ cup sugar
1 egg
½ cup raspberry yogurt (or sour cream)

2 cups flour
1 tsp. baking powder
1 jar (about 1 cup) raspberry jam

Cream butter and sugar. Add egg and beat well. Add flour and baking powder alternately with yogurt to egg/butter sugar mixture. Mix well. Spread half of batter in a greased 9x9-inch pan. Spread with jam and put rest of batter on top. Bake at 350 degrees for 30–35 minutes. When cool, ice and cut into squares.

ICING

⅓ cup soft butter
1 lb. sifted powdered sugar
5 T. milk

1 tsp. vanilla
A few drops of red food coloring

Blend together butter and sugar. Add milk and vanilla and food coloring Stir until smooth (I use an electric mixer). Thin with more milk if necessary.

Yield: this amount covers a double batch of bars

"When I first started cooking," Kathy told us, "I had mashed potatoes. I had never paid a lot of attention to what my mother did with them. I knew she kept the water, but didn't know just what she did with it. So, I decided she must put ι back in the mashed potatoes. Needless to say I soon learned this was wrong and I was supposed to put the water in the gravy."

Kathy's Yogurt Bars have won blue ribbons for five years at the fair. She also won the Dairy Sweepstakes and these bars were part of her entries.

While her mother taught her the basics, Kathy "learned mostly by trial and error plus cookbooks and recipes from family and friends."

ESTHER CORNELIUS
PALMER, ALASKA

FIRST PRIZE, SUGAR COOKIES
ALASKA STATE FAIR

PRESSED SUGAR COOKIES

2 cups unsifted flour	2 eggs
1 cup butter	1 cup white sugar
1 tsp. cream of tartar	1 tsp. nutmeg
1 tsp. baking soda	1 tsp. vanilla

Mix flour, butter, soda, and cream of tartar as you mix pie crust. Beat eggs, add sugar, nutmeg and vanilla, then add to flour mixture, and mix together. Roll small amounts in your hand and put on cookie sheet. Press down, using a round glass dipped in sugar. Bake in oven at 350 degrees till light brown. I bake them on the middle shelf. Real butter makes a lot of difference in the taste of these cookies. They are very good to make and very tasty.

Yield: around 60 cookies, depending on how large you make them

 A Norwegian-American, Esther Cornelius has always been around good cooks. "My mother was a great Scandinavian cook," she says. Although she learned to cook when she went to work at age fourteen on a farm in North Dakota, she also learned "quite a few points from my son who is a chef and maitre d'.

"The main thing," she advises about pastry and bread baking, "is not to use too much flour. And cookies taste blah without butter."

MRS. GORDON L. COWLEY

ST. JOHNS, ARIZONA

FIRST PRIZE
APACHE COUNTY FAIR

PECAN COCONUT SQUARES

½ cup solid shortening
1 cup flour
½ cup dark brown sugar

Mix well in medium-sized mixing bowl. Pat firmly into greased 12x12-inch square pan. Bake in 325-degree oven for 25 minutes. While baking beat 2 eggs really well, add 1 cup brown sugar, ½ teaspoon baking powder, ½ teaspoon salt, 1 teaspoon vanilla. Beat until well blended. Add ½ cup coconut tossed in 2 tablespoons flour and 1 cup chopped pecans. Pour over crust, bake 25 minutes, cut into *small* squares—this is rich!

 Mrs. Cowley not only won first prize with this recipe, she also won the most points in baking at the fair. She told us she learned to cook in her mother's "range restaurant" when she was twelve and thirteen. "I made all the pancakes for her," she says.
She tells a "sad-smile" story on herself: "In 1936 when times were bad, I had saved one pound of walnuts in the shell. When I finished cracking them I poured the walnuts in the wood stove and kept the shells."

DAN CURD
MADISON, WISCONSIN

FIRST PLACE, COOKIES
WISCONSIN STATE JOURNAL CONTEST

COFFEE RUM COOKIES

¾ cup unsalted butter
1 cup sugar
1 egg
1 T. instant coffee
1 T. dark rum

2½ cups plus 2 T. flour
2 tsp. baking powder
½ tsp. salt
½ cup almonds, chopped fine

Preheat oven to 350 degrees. Cream butter and sugar until light and fluffy. Beat egg with instant coffee and rum. Add to the creamed butter and sugar, beating until well combined. Mix dry ingredients and gradually stir into the other mixture. Shape into a ball and chill at least 1 hour.

Roll out ⅛-inch thick and cut into 2-inch diamonds with a cutter or a pastry wheel. Bake on ungreased cookie sheets for 8–10 minutes. Remove from sheet and cool on wire racks.

Yield: 3 dozen

Dan Curd's Cornish Chicken (page 61) and California Fruit Salad (page 102) are great, too.

GENEVIEVE CZERMENDY
DETROIT, MICHIGAN

ITALIAN COOKIES

Cook apple filling ahead and refrigerate till ready to use, or may be put in canning jars.

FOR THE DOUGH:

8 cups flour	10 eggs
1 cup sugar	¾ cup milk
8 tsp. baking powder	1 T. vanilla
1 lb. solid shortening	

Mix flour, sugar, baking powder. Add shortening and blend as for pie crust. Add eggs, milk, and vanilla together and blend. Knead till smooth, cover, let stand for 2 hours. Roll dough on floured board to thin 7x12-inch strips. Put filling in the center of the strips and lap sides of dough over and roll over cut side down. Cut into 2-inch widths or desired size. Place crosswise on greased cookie sheet.

Bake at 375 for 15 minutes.

APPLE FILLING

5 lbs. apples, diced
1 cup sugar (adding 1 cup sugar
    extra for the pot)

Place in pot, and cook till thick. (Looks like candied apples.) Cool and store in canning jars till ready to use.

NOTE: If desired, add chopped nuts, candied cherries, or candied pineapple.

"Cookbooks, a year at high school cooking class and Bob Allison's 'Ask Your Neighbor' radio program" instructed Genevieve in cookery. She has been cooking for 42 years and is our first prizewinner to give credit to a radio program.

EDWARD DUFURRENA
McDERMITT, NEVADA

PINEAPPLE COOKIES

1 cup shortening	2 well-beaten eggs
1 cup brown sugar	4½ cups flour
1 cup white sugar	½ tsp. baking powder
½ tsp. salt	½ tsp. soda
2 tsp. vanilla	½ cup chopped nuts
1 cup crushed pineapple	

Cream shortening and sugars. Add salt, vanilla, eggs and pineapple. Mix well. Sift together flour, soda, baking powder. Mix with above mixture. Add nuts. Drop onto cookie (greased) sheet. Bake at 350 degrees until done.

NOTE: Easy to freeze, and taste better after allowed to set a day or two.

 Edward DuFurrena learned to cook in 4-H. Ladies take heed! So many of our male prizewinners were 4-H cooks that we recommend this training for all boys (and girls). Edward describes his kitchen as "compact and easy to cook in."
Now twelve, he has been cooking for three years, and he helps "my mom cook for Dad, Mom and myself."

LAZY SUGAR COOKIES

½ cup butter or margarine
½ cup other shortening
½ cup sugar
½ cup powdered sugar
1½ tsp. vanilla

1 egg
½ tsp. cream of tartar
½ tsp. soda
½ tsp. salt
2¼ cups flour

Cream shortenings and sugars together. Add vanilla, egg, cream of tartar, soda, and salt. Mix well. Add flour and mix in. Roll dough into balls. Flatten on cookie sheet with a glass dipped in sugar. Bake in a 350–375-degree oven for 10 to 12 minutes.

Seventeen-year-old Lora DeMoss learned cooking skills from "my mom and 4-H too."

Lora has good advice for all of us: "Never be afraid to try a new recipe, technique, utensils, and ingredients. Be open-minded in serving food. Make everybody feel the joy you feel in preparing all types of food. Make cooking and serving a pleasant experience."

APPLESAUCE RAISIN BARS

1 cup sugar	2 tsp. soda
¾ cup shortening	1 cup raisins
2 cups sweetened applesauce	Pinch salt
2 eggs	1 tsp. vanilla
2 cups flour	1 cup nuts
½ tsp. cinnamon	

Combine sugar and shortening. Add eggs and applesauce, then raisins and dry ingredients. Add nuts and vanilla. Bake in jelly roll pan, greased and floured, for 30 minutes in 350-degree oven. When cool frost with Caramel Frosting.

CARAMEL FROSTING

1 cup brown sugar	¼ cup milk
1 stick margarine	2 cups powdered sugar
¼ tsp. salt	

Boil sugar, margarine, and salt for 2 minutes. Remove from heat, add milk. Bring to boil again. Take off heat and add powdered sugar. Stir till smooth.

"I love recipe books and never can pass up the temptation of just one more," says Joyce Dubois. "I feel if you find just one good recipe that your family likes, it is well paid for."

Mrs. Dubois is a prizewinner at the South Dakota State Fair. She says modestly, "I've had pretty good luck." We think it's more than luck—her fudge recipe was in the winning candy jar presented to the governor, and also won first place in the Candy Division.

Her Applesauce Raisin Bars are "family favorites as well as being first-place winners at the fair."

MEXICAN WEDDING CAKES

1 cup butter
½ cup powdered sugar
¼ tsp. salt

1 tsp. vanilla
2 cups sifted all-purpose flour
Powdered sugar

Cream butter; add sugar gradually. Blend in salt, vanilla, and flour. Mixture is stiff. Pinch off small pieces of dough; place on ungreased cookie sheets. Bake at 400 degrees about 10 minutes. Roll in powdered sugar while hot.

Yield: about 5 dozen

In her large, newly remodeled kitchen, Ruth prepares meals for seven every day. She gives credit to her mother for teaching her to cook, as well as to 4-H during grade school years.

Ruth advises, "Always read your recipe and check to make sure you have all the ingredients before putting anything in your pan." She has also won blue ribbons for her Lazy Daisy Cake (see page 221) and her rhubarb and cherry pies.

BECKY FAHY
MINOT, NORTH DAKOTA

CHOCOLATE CHIP COOKIES

⅔ cup butter (not margarine)
⅔ cup shortening
1 cup brown sugar
1 cup white sugar
2 eggs

2 tsp. vanilla
1 tsp. soda
1 tsp. salt
2 cups flour
6 oz. chocolate chips

Preheat oven to 325 degrees. Cream butter, shortening, and sugars together thoroughly until light and fluffy. Add eggs and vanilla and mix thoroughly. Sift dry ingredients and add very gradually to other mixture until well blended. Stir in chocolate chips. Drop by uniform-size spoonfuls onto a shiny cookie sheet— do not roll with hands. Bake on lower rack of oven for 5 minutes and then raise to upper rack to finish until golden brown (about 4–5 more minutes).

Remove with turner to a cooling rack (not waxed paper or flat surface). Put next batch on cool cookie sheet and bake. Store in tightly covered container. If you like the cookies soft, put a slide of bread in the storage container or take them out of the oven a little earlier.

 "I tried these cookies over and over for a high school boy friend until I finally got them right. Now when I make them, it's like therapy—a calming, relaxing influence—remembering all the people who have enjoyed them." Isn't that a nice way to think about cookie baking?

Becky learned "at home from my mother who is an excellent farm wife and cook and in college home ec classes. She told us her kitchen was "full of 3 generations of ovens—wood stove, electric, and microwave."

SKYE ANN GOVER
REDMOND, OREGON

BLUE RIBBON
DESCHURES COUNTY FAIR

CHOCOLATE CHIP COOKIES

1⅓ cups solid shortening
1 cup sugar
1 cup packed brown sugar
2 eggs
2 tsp. vanilla

3 cups flour
1 tsp. soda
½ tsp. salt
1 cup nuts
1 cup chocolate chips

Heat oven to 375 degrees. Mix shortening, sugars, eggs, and vanilla thoroughly. Stir dry ingredients together. Blend in. Mix in nuts and chocolate chips. Drop rounded teaspoonfuls of dough about 2 inches apart on ungreased baking sheet. Bake 8–10 minutes or until delicately browned (cookies should still be soft). Cool slightly before removing from baking sheet.

Yield: approximately 5 dozen cookies

One of our youngest winners, six-year-old Skye Ann has been cooking since she was five. She learned "from my mom. In our home." Skye has won blue ribbons for the past two years for her cookies.

When we asked Skye to describe her kitchen she said, "It's pretty."

FERN HARMON
GRANGER, IOWA

HONEY LEMON SPECIALS

½ cup (1 stick) butter or
    margarine
½ cup sugar
½ cup honey
1 egg

1 tsp. grated lemon rind
2 cups sifted all-purpose flour
¼ tsp. baking powder
¼ tsp. salt
1 cup wheat germ (save ½ cup)

Beat together butter or margarine, sugar, and honey until fluffy in large bowl with electric mixer. Add egg and lemon rind; beat well.

Sift flour, salt, and baking powder. Stir into butter-sugar mixture. Add ½ cup of the wheat germ. Refrigerate 1 hour or longer.

Shape dough into 1-inch balls; roll in remaining wheat germ. Place on ungreased cookie sheets. Flatten slightly with finger.

Bake at 350 degrees for 8 minutes, or until edges are lightly browned. Remove with spatula to wire racks to cool.

Yield: 4 dozen cookies

DONNA L. JANSEN
BOULDER, COLORADO

COCOA ZUCCHINI BROWNIES

2 cups flour
1½ cups sugar
1 tsp. salt
½ cup cocoa
1½ tsp. soda
2 eggs

½ cup chopped nuts
2 tsp. vanilla
2 cups zucchini (peeled and shredded)
½ cup vegetable oil

Sift dry ingredients together and combine with rest of ingredients. Spread dough in greased 9x13-inch pan and bake 30 minutes in 350-degree oven.

Donna's large, convenient kitchen "now sports a new range and oven." See page 288 for her Strawberry Ice Cream Pie.

WAUNITA JAY
OKLAHOMA CITY, OKLAHOMA

FIRST PLACE, GOVERNOR'S
COOKIE JAR
OKLAHOMA STATE FAIR

SKILLET DATE COOKIES

½ cup oleo-margarine
1 cup dark-brown sugar
1 8-oz. pkg. chopped dates
1 whole egg, beaten well
3 cups Rice Krispies cereal

1 tsp. vanilla
1 cup chopped nuts (pecans
  best!)
Angel-flake coconut (takes
  about 2 cups)

Place oleo, brown sugar and dates in heavy skillet (I use a cast-iron) on *medium* heat. Cook until oleo and sugar are dissolved, stirring constantly for at least 10 minutes. Remove from heat and stir in beaten eggs. Return to heat and stir well for 5 minutes. Remove from heat and stir in Rice Krispies, vanilla and nuts. Butter hands and scoop up a teaspoon of mixture at a time, roll into ball and roll in flaked coconut. I have colored the coconut with 2–3 shades of food-coloring, by shaking coconut in either jars, or empty oleo containers and adding a few drops food-coloring. The different-colored candy-balls are lovely, arranged on a plate. This recipe is quick and easy.

Yield: 3–4 dozen cookies

"I had hurriedly put away groceries in anticipation of soon-to-arrive, unplanned-for dinner guests. I got out onions and celery to sauté, and could not locate the butter I had just bought to use for sautéing. Finally—found it under kitchen sink alongside the soap I'd bought." Haven't we all done something like that?

Waunita cooks for "my husband and frequently for our five children and their spouses and six grandchildren." She learned to cook by "taking cooking class in high school. I got tips from my mother-in-law and sister, from lots of cookbooks, magazines and newspaper recipes, also from exchanging with friends."

She advises: "For anyone who loves to bake and has lots of patience, I highly recommend a beginners' cake-decorating course. I finished this past December, and just loved it. I hope to work in the advanced courses soon."

MRS. NORMAN KELLEY
PARAGOULD, ARKANSAS

DROP COOKIES

½ cup of butter or oleo
1 cup shortening
1 cup sugar
1 egg
1 tsp. vanilla

2 T. milk
2½ cups of sifted flour
½ tsp. soda
¼ tsp. salt

Drop by teaspoonfuls on ungreased cookie sheet. Press out with glass dipped in granulated sugar. Bake at 350 degrees for 10 to 12 minutes or until brown.

A cook "all of my life," Mrs. Kelley learned "by watching other people and taking down recipes from friends."

ROBIN L. KREVITSKY
PHOENIX, ARIZONA

FIRST PRIZE
ARIZONA STATE FAIR

ONE-BOWL BROWNIES

½ cup margarine	¼ tsp. salt
1 cup sugar	¼ cup cocoa
2 eggs	¾ cup flour
1 tsp. vanilla	1 tsp. baking powder

Put all ingredients in large mixing bowl. Beat with mixer at low speed (3 minutes) or by hand. Cook in greased 6x10-inch pan in a 350 degree oven for 30 minutes. Cool and frost (1 cup powdered sugar, 1 tablespoon cocoa, 2 teaspoons butter, ½ teaspoon vanilla, 1 tablespoon evaporated milk).

NOTE: You can double the recipe and use a 9x13-inch pan. A trick I use that the judges like is to put a layer of nuts on the batter after I pour it in the pan, then frost over the nuts when the brownies are cooled.

Twenty-year-old Robin says she cooks "usually for myself or a boy-friend," and she gives credit to her home ec teacher for teaching her to cook and giving her this prizewinning recipe.

Robin has been cooking since she was eight years old; her recipe has won four blue ribbons! Her younger sister, Suzy, is also a prizewinner (her recipe for Gingersnaps follows).

Suzy Krevitsky
Phoenix, Arizona

GINGERSNAPS

¾ cup shortening
1 cup brown sugar (packed)
1 egg
¼ cup molasses
2¼ cups flour
2 tsp. soda

1 tsp. cinnamon
1 tsp. ginger
½ tsp. cloves
¼ tsp. salt
Granulated sugar

Mix thoroughly shortening, brown sugar, egg, and molasses. Blend in remaining ingredients, except granulated sugar. Cover with foil and chill for 1 hour.

Heat the oven to 350 degrees. Shape the dough by teaspoonfuls into balls. Dip the tops into the sugar. Place the balls sugar side up 1 inch apart on non-greased cookie sheet. Bake 8–10 minutes or just until set. Remove from sheets onto spread-out newspaper on a counter or table. Now eat!

 "My mom taught me to bake cakes, cookies, and main dishes when I was seven or eight. My dad has been teaching me how to bake bread, rolls, and yeast items for about four years. I've learned all my cooking at home," says Suzy, "with the exception of camping cuisine, which I can credit to my Girl Scout adventures."

Eighteen-year-old Suzy has piled up a lot of wins at the Arizona State Fair since she began entering in 1971, including a rosette for having the most points in the Junior Division. She sent us a cute drawing along with some good hints and advice for other cooks:

1. Have all of your ingredients handy, but don't try to be perfectly organized.
2. Don't get discouraged by mistakes—"If at first you don't succeed..."
3. Lay down paper towels under anything you measure and then you can throw away your mess!
4. Fill your sink with hot, soapy water before you begin and just toss in utensils as you dirty them.
5. No matter how tired you may be, *clean up the kitchen as soon as you're through baking!* It's always nicer to collapse knowing that you're done with your work.
6. Let your kids watch and help you cook. Never discourage them in anything, for that matter!
7. Don't make cooking a chore—you'll never have any fun that way!

LEORA McCLUNG
LEWISBURG, WEST VIRGINIA

FIRST PLACE, GOVERNOR'S COOKIE JAR
WEST VIRGINIA STATE FAIR

FRUIT CAKE COOKIES

1 cup butter
2 cups dark brown sugar
4 eggs
1 lb. English walnuts (coarsely chopped)
1 lb. pecans (coarsely chopped)
1 box white raisins
1 box dark raisins
½ lb. green candied cherries

½ lb. red candied cherries
1 cup whiskey
½ lb. candied pineapple
1 tsp. cinnamon
1 tsp. nutmeg
1 tsp. soda
3 cups flour (save 1 cup to dredge fruit and nuts)

In large bowl cream butter and sugar. Add eggs, beat well. Slowly add whiskey and dry ingredients together. Add flour-dredged fruit and nuts. Work well with hands. Chill overnight. Drop by teaspoons on greased cookie sheets. Bake at 325 degrees for 20 minutes or until delicately browned. Cool. Store in airtight containers.

NOTE: These cookies freeze well.

Leora learned to cook from "my mother and grandmother and from a collection of good cookbooks."

She says her worst mistakes come from "doing too many things at one time and burning things."

Winner of the coveted Governor's Cookie Jar award, Leora had to fill a one-gallon clear glass jar with not less than nine kinds of cookies. The fancy assorted cookies were made from different kinds of batters and doughs. Along with the tightly sealed jar each contestant had to submit one of each kind of cookie in a small box for the judge. The winner presents her jar to the governor in person.

Leora showed us a picture of Governor John D. Rockefeller getting his prize (Lucky Guv!) with Leora at his right. We were delighted to see another of our prizewinners, Carol Spence, in the same picture—she won the First Lady's Candy Box Award!

See Carol Spence's recipe for Santa's Whiskers page 342.

JANICE ANN MCCRATH

SOUTH LYON, MICHIGAN

PINEAPPLE COCONUT MERINGUES

3 egg whites
1 cup sugar
¼ tsp. salt
1 tsp. vanilla

¾ cup shredded coconut
¾ cup chopped candied pineapples (red-green)

Heat oven to 300 degrees. Blend egg whites, sugar, salt, and vanilla in top of double boiler. Place over boiling water. Beat with beater until mixture forms stiff peaks, scraping bottom and sides of pan with rubber scraper. Immediately stir in coconut and pineapple.

Drop teaspoonfuls on lightly greased baking sheets. Bake 12–15 minutes or until lightly browned. Remove from sheets immediately.

Yield: about 3 dozen

After twelve years of working, Janice McCrath went back to school to become a dietitian. She advises others to "be adventurous in your cooking; try anything, adjusting the ingredients to your own taste."

Janice told us her kitchen was "small, well equipped, comfortable, and exciting." She told a story on herself that maybe we shouldn't make public: "The almond bundt cake I made for a party at Eastern Michigan University, where I am treasurer of the Home Ec Club, had a two-inch tunnel running around the total circumference. Thank God I caught it before it was served!"

MARGIE McGLACHLIN
SEDGWICK, KANSAS

GOVERNOR'S COOKIE JAR
FIRST PLACE, BREAD BASKET
KANSAS STATE FAIR

LEMON LASSIE COOKIES

FILLING

2 eggs, slightly beaten	¼ cup lemon juice
½ cup sugar	1 tsp. salt
1 T. grated lemon rind	1 cup coconut

Combine all ingredients except coconut; cook over low heat, stirring constantly, until thick. Remove from heat; add coconut. Set aside to cool.

BATTER

2¼ cups flour	½ cup butter
1 tsp. cinnamon	1 cup sugar
½ tsp. baking soda	1 egg
¼ tsp. salt	¼ cup light molasses

Combine flour, cinnamon, soda, and salt.

Cream butter and sugar; blend in egg and molasses. Beat until fluffy. Add dry ingredients gradually, mixing thoroughly.

If desired, chill dough for easier handling. Divide into 4 parts. Shape each part into 15-inch roll on lightly floured surface. Flatten to 15x2½-inch strips. Spread one-fourth filling down center of each strip. Fold strips in half lengthwise; seal edges. Cut into 1½-inch bars and place on ungreased cookie sheet. Bake at 350 degrees 12 to 15 minutes.

Yield: 3–4 dozen cookies

Margie learned to cook at home when she was ten. "I was taught by my mother," she told us. She works in a "very handy, well-equipped kitchen."

She said the "Lemon Lassie Cookies were the most unusual ones" included in her Governor's Cookie Jar.

Try Margie's Cheese Sesame Rolls (page 134).

COOKIES   333

BEST BUTTER COOKIES

Sift together in large mixing bowl, 3 cups flour, 1 teaspoon soda, and 2 teaspoons cream tartar. All measurements are to be level. Mix into the flour mixture 1 level cup of butter. Blend thoroughly until grainy, as though making pie crust. In a small bowl, beat 2 eggs until light and add 1 level cup of sugar. Mix together thoroughly. Add to the flour mixture and mix until it is easy to handle. Roll out thin (with a "stockinged" rolling pin) and cut with cookie cutter. Bake in a 350-degree oven.

 North Dakota's Governor's Cookie Jar has six kinds of cookies in it, and Nellie Marie Nelson's Best Butter Cookies were one of the six chosen. These butter cookies have won her more blue and purple ribbons than we have room to list.

Nellie cooks for two to ten people, because "I am a farm wife and we have hired help." Now a champion baker, with two modern well-equipped kitchens (one in town and one at the farm), she can laugh about the time she used 1½ cups salt in place of 1½ cups sugar while making a chocolate cake. "When I took the cake from the oven, it had a gray appearance and was heavy as lead. It tasted like the Dead Sea." She was only thirteen then—but she's never forgotten that cake.

SARAH C. PATTERSON
SEDALIA, MISSOURI

ARCHWAY COOKIE AWARD
SWEEPSTAKES, BAKING
MISSOURI STATE FAIR

DATE PINWHEEL COOKIES

½ cup margarine
½ cup brown sugar
½ cup granulated sugar
1 egg

½ tsp. vanilla
2 cups flour
½ tsp. soda
½ tsp. salt

Mix and chill. Divide in half. Roll each half 12x8x¼ inches. Spread half of Date Filling on each strip. Roll like jelly roll. Chill overnight. Bake on greased cookie sheet at 400 degrees.

Yield: 5 dozen cookies

DATE FILLING

1 lb. dates (cut up)
½ cup sugar
½ cup water

Cook and stir until thick. Cool. Add ½ cup nuts, chopped fine.

 Sarah works in her modern, convenient kitchen, creating all kinds of prizewinning baked goods. She has won Sweepstakes in Baking with Lard as well as Baking.

CLAIRE PELLETIER
NORTH CONWAY, NEW HAMPSHIRE

SHEET GINGERBREAD

2 cups flour	1 cup hot coffee
1 cup sugar	½ cup soft butter
1 tsp. soda	½ cup shortening
1 tsp. cinnamon	½ cup molasses or dark corn
1 tsp. ginger	syrup
1 tsp. cloves	1 tsp. vanilla
⅛ tsp. salt	2 eggs

Preheat oven to 350 degrees. Grease and flour 13x9-inch pan. Combine all ingredients. Beat until smooth at medium speed. Pour into greased pan. Bake 25–30 minutes until top springs back when touched lightly in the center.

FROSTING

¼ cup butter	½ tsp. vanilla
1½ cups powdered sugar	2–3 T. water

In small saucepan over low heat cook butter until light golden brown, stirring constantly. Add remaining ingredients, blend until smooth. Frost when gingerbread is cool.

Claire's delicious German Coffee Cake is on page 197.

PEANUT BUTTER COOKIES

1¼ cups sifted flour
¼ tsp. salt
1 tsp. cinnamon
½ tsp. soda
½ cup butter or margarine
   (room temperature)

½ cup packed brown sugar
½ cup granulated sugar
½ cup creamy-style peanut
   butter
1 egg
1 tsp. vanilla

Cream butter, peanut butter, sugars, and egg thoroughly. Sift flour. Blend all dry ingredients; stir in. Roll teaspoonfuls of dough into balls; place on greased baking sheets. Flatten and crisscross with floured fork. Bake in moderate oven (350 degrees) about 10 minutes or until done. Cool.

Yield: about 3 dozen cookies

"Once I made my favorite meal," ten-year-old Lori told us: "Vegetable soup, green salad, French bread, and chocolate cake. My two older brothers (Mike, age thirteen, and David, sixteen) both grabbed their throats like they were poisoned when they tasted my soup. They always like to tease me when I cook something but they always eat it and come back for more."

Lori has been cooking for two years. She won a first-premium blue ribbon at the El Dorado County Fair for her Peanut Butter Cookies. Her blue ribbon entitled her to enter the California State Fair, where she got a blue first-award ribbon. She says she is learning to cook by joining 4-H, "and my mother is teaching me."

MARY PROUTY
BRYANT, SOUTH DAKOTA

FIRST PLACE, COOKIES
ARCHWAY COOKIE AWARD
SOUTH DAKOTA STATE FAIR

CHOCOLATE PINWHEELS

Sift together 1¾ cups sifted all-purpose flour, ½ teaspoon baking powder, ¼ teaspoon salt.

Cream ½ cup butter or margarine gradually. Add ½ cup sugar, creaming well.

Blend in 1 unbeaten egg and 1 teaspoon vanilla. Add the dry ingredients gradually, mix thoroughly.

Place half of dough on waxed paper, blend 1 square melted unsweetened chocolate into remaining dough. Chill dough for easier handling, about 1 hour.

Roll out light dough on floured waxed paper to a 15x7-inch rectangle. Repeat with chocolate dough. Place chocolate on top of light dough. Roll up as for jelly roll, starting with 15-inch side. Wrap in waxed paper. Chill at least 2 hours. Cut into ½-inch slices, place on ungreased baking sheet.

Bake in moderate oven (375 degrees) for 7 to 10 minutes or till lightly browned.

Yield: about 4 dozen

See also Mary's Apricot Bread (page 198).

SHARON REYNOLDS
MINOT, NORTH DAKOTA

FIRST PLACE, COOKIES
NORTH DAKOTA STATE FAIR

CANDY COOKIES

Cream ¾ cup butter and ¾ cup powdered sugar with electric beater. Add 1 teaspoon vanilla, 2 tablespoons evaporated milk, and ¼ teaspoon salt to cream mixture. Blend in 2 cups flour. Chill this mixture for ½ hour. Roll out half the dough at a time on a floured 12x8-inch surface. Trim the sides and cut into rectangles or squares. Place on ungreased cookie sheet. Bake at 325 degrees for 12–16 minutes.

Yield: 3–4 dozen cookies

Cool and spread with 1 teaspoon Caramel Filling on each and top with ½ teaspoon Chocolate Icing.

CARAMEL FILLING

Combine in a double boiler ½ lb. light caramels and ¼ cup evaporated milk. Heat till caramels melt, stirring occasionally. Remove from heat and stir in ¼ cup butter, 1 cup powdered sugar, and 1 cup chopped pecans.

CHOCOLATE ICING

Melt 1 6-ounce package (1 cup) semisweet chocolate chips with ⅓ cup evaporated milk over low heat. Stir in 2 tablespoons butter, ½ cup powdered sugar, and 1 teaspoon vanilla.

"When I was eight I made my first milk gravy and fed it to the baby. The gravy was so thick the baby's mouth was glued shut. My dad had to pry it open." Sharon was just learning to cook then, she says. "I learned to cook for hired men; we lived on a farm and my mother worked in the fields, so someone had to cook. I was delegated."

Now, she says, "We live in a trailer so my kitchen is quite small, although we do have good cupboard space. My refrigerator and stove are close to my sink and since I'm in the kitchen most of the time I've made it a bright, cheery place."

MRS. RICHARD RITTER
EPHRATA, PENNSYLVANIA

WHOOPIE PIES

CREAM TOGETHER:

  1 cup solid shortening
  2 cups granulated sugar
  2 eggs

MIX IN:

  1 cup milk
  2 tsp. vanilla

ADD TO MIXTURE:

  4¼ cups flour
    1 cup cocoa
    1 tsp. salt

Add and stir until mixed 1 cup hot water with 2 teaspoons baking powder. Drop by spoon on ungreased cookie pan. Bake at 375–400 degrees for 6–8 minutes.

ICING

2 egg whites, beaten
4 T. flour
2 T. vanilla

3 cups 10X sugar
2 cups solid shortening

Mix and spread between 2 halves of cookies.

Mrs. Ritter says, "I first entered Whoopie Pies in 1970 and have won every year since then—five firsts, four seconds, and one third." She adds, "First time I made these cookies I greased the cookie pan and they all slid together into one large cookie."
  She cooks for her husband and two sons, and has "been cooking seriously for 14 years."

JOSEPHINE SMITH
WICHITA, KANSAS

ARCHWAY COOKIE AWARD
KANSAS STATE FAIR

TROPICAL FRUIT COOKIES

1 cup margarine	4 cups all-purpose flour
1 cup granulated sugar	¼ tsp. salt
1 cup brown sugar	½ tsp. baking soda
3 eggs (well beaten)	1 tsp. vanilla

Cream shortening, add sugar gradually, creaming well. Add eggs and mix thoroughly. Sift together dry ingredients and add to first mixture. Blend thoroughly.

Divide dough into 2 parts and chill for easier handling. Divide each ball into halves. Roll each section on floured waxed paper and spread with Tropical Filling. Roll up jelly roll fashion. Place in freezer until it will slice nicely. Slice ¼-inch thick.

Bake at 350 degrees for 12 minutes.

TROPICAL FILLING

1 lb. chopped dates	½ cup nuts, chopped fine
¼ cup crushed pineapple	1 cup water
1 cup granulated sugar	

Combine all the ingredients and cook over low heat, stirring, until thick. Cool.

Mrs. Smith is the sister of another prizewinner in our book, Doris Barb (see Bran Bread page 164, and Butterscotch Oatmeal Chips page 307). "I grew up on a farm. When I was a girl, we always had good staples to use in cooking. My mother taught me to cook as I helped her; she always had several to cook for besides our family. My father always had hired help, so that took a lot of preparation of foods."

Mrs. Smith was married 54 years before her husband passed away. "I got to make our fiftieth-anniversary cake," she says proudly.

She has two sons, six grandchildren, and two great-grandchildren. "I started taking entries to the baked foods department at the Kansas State Fair in 1953 and have not missed a year since. In 1953 I took only a few entries, and each year I have taken a few more." Mrs. Smith has won the Governor's Cookie Jar Award twice and the Archway Cookie Award twice. She has more than 600 ribbons, 200 blue, and 19 sweepstakes.

She says, "Even though I am seventy-seven years old I still will enjoy taking my baked foods to the state fair."

See her Holiday Bread (page 150).

CAROL SPENCE
SINKS GROVE, WEST VIRGINIA

FIRST PRIZE
GOVERNOR'S COOKIE JAR
WEST VIRGINIA STATE FAIR

SANTA'S WHISKERS

1 cup butter or margarine,
   softened
1 cup sugar
2 T. milk
1 tsp. vanilla

2½ cups all-purpose flour
¾ cup maraschino cherries,
   chopped fine
½ cup pecans, chopped fine
¾ cup flaked coconut

Cream together butter and sugar, blend in milk and vanilla. Stir in flour, maraschino cherries, and pecans. Form dough into 2 8-inch rolls. Roll in flaked coconut to coat outside. Wrap in waxed paper and chill thoroughly. Cut in ¼-inch slices. Bake on ungreased cookie sheet at 375 degrees about 12 minutes.

 "My mother left me alone as a very young girl in the kitchen to bake a spice cake. I used whole allspice instead of ground. The whole family had a laugh over the little brown balls in the cake." A first-prize winner many times, Carol doesn't make those mistakes anymore. Her recipes have been chosen for the First Lady's Candy Box and the Governor's Cookie Jar.

Cooking in what she calls "my topsy-turvy kitchen," Carol regularly cooks for four.

MARIE SNOW
ASOTIN, WASHINGTON

BUTTERMILK BROWNIES

BATTER

1 cup margarine	1 tsp. soda
⅓ cup cocoa	½ tsp. salt
1 cup water	2 eggs, slightly beaten
2 cups flour	½ cup buttermilk
2 cups sugar	1½ tsp. vanilla

Bring to boil margarine, cocoa, and water. Combine dry ingredients and add eggs, buttermilk, and vanilla. Blend in cocoa mixture. Bake in greased 11x15-inch pan at 375 degrees for 20 minutes. Frost while hot.

FROSTING

¼ cup margarine	2½ cups sifted powdered sugar
3 T. cocoa	1 tsp. vanilla
3 T. buttermilk	1 cup chopped walnuts

Bring margarine, cocoa, and buttermilk to a boil. Stir in sugar and vanilla and fold in nuts.

See her Almond Chicken (page 73).

TAYA SPRATLING
KEYES, CALIFORNIA

MOLASSES COOKIES

¾ cup shortening
1 cup sugar
¼ cup molasses
2 tsp. baking soda
½ tsp. cloves

½ tsp. salt
1 egg
2 cups sifted all-purpose flour
1 tsp. cinnamon
½ tsp. ginger

Cream together shortening and sugar. Add molasses and egg, beat well. Sift together flour, soda, cinnamon, cloves, ginger, and salt. Add to first mixture. Mix well; chill about 1 hour. Place on cookie sheet by teaspoonfuls about 3 inches apart. Bake at 375 degrees for 8 to 10 minutes.

Yield: 3 dozen cookies

Thirteen-year-old Taya Spratling told us, "I'm single and I cook for fun."

PEGGY STUART
LEWISBURG, WEST VIRGINIA

FIRST PRIZE
WEST VIRGINIA STATE FAIR

APPLE STRIPS

Sift together 2½ cups flour, ½ teaspoon salt, and ¼ cup sugar into mixing bowl.

Cut in ¼ cup butter or margarine and ½ teaspoon grated lemon rind until particles are size of small peas.

Sprinkle 5–6 tablespoons cream (sweet or sour) over mixture, tossing lightly with fork until dough is moist enough to hold together. Divide dough in half. Form into 2 balls.

Roll out half of dough on waxed paper to 15x10-inch rectangle. Turn over onto ungreased jelly roll pan or baking sheet. Peel off paper.

Bake in moderate oven (350 degrees) 15 minutes.

FILLING

Pare and cut 4 cups apples (4 medium) into ¼-inch cubes. Add ⅓ cup of raisins, ¼ cup sugar, 1 tablespoon flour, ¼ teaspoon cinnamon, and 3 tablespoons lemon juice. Spread over baked crust.

Roll out remaining dough into 15x10-inch rectangle on waxed paper. Turn over on apple filling. Brush with slightly beaten egg and sprinkle with sugar.

Bake in moderately hot oven (400 degrees) 25–30 minutes until golden brown. Cool slightly and cut into desired shapes.

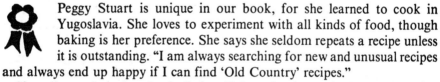 Peggy Stuart is unique in our book, for she learned to cook in Yugoslavia. She loves to experiment with all kinds of food, though baking is her preference. She says she seldom repeats a recipe unless it is outstanding. "I am always searching for new and unusual recipes and always end up happy if I can find 'Old Country' recipes."

She tells us about her Apple Strips: "My recipe is an old European recipe which with good tart apples makes a very different kind of dough. Cut in the shape of diamonds it makes quite a large amount of dessert, and is certainly inexpensive for our time."

BUTTERSCOTCH BARS

¼ cup butter
1 cup light brown sugar
(packed)
1 egg
¾ cup all-purpose flour

1 tsp. baking powder
½ tsp. salt
½ tsp. vanilla
½ cup walnuts, coarsely
chopped

Heat oven to 350 degrees. Melt butter over low heat. Remove from heat; stir in sugar until blended; cool. Stir in egg. Stir flour, baking powder, and salt together; blend in. Mix in vanilla and walnuts. Spread in well-greased 8x8-inch square pan. Bake 25 minutes. Do not overbake! Cut in bars while still warm.

Robin tells about herself better than we can.

"I am seventeen years old and a senior at Moravia High School. I started exhibiting at the Iowa State Fair at the age of fourteen, in the Beginners' Division. The next year I was fifteen, so I had to go in the Adult Division. I was really nervous that year because I had to compete with people with a lot more experience, and also my grandmother. My mother told me not to expect any blue ribbons, but surprise! I got the Sweepstakes in Cookies, since I had the most blue ribbons in the Cookie Division. The next year I got Sweepstakes in Cookies and also won a cookbook. This year I got Sweepstakes in Cookies, won a cookbook, and got runner-up in Archway, which is the best cookie of the fair for that year.

"I had never exhibited at any other fair before. My mother and grandmother are State Fair Champions in baking. So it was a great honor for me to win over my grandmother three years straight in the Cookie Division."

Robin adds, "These bars won me a blue ribbon at the 1978 Iowa State Fair. They were also my runner-up in Archway."

A PERFECT BAR HINT

Mix bar cookie dough as recipe directs. With spatula, spread dough evenly in greased square or oblong pan. Bake minimum time in preheated oven.

To test for doneness: bake fudgy-type bars until top has a dull crust. Bake cakelike bars until toothpick stuck in center comes out clean.

Perfect bar cookies have: uniform shape; rich, moist eating quality; thin delicate crust; appealing flavor.

DONNA TATOM
CLACKAMAS, OREGON

JOHNNY APPLESEED UPS

2 cups chopped apples	½ tsp. salt
1 cup sugar	1 tsp. soda
1 egg	1 tsp. cinnamon
¼ cup cooking oil	½ cup raisins
1 tsp. vanilla	3 T. 7-Up
1 cup flour	¼ cup oats

Mix together in approximate order given. Spread in 9x13-inch cake pan or cookie sheet. Preheat oven to 350 degrees. Before putting cookies in oven, spread oats over cookie mix. Bake for 20 minutes. When cookies are cool, sprinkle with powdered sugar. Cut into squares.

 "One day while I was making jam the door was left open. When I turned around I was being watched by our large goat, the lamb, and a very confused chicken. I must say they liked the overcooked jam (it wasn't a blue-ribbon winner)." What a trio of judges!

Donna says her kitchen is the "hub of our home. Our three boys and an assorted number of baby animals are fed and loved here."

Donna is a descendent of the famous apple-growing pioneer. In his honor she created Johnny Appleseed Ups.

HONEY NEWTONS

FILLING

½ lb. dried figs, chopped fine
1 cup plus 3 T. water

½ cup honey
2 tsp. lemon juice

Combine ingredients and simmer gently, stirring. Cook until consistency of marmalade, approximately 15 minutes. Set aside to cool.

COOKIE DOUGH

1 cup butter
2 cups grated Cheddar cheese
   (½ lb.)
2 cups sifted all-purpose flour

Cream butter, add cheese (room temperature), and cream until well blended. Stir in flour, mix well, and chill.

Roll dough ⅛-inch thick on lightly floured board. Cut in 2-inch circles. Put one-half of the circles 1 inch apart on lightly greased baking sheet. Place 1 teaspoon filling in center of each cookie. Top each with another circle of dough. Press edges with fork to seal. Prick cookie tops in several places. Bake at 350 degrees for 15 minutes or until lightly browned. Remove to racks to cool.

Yield: 3½ dozen cookies

Try Marge's Antipasto (page 442).

VIRGINIA WIEDENFELD
RICHLAND CENTER, WISCONSIN

CHOCOLATE CHIP OATMEAL COOKIES

1½ cups flour	2 eggs, unbeaten
1 tsp. soda	1 tsp. hot water
1 tsp. salt	6 oz. chocolate chips
1 cup shortening	2 cups oatmeal
¾ cup white sugar	1 tsp. vanilla
¾ cup brown sugar	

Measure flour, add soda and salt. Cream shortening until fluffy. Add sugars, cream well. Beat in eggs, add hot water, add dry ingredients. Add chocolate chips and oatmeal. Mix well. Add vanilla. Roll into balls and place on greased cookie sheet. Smash somewhat with a fork. Bake at 350 degrees for 10 minutes.

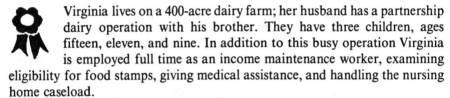 Virginia lives on a 400-acre dairy farm; her husband has a partnership dairy operation with his brother. They have three children, ages fifteen, eleven, and nine. In addition to this busy operation Virginia is employed full time as an income maintenance worker, examining eligibility for food stamps, giving medical assistance, and handling the nursing home caseload.

Besides various cooking and canning awards, she has shown her garden vegetables, and won many prizes for her efforts.

GENEVIEVE WOMBACHER
IOWA CITY, IOWA

GRAND PRIZE
DES MOINES STATE FAIR

KOLACHES

2 cups lukewarm milk
½ cup sugar
1 T. salt
½ cup melted oleo or butter
3 envelopes dry yeast

½ cup lukewarm water
3 egg yolks
1 whole egg
5–6 cups flour

In small mixing bowl dissolve yeast and 1 tablespoon sugar in water and set aside to work. Put lukewarm milk in large mixing bowl (at least a gallon in size) and add sugar, salt, beaten eggs, and shortening. Mix well, then beat in 3 cups flour and mix well; add yeast mixture and mix well again and then add enough flour to make a soft dough. When dough is mixed well, grease the top and cover, put in a warm place, and let rise until doubled in bulk. When dough is risen make balls the size of small walnuts and put 12 on greased cookie sheet and let rise for about 10 minutes, then push centers down and out and fill with filling you desire. Let rise again for about 10 minutes, then bake in 400-degree oven until brown, 7 or 8 minutes. Take from oven and grease with melted oleo and let cool on rack.

The kinds of filling I use include prune, apricot, peach, pineapple, cherry, poppy seeds, ground nuts, and applesauce.

Yield: 5 dozen

"I learned to cook from my mother and have cooked and baked ever since I can remember," Genevieve says. With seven children raised and twenty-four grandchildren to enjoy her cooking, Genevieve now manages a hot-lunch program and cooks for 400 every day."

CANDY WYNNE
NORMAN, OKLAHOMA

FUDGE BROWNIES

½ cup butter or margarine
1 cup sugar
1 tsp. vanilla
2 eggs
1 1-oz. sq. unsweetened
   chocolate, melted

3 T. powdered cocoa
½ cup sifted all-purpose flour
½ cup chopped pecans
3 Hershey Bars (plain)

Blend all ingredients except candy bars. Pour into greased 8x8x2-inch pan. Bake at 325 degrees for 30–35 minutes. When brownies are done take out of oven, lay candy bars on top, and wait a minute before spreading as a frosting. Cut, decorate each piece with pecans.

"I started cooking at home when I was nine years old," Candy says, "but after having four children I progressed very rapidly." She cooks for six on a daily basis.

A hint that you might like to try: "Pan coating—one cup Crisco and ½ cup flour mixed together and put in small bowl. Keep in refrigerator. This makes a frypan work like teflon. Use it for cakes, muffins, etc."

Candy told us, "My first pan of gravy stuck a coupon from the flour sack to my cabinet that an S.O.S. pad couldn't remove! We ate it though. My gravy has stuck us together for years!"

CHAPTER TWELVE

CANDY

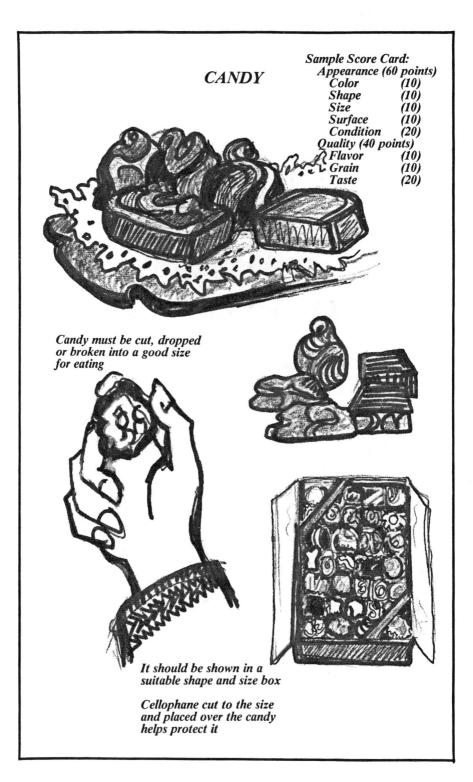

CANDY

Sample Score Card:
Appearance (60 points)
Color   (10)
Shape   (10)
Size   (10)
Surface   (10)
Condition (20)
Quality (40 points)
Flavor   (10)
Grain   (10)
Taste   (20)

Candy must be cut, dropped or broken into a good size for eating

It should be shown in a suitable shape and size box

Cellophane cut to the size and placed over the candy helps protect it

COLEEN ADDY
ROSWELL, NEW MEXICO

GARLIC PECANS

1 lb. shelled pecan halves	1½ tsp. seasoned salt
¼ cup butter or margarine	½ tsp. onion powder
2 tsp. garlic salt	½ tsp. celery salt

Heat electric skillet to 250 degrees. Melt butter or margarine. Add nuts and seasonings. Toast 30 to 40 minutes, stirring often.

Spread on paper towels to drain and cool. Store in a covered container. Coleen says they taste better if refrigerated and eaten while cold.

HARD CANDY

½ cup water	2 cups sugar
½ cup white corn syrup	Pinch salt

Bring water and syrup to a rolling boil. Remove from heat, add sugar and salt, stir until dissolved.

Bring mixture to a rolling boil, cover with a tight lid, boil for 3 or 4 minutes to remove sugar crystals from sides of pan. Boil to a hard-crack stage (310 degrees sea level) *without stirring* (watch closely so it doesn't scorch).

Add food coloring and oils for flavoring. Let boil up a minute after adding flavoring (it will sugar if stirred).

Pour into buttered pans and cut before it gets cold.

NOTE: Get oil flavorings at the drugstore. Cinnamon, peppermint, cloves, lemon, orange, and anise are good. Add oils by drops, as they are quite strong.

Coleen has been a prizewinner for her candies over the years. However, she gave up entering the fairs, substituting candy-making demonstrations for all the Extension Clubs in Chaves County.

About this recipe she says, "Try my original recipe for Garlic Pecans. It is different, unusual; and I think you'll enjoy and like—most everyone does."

Some more winners from Coleen: Spring Time Dip (page 3), Chicken Tortilla Pie (page 57), Mexican Corn (page 79), Garlic Pecans (page 355), and Hard Candy (page 355).

SOPHIE BURDEN
WICKENBURG, ARIZONA

CHRISTMAS RUM SQUARES

1 cup flour
2 tsp. baking powder
¼ tsp. baking soda
½ tsp. salt
½ cup sugar
¾ cup milk
1 egg, beaten
1 T. grated orange rind

1 T. melted shortening or
  salad oil
½ cup unsifted whole wheat
  flour
2 sq. semisweet chocolate,
  melted
1 cup diced dried fruits
Rum

Heat oven to 375 degrees. Sift first 5 ingredients. Combine milk and next 3 ingredients; add melted chocolate. Stir in the flour mixture, then combine the whole wheat flour and dried fruits. Mix well.

Pour into well-greased 9x5x3-inch loaf pan. Bake for 50 minutes or until done.

Cool slightly and cut in small squares. Pour rum over the whole thing—just keep pouring until it seems pretty well soaked up but not soggy. Then quickly put in aluminum foil and freeze until ready to use.

NOTE: I added a teaspoonful of vanilla and wrapped them in little separate balls. People sure raved!

A few more great dishes by Sophie Burden: Dad Fletcher's Tamale Pie (page 23), Real Spanish Rice (page 81), Dana's Charros Beans (page 81), Strawberry-Rhubarb Salad (page 101), Tomato Aspic (page 101), Remuda Beer Biscuits (page 169), and Christmas Rum Squares (page 356).

LORI BURROW
LOWREY CITY, MISSOURI

FIRST PRIZE, FUDGE
MISSOURI STATE FAIR

FUDGE

3 cups sugar
¾ cup margarine
⅔ cup evaporated milk
1 12-oz. pkg. semisweet
    chocolate bits

1 7-oz. jar Kraft Marshmallow
    Creme
1 cup chopped nuts
1 tsp. vanilla

Combine sugar, margarine, and milk in heavy 2½-quart saucepan. Bring to a full boil, stirring constantly. Continue boiling 5 minutes over medium heat, stirring constantly to prevent scorching. Remove from heat, stir in chocolate pieces until melted. Add Marshmallow Creme, nuts, and vanilla. Beat until well blended. Pour into greased 9x13-inch pan. Cool at room temperature. Cut into squares.

Yield: approximately 3 pounds

Lori has been a 4-H member for eight years, and has taken cooking every year. Now, she says, "I enjoy just doing it."

REESA BYRD
ENTERPRISE, ALABAMA

GRAND PRIZE
NATIONAL PEANUT FESTIVAL
DOTHAN, ALABAMA

PEANUT BUTTER CANDY

2 sticks oleo	1 lb. confectioners sugar
1½ cups plain or crunchy peanut butter	1 14-oz. pkg. caramels
1½ cups graham cracker crumbs	½ stick oleo
	Salted peanuts

Melt 2 sticks oleo with 1½ cups plain or crunchy peanut butter and stir until well blended.

Pour this mixture into large bowl. Add graham cracker crumbs and stir well. Add confectioners sugar. Blend well and knead with hands until you can handle well. (If peanut butter is dry leave a little confectioners sugar in bottom of box—don't use it all). Spread mixture onto a large cookie sheet and roll flat with rolling pin or make into three or four logs—or you can make into 100 1-inch balls (easiest way is on cookie sheet).

Melt caramels in saucepan with oleo and stir constantly until well blended. (This can be done in top of double boiler or in oven.)

Pour immediately onto the cookie sheet and spread gently—top with crushed salted peanuts. Cut into squares immediately.

NOTE: If making the logs, put caramel mixture around the logs and roll in peanuts. If doing the balls, double quantity of caramels; be sure and roll immediately into the peanuts while caramel topping is still warm. May be necessary to shape caramel on each individual ball and then roll in peanuts immediately.

Try Reesa's "Hot Beef Dip" (page 4).

CHOCOLATE-CARAMEL SQUARES

4 oz. butter
2 oz. sugar
5 oz. self-rising flour

Cream butter and sugar; add flour and mix. Put into a 7x10¾x2-inch baking tin. Bake till light brown—20 minutes at 325 degrees.

FILLING

3 oz. butter	5 oz. condensed milk
3 oz. sugar	¼-½ lb. milk chocolate, melted
2 T. corn syrup	

Bring all but milk chocolate to a boil over low heat. Boil for 4 minutes, stirring all the time. Pour the taffy on top of the baked pastry base. Cool slightly. Melt chocolate and spread over top of taffy. When chocolate is almost set score squares to size desired.

"I started to cook after I was married. I had a *Betty Crocker Cookbook* and one or two of my mother's recipes. I now have shelves of cookbooks and recipes of all kinds, you could say I collect recipes. I've been cooking and baking for 26 years now.

"I can't think of any bad mistakes, but there have been a couple amusing things. Several years ago a little friend who was living with us came in from school this one day and asked what I was making. I told her I was making spaghetti sauce and that we were having spaghetti for supper. She stood and looked at me for a minute and then replied, 'But that's not spaghetti, spaghetti comes in a can!'

"Last year a little friend of ours was spending a few days with us. She loves gingerbread men, so we made gingerbread, she ate several. We were sitting in the family room when she said, 'I sure do love this gingerbread but it sure gives me the runs,' as she jumped up from her chair and ran to the bathroom. We all sat and had a good laugh. I now make a batch of gingerbread dough and keep it frozen in the freezer, and when she comes over for a stay we take out just enough dough to make about six gingerbread men and she takes some of them home for Mommy."

See Marla's Buttermilk Coconut Cake (page 213).

ELIZABETH COONEY
BOWIE, MARYLAND

FIVE-MINUTE (NEVER-FAIL) FUDGE

⅔ cup evaporated milk
1⅔ cups sugar
½ tsp. salt
1½ cups diced marshmallows

1½ cups semisweet chocolate chips
1 tsp. vanilla
½ cup chopped nuts

Heat milk, sugar, and salt to boiling, then cook 5 minutes, stirring constantly. Remove from heat. Add remaining ingredients and stir until marshmallows melt. Pour into buttered 9-inch pan.

"The secret of good pie crust," Elizabeth says, "is always add a little more shortening than the recipe calls for. Do not handle any more than you have to because that makes it tough."

Elizabeth has won prizes for her pies, brownies, and fruit as well as her fudge.

MARY M. COOPER
FLEMINGSBURG, KENTUCKY

FIRST PLACE, CANDY
KENTUCKY STATE FAIR

YANKEE NOODLES

1 12-oz. pkg. butterscotch
    morsels

1 5-oz. can chow mein noodles

Melt butterscotch morsels over low heat. Add noodles and mix well.
Using a teaspoon, drop on slightly greased wax paper. Cool in refrigerator.

Yield: 24–30 servings

MARY'S PEANUT BRITTLE

1 cup white sugar
½ cup light corn syrup
1¼ cups salted peanuts

1 tsp. vanilla
⅛ tsp. butter

Mix sugar, corn syrup, and peanuts in a 2-quart casserole. Cook in microwave
at Time Cook, 4 minutes, on High. Add vanilla and butter. Cook in microwave
at Time Cook, 1 minute and 5 seconds on High.
    Add 1 teaspoon soda and mix well. Spread out on greased cookie sheet and
let cool.

Yield: about 1 pound

NOTE: I use regular salted nuts, not the red-skinned peanuts. This does not
require as much butter as most recipes. Therefore it is not as hard and sticky as
some candy.

Mary Cooper learned to cook as a little girl, "by helping my grandmother, and my mother showed me her ways and secrets."
    Mary has a large, convenient kitchen. She prizes her microwave for
"saving time and energy."

DATE BALLS

Melt ¼ cup butter (oleo) in saucepan or double boiler.

ADD

> 1 lb. cut-up dates
> 1 cup sugar
> 1 beaten egg

Mix well together and cook over low heat until dates are quite smooth, at least 15 minutes. Let cool.

STIR IN

> ½ cup chopped nuts   Pinch salt
> 2 cups Rice Krispies   1 tsp. vanilla

Shape into balls. Roll in shredded coconut or granulated sugar (I prefer sugar). These are better set overnight, as flavor is better.

Try Beatrice Dyer's Tuna Casserole (page 31), too.

ELENA ECKLEY
SWANTON, OHIO

FIRST PRIZE, DIVINITY
FIRST PRIZE, CANDY
OHIO STATE FAIR

COCONUT FONDANT

2½ cups sugar	¼ tsp. cream of tartar
2 T. butter	1 T. corn syrup
½ cup milk	1 cup baking refined coconut
½ cup whipping cream	2 T. coconut extract

Combine sugar, butter, milk, whipping cream, and cream of tartar in a heavy, large pan. Stir until sugar is dissolved. Place on high heat. Bring to a boil, then gently lower candy thermometer into boiling syrup. Lower heat slightly. Cook without stirring, wiping crystals from sides of pan with a wet basting brush, until candy reaches 236 degrees. Pour on cold slab. When heat is no longer coming from the mass of candy, test it with your finger· if the dent left by your finger fills in very slowly it is lukewarm and ready to work. Put the extract on the mass and sprinkle the coconut on it. Work the mass with the spatula until it turns from transparent to opaque and the mass forms a ball. Knead with your hands until smooth and creamy. This fondant is best if left tightly wrapped with plastic wrap for a week or so before chocolate dipping.

Melt chocolate in the top of a double boiler. Form fondant in little balls for hand dipping. Or chocolate-coat plastic molds—put filling in, then close candy with additional chocolate. Release finished piece from mold when chocolate is set.

This seems like a time-consuming project but the end product is far superior to any commercial product. I have made many other flavors using the basic fondant recipe and procedure and I have won many prizes.

DIVINITY

3 fresh egg whites	3 T. corn syrup
2 cups sugar	1 cup chopped walnuts
½ cup water	½ tsp. vanilla

Beat the egg whites until stiff and set them aside. Put sugar, water, and syrup into a pot on the stove at medium heat and stir. Wash the sugar crystals down from the sides of the pot with a damp basting brush. Cook to 236 degrees. Then take ⅓ cup of this syrup and add it slowly to the egg whites, beating continuously at medium speed. Cook the remaining syrup to 264 degrees. Add this to the egg whites and the 236-degree syrup, still beating continuously at medium speed. Keep beating 12–15 minutes longer, until the batch looks dull. Remove beater; add the chopped walnuts and vanilla. Spoon the batch out in teaspoon-sized pieces onto a baking sheet with waxed paper. When the pieces are set (in a few hours) store in a Tupperware container. This will keep them fresh and tender for weeks.

For best results the beating speed should never exceed medium. Divinity is tricky, sticky candy to make in the warm, humid summers in Ohio. This recipe works well, in spite of the humidity.

Elena Eckley is an educational media specialist in a large rural high school. She is 26 years old, has been married three years, and has no children. She writes: "I learned to bake by trial and error. However, my family background was conducive to good baking: my grandparents and my father owned a bakery for many years in the 1940s and early fifties but sold it when I was three. My mother and father always baked at home and they are my best critics. My kitchen is 13x13 feet square and the stove and oven that have brought me at least 50 prizes in my three years of entering fairs is a 28-year-old you-clean oven. No fancy microwave or anything like that. Since I work ten months of the year I have the summer, or part of it, to enter fairs.

"I never freeze anything to be entered, one thing my father impressed upon me was the change of texture that accompanies the freezing and thawing process, and he's right. I begin by making candy fondant fillings several weeks before the fairs. These get chocolate dipped the week before tasting. Caramel turtles, peanut butter cups, and other candy is also started two weeks before competition. The Divinity is made a few days before tasting and stored in a Tupperware container in the cool cellar. This summer I made three batches of Divinity before I felt it was the best. Actually I was ready to give up after the second batch but my husband said, 'Oh, try just one more batch, you're a perfectionist,' and wouldn't you know the third time was the charm.

"The baking routine begins the day before the fair. I call it my Baking Marathon. I list all the items to be made by length of process and temperature of oven. Breads are started first since other things can be made and baked while the breads are rising. My cookies have been baked last the past few years because they are easy and I am usually quite tired after 12-plus hours of baking. (They also use the hottest temperature oven.) My preparation for the Ohio State Fair and the local Fulton County Fair also may seem crazy to some but it is a hobby to me and I will probably be entering both for many years."

MARTHA ESTRADA
BETHANY, OKLAHOMA

SECOND PRIZE, TOFFEE
OKLAHOMA STATE FAIR

TOFFEE

2 cups oleo
2 cups sugar
1 cup pecans, chopped

6 1⅜-oz. Hershey Bars
1 T. water
1 T. corn syrup

Melt oleo. Blend in sugar, syrup, and water. Cook over medium heat, stirring constantly, till hard crack stage (295–300 degrees). Use candy thermometer. Quickly stir in nuts. Pour into buttered 9x13-inch pan or large cookie sheet. While still hot, lay Hershey Bars on top. When cooled, break into pieces.

Try Martha's Italian Creamcake (page 220).

PEANUT PATTIES

2½ cups sugar
⅔ cups white corn syrup
1 cup evaporated milk

3 cups raw peanuts
1 tsp. vanilla
1 tsp. butter

Mix sugar, syrup, milk, and peanuts together in a 2-quart saucepan. Cook over low heat for 1 hour, stirring occasionally. Remove from heat and add butter and vanilla and beat with a spoon until creamy. Spoon onto waxed paper to form patties. Add red cake coloring if desired while beating.

"I guess we've all burned our dishes at one time or another," William said cryptically when we asked about his worst mistakes cooking.

He learned to cook "when I was a young boy in the eighth grade. I was living by myself." He advises other cooks, "Try new recipes, you might find one that's a winner."

HAZEL GODFREY

CRESCENT, OKLAHOMA

FIRST PRIZE

OKLAHOMA STATE FAIR

MOST WONDERFUL TOFFEE

1 cup butter or good grade oleo
1 cup sugar
3 T. water

½ cup chopped nuts
1 6-oz. pkg. chocolate chips

Cook together butter, sugar, and water in heavy saucepan, until mixture turns caramel color—300 degrees. Remove from heat and stir in half the nuts. Pour into buttered 13x9x2-inch baking dish. Sprinkle with half the chocolate chips, let stand for a few minutes until chips melt. Spread over surface of toffee. Cover with waxed paper. Turn dish over onto surface and spread remaining chocolate chips, letting melt, and then spread. Sprinkle remaining nuts on top. When cool, break into pieces and store in airtight containers.

Try Hazel's Doughnuts (page 130), Orange Raisin Pie (page 281), and Pineapple Pie (page 281).

JOYCE HAIGH
CHARLOTTE, MICHIGAN

FIRST PLACE, BEATEN CANDY
MICHIGAN STATE FAIR

HAND-BEATEN MICHIGAN MAPLE CANDY

Place large, very heavy saucepan on burner and pour in 1 quart very best grade Michigan Maple Syrup. Bring to boil and cook to 240 degrees. Watch very closely. While syrup is cooking, butter 4 metal pie pans generously. When syrup has reached 240 degrees, pour carefully into pans. Let cool till you can make a slight dent and the syrup will not stick to finger. Place a pan on wet dishcloth, and stir with a flat wooden paddle, being sure to keep in middle of pan. Keep away from sides and work in way your grandmother worked her butter. The trick is to know when to stop stirring; just hesitate and see if patty will hold its shape and not run. If it holds you've succeeded in making a great candy. You should have a large, patty-shaped candy. Let stand 20 minutes, invert pan, press, and candy will come loose. Mark on back with sharp knife and break into pieces. (We like black walnuts added just when we've almost finished stirring.) If you don't come out OK, use as brown sugar substitute.

"When I was about ten years old we went fishing back at our river and on the way to the house my mother told me to run ahead and build the kitchen fire so we could hurry supper. I did and I put in *too many* pine knots and the stove and chimney were all red hot—nearly burned the house down."

Obviously, Joyce learned to cook "at home—when barely tall enough to reach table and old wood range—from my mother." She told us her kitchen now is "modern, clean enough to be healthy, and lived in every day."

Joyce has been cooking about fifty years, and has "six fully grown children."

VERNEAL HAMILTON
RECTOR, ARKANSAS

FIRST PLACE, CANDY, COOKIES
ARKANSAS STATE FAIR

ARKANSAS MILLIONAIRE CANDY

1 8-oz. pkg. caramels
2 T. milk
2 cups pecan halves

1 12-oz. pkg. chocolate
 chips
¼–½ block paraffin

Melt caramels and milk in double boiler, stir in pecans. Drop by teaspoonful on waxed paper.

Melt chocolate chips with paraffin in double boiler. Dip caramel and pecan drops in mixture, set on waxed paper, and let cool.

A cook for 55 years, Verneal Hamilton has won many prizes with her bread, cakes, and cookies. She saves good recipes, she told us, and learned to cook as a small girl from her mother.

Verneal and her husband Lawrence live on 198 acres, three miles from Rector, Arkansas, where they raise Hereford beef cattle. They have two children and three grandchildren. Verneal says, "I have never worked for the public. I take care of home, garden, and yard." She is active in a number of organizations; and is so well known for her cooking skills that she acts as a judge for fairs in other counties.

Her recipe for Cheesecake is on page 230.

CREAM CHEESE MINTS

1 3-oz. pkg. cream cheese
1 lb. confectioners sugar
1 T. vanilla extract or bean

Let cream cheese come to room temperature. Mash well with a fork until creamy in texture. Work in confectioners sugar a little at a time (sifting is not required, but it will mix faster if you do). Mix well. If you are using vanilla extract add now and mix well.

All of this mixing does require quite a bit of kneading. If mixture is too dry, add a few drops of lukewarm water: if you goof and add too much water, just work in a bit more powdered sugar! Make little balls of the cream cheese mixture and roll them in granulated sugar, press in a rubber or plastic candy mold, unmold at once, and set on cake rack to dry. Keep in refrigerator or freeze. They taste much better at room temperature, so let them sit out a while before serving.

Yield: Varies according to size mold used, but you can count on at least 4 dozen unless your mold is the size of an English walnut!

NOTE: I used extract for the fair, but since then vanilla bean about 8 inches long. The aging takes more time—just check until your nose tells you the aroma is strong enough.

 Michele tells us, "My mother and my maternal grandmother taught me to cook, and taught me well! When I was three my mother introduced me to the fine art of mashing potatoes and I, in turn, introduced her to instant textured walls."

When we asked Michele how many she cooks for, she said, "As many as I can get to come and eat. As a rule, my husband and myself.

"My worst mistake? Gourmet vanilla scrambled eggs—went a little too heavy on the vanilla and blew brunch for four guests! My husband and I weren't married and I was really trying to impress him."

About her prizewinning Cream Cheese Mints Michele said, "The judges would shudder if they knew how simple."

MILLICENT GIBSON
GRACE, IDAHO

NUT ROLLS

3 cups sugar	⅛ tsp. salt
1 cup water	1 stick butter
1⅓ cups light corn syrup	1 tsp. vanilla
2 egg whites stiffly beaten	

Combine ¾ cup sugar, ⅔ cup corn syrup, and ¼ cup water. Put in a small saucepan and stir over medium heat until dissolved. Stop stirring. Boil to 238 degrees on thermometer. Pour syrup over beaten egg whites. (I use my small mix-master bowl.)

Beat constantly until nearly cool.

After the ingredients are well blended in mixer beat with spoon by hand. Butter large bowl of mixer and spoon into large bowl while you cook the second step.

Combine 2¼ cups sugar, ⅔ cup light corn syrup, ¾ cup water. Put on stove over medium heat and stir until dissolved. Cook to 258 degrees. Pour in slow stream into first batch, beating all the time until all syrup is used. Stir in stick of butter with wooden spoon. Add vanilla. Stir until well blended. Let stand in bowl, beating occasionally, until fairly stiff. Line a 9x9-inch pan with buttered waxed paper. Pour in nougat mixture and press down with fingers. Let stand several hours until set. Cut into 16 bars.

CARAMEL COATING

2 cups sugar	2 cups whipping cream
1 cup white syrup	2 lbs. shelled pecans or walnuts
¾ stick real butter	

Mix sugar, syrup, and a little of the cream. Place over low heat and stir to keep from burning. When boiling add butter. Add a little cream at a time, stirring after each addition until all cream is used. Cook to 242 degrees.

Remove from heat and let cool for 3 or 4 minutes. With 2 forks dip logs in caramel mixture, drain a second, then roll in pecans, walnuts, or cashew nuts.

Yield: 16 rolls or about 5 pounds of candy

NOTE: I put a small quantity of nuts in a 9-inch dipper to roll candy in. Add more nuts to pan as needed. I got Sweepstakes on this candy. Our altitude is about 5300 feet.

Millicent works in her convenient kitchen with lots of appliances; even so, she once sprinkled salt on cinnamon rolls instead of sugar.

Millicent and her husband, Lawrence, raise a large garden, and each year she puts up several hundred jars of jam, pickles, vegetables, and fruit. She has been cooking for 52 years, and she learned "in my home, trial and error and recipes from friends."

REFRIGERATOR CRISPS

1 cup shortening	½ tsp. salt
½ cup granulated sugar	½ tsp. soda
½ cup brown sugar	1 tsp. ground cinnamon
1 egg	¼ tsp. ground nutmeg
2 T. milk	¼ tsp. ground cloves
2¼ cups sifted all-purpose flour	½ cup walnuts, chopped fine

Cream together shortening and sugars; add egg and milk; beat well. Sift together dry ingredients; stir into creamed mixture. Add nuts. Shape into rolls 2½ inches in diameter. Wrap in waxed paper; chill well.

Slice about ¼-inch thick. Place 1 inch apart on lightly greased cookie sheet. Bake in moderate oven (375 degrees) 5–7 minutes or until delicately browned. Remove at once to rack.

Yield: 6 dozen

"I still consider my cooking talents to be forming, but I have had exposure to some good cooks while growing up. Some of the earliest holidays I remember were celebrated at my grandmother's house. My maternal grandmother came from Hungary at fourteen, married, and raised seven children. She cooked good basic food as well as excellent pastries and other delicacies. Many of my aunts and uncles were raised on a farm where my grandmother also canned foods to feed her large family through the winters.

"An old custom was to cook the dinner when a friend's child married and then when your child married, the favor was reciprocated. My grandmother did this on a regular basis. I even now have friends who comment when they know a wedding will be 'a good Hungarian wedding' that the food will be good. I remember hearing my mother and grandmother talking when I was a child about my mother's wedding. They made noodles for weeks ahead of time for soup. They rolled stuffed cabbages and really prepared for a feast. For my own wedding, my aunt, uncle, mother, and myself made a traditional Hungarian nut torte for my wedding cake. We did it a week ahead of time and froze it. My mother then thawed and decorated it a day before the wedding.

"By the time I was old enough to begin to really cook on my own, my grandmother had died, but through my mother and aunts, I've learned the confidence to try almost anything. My early cooking was watching them cook. When my mother went to work, I was a teenager and began preparing meals, first under instructions my mother would leave for me to do after school and as I became more confident, I would just try on my own.

"My mother had been entering things in the Michigan State Fair since I was little. I tried the junior divisions at nine. After I entered the 4-H Club, I also tried county fairs. I enjoy just trying to place. Many years I've spent the night before baking is due at state fair, up finishing, trying to make things just right.

"I think anyone who cooks has had their share of funny and bad occurrences. My husband still jokes at my early attempts to make chocolate pudding (it sat in the freezer for three days in my attempt to thicken it; it never did!). When I asked him to recall the worst thing that ever happened while cooking, he said, 'Tell them about setting the kitchen on fire when you melted wax for your jam.' We laugh about it now, but I was scared to death then. I had put the wax on to melt and he called me to come see something on T.V. I stood watching for what I thought was a minute, when this orange glow caught my eye from the side. I went back to the stove and flames were leaping up. The smoke alarm went off at that minute too, which set my daughter howling. I was yelling for my husband, who quickly came and picking the whole mess up with potholders, heaved it out the back door. He was fire chief at the time and all he could say was, 'Boy, am I glad we didn't have to call out a fire truck for this!'"

JOY S. JONES
SEYMOUR, TENNESSEE

FIRST PRIZE
TENNESSEE VALLEY AGRICULTURAL
AND INDUSTRIAL FAIR

DIVINITY

2 cups sugar
½ cup light corn syrup
½ cup hot water
¼ tsp. salt

2 egg whites
1 tsp. vanilla
½ cup chopped nuts

In a 2-quart saucepan, combine sugar, corn syrup, hot water, and salt. Cook and stir till sugar dissolves and mixture comes to a boil. Cook to hard-ball stage (250 degrees) without stirring. Wipe crystals from sides of pan with fork wrapped in paper towel or put lid on briefly and crystals will dissolve. Remove mixture from heat. Beat egg whites till stiff peaks form.

Slowly pour *hot* syrup over beaten whites, beating constantly with mixer at high speed (I beat the last few minutes by hand). Add vanilla and continue beating till mixture loses its gloss.

Add nuts. Drop by teaspoon onto waxed paper. I add bits of candied cherries or put a pecan half on top.

NOTE: It's best *not* to make divinity on a damp or rainy day.

CANDY   375

ENGLISH TOFFEE

1 cup oleo	1 cup slivered almonds
2 cups sugar	½ cup chopped pecans (salted)
⅓ cup water	2 T. light corn syrup
1 large bar milk chocolate	

Melt butter in heavy pan. Add sugar, water, syrup. Add almonds, cook to hard crack stage (290 degrees). Pour onto buttered cookie sheet. Melt chocolate bar in double boiler; spread on thoroughly cooled toffee. While chocolate is still unset, sprinkle warm roasted pecan meats on top. Let stand till chocolate is completely set; then break into bite-size pieces.

BLUE RIBBON CARAMELS

1 cup oleo or butter	Pinch of salt
1 lb. brown sugar	1 tsp. vanilla
1 cup light corn syrup	
1 14-oz. can sweetened condensed milk	

Melt butter in heavy pan. Add sugar, salt, stir thoroughly. Stir in syrup, mix well. Gradually add milk, stirring constantly. Cook. Stir over medium heat to firm ball stage (245 degrees). Takes 12–15 minutes. Remove from heat, stir in vanilla. Pour into a buttered 9x9- or 7x11-inch pan, cool. Cut into squares. Wrap each piece in waxed paper.

Yield: 2½ pounds

NOTE: For chocolate caramels add 1 square (1 ounce) baking chocolate alternately with the addition of the milk. (Chopped nut meats may also be added after cooking if desired.)

For many years Janet Koplinski made, wrapped, and boxed her favorite candies as presents for family friends. Now she is winning blue ribbons. Making candy at the Koplinski house is a fun time. Her two boys, Scott and Brian, "help me wrap the caramels and they like to put them in the boxes." Her husband likes to help too; in fact, Janet laughs, "He likes to put his fingers into the candies as they go in the boxes."

What's her favorite? After making so much, Janet confesses she hardly eats it at all anymore, "but I would say my all-time favorite is English Toffee."

Susan Murley
Louisville, Kentucky

CARAMELS

2 cups granulated sugar
2 cups light corn syrup
2 cups evaporated milk
1 stick (½ cup) butter

Pinch of salt
1 tsp. vanilla
¾ cup chopped nuts (optional)

Mix sugar and syrup in large, deep, heavy pan. Bring to slow boil, turn up heat, and begin adding milk in thin stream so that mixture never stops boiling. Add butter and stir constantly for about 30 minutes before testing in cold water. Must make firm ball (about 242 degrees). Add vanilla and nuts. Pour into 9-inch buttered pan. Cool. Use knife around edges, turn over, and knock out. Cut in small pieces and wrap in waxed paper or plastic wrap.

Susan says, "It's a wonder these caramels won a prize at all. For the family I wrap them in waxed paper, but for something special I went to the candy supply store and purchased colored foils without giving a thought as to what I was putting into them. I'm surprised the judges could get through the wrappings to taste them!"

Try Susan's Pumpkin Bread (page 191).

MRS. OSWALD MYRAN

WESSINGTON SPRINGS,
SOUTH DAKOTA

BLUE RIBBON
SOUTH DAKOTA STATE FAIR

BEST EVER FUDGE

8 T. butter
3 1-oz. pieces of chocolate
4 cups sugar
1 pt. half and half

Cream of tartar
2 tsp. vanilla
1 lb. or 2 cups walnut meats,
    coarsely chopped

Melt butter and chocolate together slowly, stirring constantly. Take off heat and stir in sugar, then add cream and stir well. Raise heat on high and when mixture boils shake in a pinch of cream of tartar (2 shakes), then turn heat down till it barely boils (just bubbly). Boil 20 to 30 minutes. Stir gently only a couple of times to scrape sides of pan. Start testing for doneness after 20 minutes by dropping small amount of mixture into cool water. When water remains fairly clear and fudge can be picked up between fingers remove pan from heat.

Cool slowly in a cool place (but *not* in cold water) until completely cool (mixture may look stiff). Stir and pull mixture until it thickens. Add vanilla and nutmeats. Pour onto large buttered platter. Place in cool place until firm and cut into squares.

Try Mrs. Myran's Honey Graham Bread (page 139), Beet Pickles (page 426), and Watermelon Pickles (page 426).

PEANUT BRITTLE

3 cups sugar	½ tsp. salt
1 cup corn syrup	1 T. butter
½ cup water	1 tsp. vanilla
2 cups raw Spanish peanuts	2 tsp. baking soda

Boil sugar, corn syrup, and water to 250 degrees. Add nuts, salt, and butter all at once and cook to 300 degrees—peanuts begin to brown, the skins pop, and the syrup turns a yellow brown. Remove from heat. Immediately stir in vanilla and soda. Pour quickly in a ribbon down the center of 4 buttered cookie sheets. Candy will foam. Do not spread out in pans with spoon, but as soon as you can slip a knife under edges and get hold of them, carefully pull candy out thin toward edges of pans. Work quickly as it sets and hardens.

 Beth has only been entering the fair competitions for two years, but she has already won two firsts and a second.

GLORIA SHOBER
EPHRATA, PENNSYLVANIA

FIRST PRIZE
EPHRATA COUNTY FAIR

WALNUT PENUCHE

2½ cups confectioners sugar
1 cup walnuts, cut up
½ cup butter or margarine

1 cup brown sugar
¼ cup milk

Butter 8-inch square pan very lightly. Place butter in saucepan and melt slowly over low heat. Stir in brown sugar. Let boil for 2 minutes, stirring all the time. Slowly add the milk and let it cook until the mixture boils. Remove from heat and allow to cool. Add sugar slowly and beat the mixture until it looks like fudge. Add nuts. Spread in pan and refrigerate until stiff—approximately ½ hour. Will be *soft* and *rich*.

Try Gloria's Moravian Coffee Cake (page 200).

CINDY STALNAKER
SUMMERSVILLE, WEST VIRGINIA

FIRST PRIZE, DIVINITY
WEST VIRGINIA STATE FAIR

DIVINITY

2⅔ cups sugar
½ cup water
2 tsp. vanilla

⅔ cup light corn syrup
2 egg whites
Whole pecans (optional)

Heat sugar, corn syrup, and water in 2-quart saucepan over low heat, stirring constantly, until sugar is dissolved. Cook, without stirring, to 260 degrees on candy thermometer or until small amount of mixture dropped into very cold water forms a hard ball. Or drop mixture from a spoon; if it spins a thread it's ready. Remove from heat.

Beat egg whites until stiff peaks form; continue beating while pouring hot syrup in a thin stream into egg whites. Add vanilla; beat until mixture holds its shape and becomes slightly dull (mixture may become too stiff for mixer). Drop mixture from tip of buttered spoon onto waxed paper. Put a whole pecan on top of each one if desired.

Yield: about 4 dozen candies

NOTE: Use 1 tablespoon less water on humid days. *For best results don't make on rainy or humid days.*

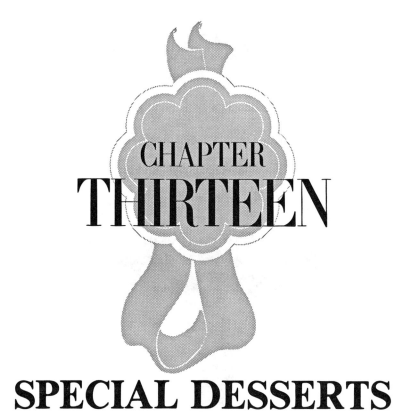

CHAPTER THIRTEEN

SPECIAL DESSERTS

SPECIAL DESSERTS—You are the judge

TAMMIE BIERIG
OKEENE, OKLAHOMA

CHERRY KUCHEN

BATTER

2 cups flour	½ cup oil
3 tsp. baking powder	2 eggs
½ cup sugar	½ cup milk
½ tsp. salt	½ tsp. vanilla
1 pkg. yeast	1 can of cherry pie filling

Combine the first 9 ingredients. Blend until moistened at low speed and then increase to medium speed for about 2 minutes. Spread cherry pie filling over the top of the batter.

TOPPING

1 cup sugar	¼ cup butter
1 cup flour	¼ cup chopped nuts

Combine sugar, flour, butter, and nuts. Sprinkle over the top of the cherry pie filling. Bake at 350 degrees until golden brown—about 35 to 40 minutes.

Try Tammie's Gourmet Potatoes (page 80).

DEBORAH BUXTON

SOUTH LYNDEBORO,
NEW HAMPSHIRE

Here is a "very colorful and refreshing dessert" from a New Hampshire prizewinner, Deborah Buxton.

SHERBET WATERMELON SURPRISE DESSERT

1 12-oz. pkg. chocolate chips
1 qt. softened lime sherbet
1 qt. softened raspberry sherbet

Line lettuce crisper bowl with 1 inch of lime sherbet—freeze till firm. Add
chocolate chips to raspberry sherbet and mix together. Fill the center of the lime
sherbet with the raspberry sherbet and freeze till firm. Just before serving dip
crisper in warm water to loosen. Remove sherbet and slice like a watermelon!
It's a very colorful and refreshing dessert.

Debbie's Sautéed Green Beans with Onions are on page 83, and her Raisin
Bran Muffins are on page 171.

A. CARMAN CLARK
UNION, MAINE

SLUMP AND GRUNT

The ingredients are the same for both Slump and Grunt and Blueberry Cakes, but the method of preparation differs. Both are hearty and delicious and should be served while warm with a pitcher of thick cream or with whipped cream, slightly sweetened and flavored with a dash of nutmeg.

½ cup water	2 tsp. baking powder
1 qt. blueberries	½ tsp. salt
1 cup sugar	¼ cup sugar
2 T. butter	½ cup milk
1 cup flour	

SLUMP

In a deep skillet or wide-bottomed saucepan put the water, butter, berries, and 1 cup sugar. Bring to the boiling point.

Mix the remainder of the ingredients to a stiff batter. Spoon over the berries as dumplings. Cover tightly and simmer for 12 minutes. Do not remove the cover during this cooking time.

GRUNT

Preheat oven to 400 degrees. Grease a deep baking dish or casserole and put the berry mixture into it and put in the oven while mixing the topping dough.

Blend the butter into the flour. Add the rest of the ingredients. Spoon over the hot berries and bake for 20 minutes.

BLUEBERRY CAKE

In Maine, a blueberry cake is most often a kind of hot bread. You place a pat of butter on top of your serving and watch it melt and run down while you are cutting your meat, then you eat it while it's still hot.

THE HOT BREAD TYPE OF BLUEBERRY CAKE:

1 egg	1¾ cups flour
¼ cup sugar	3 tsp. baking powder
2 T. butter	1 cup milk
1 tsp. salt	2 cups blueberries

Beat egg, sugar, butter, and salt together. Add flour, baking powder, and milk and mix well. Fold in 2 cups of blueberries. Bake at 375 degrees for about 35 minutes. Serve hot.

"At age 15," says Carman, "I needed money for my college fund. I could read. I had a cookbook, so I took a job as cook for the summer in the Adirondacks in New York." Today, Carman reads cookbooks for adventure and experiment. She had the top Blueberry Exhibit at the Maine Blueberry Festival.

Carman told us that "This old-time recipe of Maine is supposed to have derived its name from the recurring behavior of the menfolk when this dessert was served. Instead of getting back to the farm work, they were inclined to 'slump' into a porch chair and 'grunt'."

RENAE ECCLESTON
FOWLER, KANSAS

COCA-COLA CUPCAKES

2 cups flour
2 cups sugar
2 sticks of oleo
3 T. cocoa
1 cup Coca-Cola

½ cup buttermilk
2 beaten eggs
1 tsp. vanilla
¼ tsp. salt

Combine flour and sugar. Heat to boiling the oleo, cocoa, and Coca-Cola and blend with flour mixture. Add remaining ingredients and blend in. Batter will be runny. Pour into paper-lined cupcake papers in muffin tins. Bake (350 degrees) for 15 minutes on lower rack in oven.

FROSTING

Boil 1 minute—1 cup sugar, ½ cup condensed milk or light cream, ¼ cup oleo, 1 square chocolate, add 1 teaspoon vanilla. Cool partway and beat till thick.

Renae's Whole Wheat Cottage Cheese Rolls and Home-Style Brown English Muffins are on page 124.

EMILY HELLER
LIVONIA, MICHIGAN

FIRST PRIZE
PINEAPPLE GROWERS' CONTEST
HONOLULU, HAWAII

PINEAPPLE CHOCOLATE DESSERT

1 1-lb., 4-oz. can crushed
    pineapple
⅓ cup plus 1 T. unsweetened
    cocoa powder
2¼ cups all-purpose flour
1 cup light brown sugar
    (packed)
⅔ cup granulated sugar
⅔ cup shortening

½ cup plus 2 T. buttermilk
3 large eggs
2 tsp. pineapple extract
1½ tsp. salt
1 tsp. baking powder
1 tsp. baking soda
Deluxe Buttercream
Chocolate Fudge Frosting

Drain pineapple, saving syrup. Heat ¼ cup syrup, add cocoa, and stir until smooth. Place in large bowl with flour, sugars, shortening, buttermilk, eggs, pineapple flavoring, salt, baking powder, and soda. Beat 1 minute on low speed, scraping bowl. Beat 2 minutes on medium speed. Add drained pineapple, and beat 1 minute on medium speed. Spread batter evenly in well-greased, lightly floured 9x13x2-inch baking pan. Bake in moderate oven (350 degrees) 40 to 45 minutes, or until cake tests done.

Remove from oven and cool on wire rack, then chill in refrigerator. Prepare Deluxe Buttercream and spread over chilled cake. Chill, preferably 10 minutes in freezer. Spread Chocolate Fudge Frosting over chilled Buttercream. Chill in refrigerator until set, about 30 minutes. Bring to room temperature before serving.

Yield: 12–16 servings

DELUXE BUTTERCREAM

In a small bowl, beat 1 chilled egg white, ½ teaspoon vanilla, and ¼ teaspoon salt until stiff. Beat in ¼ cup powdered sugar. Set aside. In small mixer bowl, beat ½ cup softened butter with 1 cup powdered sugar at low speed 1 minute or until fluffy. Add ⅓ cup sweetened condensed milk and beat ½ minute. Add egg white mixture and beat ½ minute, or until well blended. Stir in an additional ¼ cup powdered sugar. Spread evenly over the well-chilled cake. Return to refrigerator or freezer to chill before adding Chocolate Fudge Frosting, but do not freeze.

CHOCOLATE FUDGE FROSTING

Heat ⅓ cup plus 1 tablespoon evaporated milk, but do not boil.. Remove from heat. Stir in 1 cup light brown sugar (packed), ½ teaspoon vanilla, and ¼ teaspoon salt. Let rest several minutes, stir and let rest again, repeating until sugar is dissolved and forms a syruplike honey. Do not beat. Warm 2 teaspoons oil over low heat, add 1 6-ounce package semisweet chocolate pieces, and stir until chocolate is completely melted. Remove from heat, add to brown sugar mixture, and stir vigorously until well blended and smooth. Quickly spread over chilled Buttercream. Refrigerate 30 minutes to set frosting. (This cake keeps well for two or three days, or may be frozen for a week or so.)

Emily Heller won over more than 70,000 other entries in the Pineapple Growers' Contest—now, that's competition! She grew up in Bucyrus, Ohio, and learned to cook in her mother's farm kitchen.

Here is advice from this champion: "Experiment every day; never cook the same item the same way. Keep a large notebook recording changes just as though you were working in a lab. If your ideas are *very* strange, just make small amounts—don't be wasteful."

Emily is a housewife and an accountant in her husband's dental office. She takes competition cooking seriously, and has been a finalist in the Pillsbury Bake-Off.

ELIZABETH HERNANDES
ANCHORAGE, ALASKA

ALASKAN HONEY

Boil 10 cups sugar, 1 teaspoon alum, and 2½ cups water for 8 minutes. Remove from heat and add 48 clover blossoms and 18 fireweed blossoms. Leave in syrup until it turns a golden amber color (10–15 minutes). Remove blossoms and pour into jars.

Yield: 8 cups

Liz says, "Thought you might like this true Alaskan recipe! Makes great gifts." She won third prize with this Honey recipe at the Alaska State Fair.

Try Liz's Butter Rolls (page 133).

BUTTERY WALNUT CAKES

1 cup butter	2 tsp. baking powder
¾ cup white sugar	1 tsp. vanilla
1 egg	1 cup walnuts, chopped fine
2½ cups all-purpose flour	Apricot preserves (optional)
¼ tsp. salt	

In large bowl cream butter and sugar till fluffy. Beat in egg, stir salt and baking powder into flour. Work into butter mixture gradually. Add vanilla and stir in nuts. Chill at least 1 hour. Roll out to ⅛ inch and cut with cookie cutters or cut into diamonds with knife. If using apricot preserves (really good!) spread tops of cookies, leaving a small plain border around edge. Bake on *un*greased cookie sheet at 400 degrees between 5 and 8 minutes till edges start to brown.

Yield: 6–7 dozen

 "After I'd spent hours carefully layering batter/cheese filling/batter/etc. for a bundt cake recipe I was trying to perfect, our dog ran between my legs just as I was putting it in the oven. I flipped it upside down on the oven door." We sympathize!

Katherine learned to cook "at home. With ten children in the family my mother encouraged us in any homemaking endeavor."

She says, "With the amount of baking I do, I'd honestly have to say my kitchen is *toooooo* small." A cook for 21 years, Katherine cooks "for as few as four, as many as thirty." She advises: "Don't be afraid of new recipes. A lot of times the more complicated-looking ones are quite simple, once you get going."

PRUDENCE H. STEPHENSON
St. Paul, Minnesota

HONEY ALMOND GRANOLA

In a heavy skillet or large frying pan, mix together:

½ cup butter
⅔ cup honey
½ tsp. salt

Mix till butter has melted, then add:

2 cups old fashioned oatmeal
1½ cup coconut shreds
½ cup wheat germ
1 cup unsalted soya beans
¾ cup salted sunflower seeds

1½ cup almonds-chopped: half
 with skins on and half
 slivered almonds with
 skins off
4 T. vanilla

Mix everything thoroughly in the frying pan, then turn into large pyrex baking pan about 10x15-inches and bake at 350 degrees for 22–27 minutes, stirring frequently so mixture does not get too brown. It should be just golden for the best flavor.

After granola has cooled and been stirred again, add 1–1½ cups raisins (dark and light, if desired). Mix thoroughly and store in glass jars in the refrigerator.

Yield: about 2¼ quarts

NOTE: Very good sprinkled on vanilla ice cream.

Prudence Stephenson cooks on a twenty-nine-year-old *red* Chambers range. She has been cooking for thirty-three years. She told us about a time during her second year of baking for the Fair. Her two and a half year old son watched her bake—then he carefully put 2 cups of buttermilk through the flour sifter.

This Honey Almond Granola recipe also won First Prize and Sweepstakes from the Minnesota Beekeepers Association. Prudence's only advice to you about the recipe is, "Enjoy!!!"

LOTTE TAYLOR
JUNCTION CITY, KANSAS

LOTTE'S GERMAN APPLE SLICES

3 cups sliced and peeled
    apples (thicken as for pie)
2½ cups flour
1 cup oleo

Milk
½ tsp. salt
2 eggs, separated

Combine flour, salt, and oleo. Cut in with pastry cutter until crumbly. Beat egg yolks with enough milk to make ⅔ cup, add to flour mixture. Form into a ball.

Divide dough. Put half into a 15x9-inch glass pan. Spread with filling. Roll out rest of dough on lightly floured board and place on top of filling, seal edges. Beat egg whites with 1 tablespoon water until foamy. With pastry brush spread over top. Bake at 350 degrees for about 45 minutes or until golden brown. Cool slightly. Brush with glaze.

GLAZE

¾ cup sifted confectioners
    sugar

1 tsp. almond flavoring
2 tsp. water

APPLES FOR PIE

3 cups prepared fruit
1 cup sugar

1 T. flour
1 tsp. almond flavoring

Lotte's recipe for Cinnamon Rolls is on page 203.

GENNELL WIELAND
WEATHERFORD, OKLAHOMA

CHAMPION WASHITA COUNTY
RESERVE CHAMPION
HYDRO FAIR

STRAWBERRY ICE CREAM

4 eggs
1 T. flour
2 cups sugar
2 T. cornstarch
2 qts. milk
1 tsp. salt
2 tsp. vanilla

½ pt. cream
1 large can milnot (a type of canned milk)
½ cup white syrup
1 qt. crushed strawberries
1 T. gelatin (dissolved in 1 cup cold milk)

Beat eggs until foamy. Mix sugar, flour, and cornstarch. Add to eggs. Mix well. Heat 1 quart of the milk and add the egg mixture. Bring to a boil, stirring constantly. Be careful, as this will scorch easily. Let cool, then add rest of ingredients and enough milk to fill ice cream can ¾ full. Freeze until firm. Let set 1 hour to ripen.

Yield: 1 gallon

NOTE: This recipe may be used without strawberries.

 Here is an ice cream recipe from Oklahoma cook Gennell Wieland. She learned to cook when she was very young because "my mother was ill with a heart disease." Now she has been cooking for 45 years and cooks for two people every day.

See Gennell's recipe for Coconut Cream Pie (page 302).

MALINDA WISE
LINCOLNTON, NORTH CAROLINA

FIRST PLACE, YOUTH CATEGORY
APPLE DISH CONTEST
LINCOLN COUNTY APPLE FESTIVAL,
NORTH CAROLINA

APPLE FLOAT

2 cups applesauce
½ cup sugar
1 tsp. vanilla flavoring
3 drops almond flavoring

3 egg whites
3 tsp. sugar
¼ tsp. cream of tartar

Combine applesauce, sugar, and flavorings. In separate bowl mix egg whites, 3 teaspoons sugar, and cream of tartar. Beat egg whites and cream of tartar till soft peaks form. Add sugar, beating till stiff and peaks form and sugar is dissolved.

Gently fold egg whites into applesauce mixture. Serve in sherbet glasses with a scoop of whipped cream and cherry on top. Chill 1 hour, serve cold.

Yield: 6 servings

Malinda (eleven years old), won the Apple Dish Contest for youth and adults at the Annual Lincolnton Apple Festival. This was her first cooking contest and she won with a recipe that originated with her great-great grandmother. She said, "My mother remembers when her grandmother used to make it for her when she was a little girl." The recipe was handed down by word of mouth, "and to our knowledge was not written down until I entered it in the 1980 Lincoln County Apple Dish Contest."

CHAPTER FOURTEEN

CONDIMENTS AND PRESERVES

CONDIMENTS & PRESERVES

PRESERVES

Contain fruit or pieces of fruit in a thick transparent syrup

Color and package are important

Select the best fruit, consistency is important

PICKLES

Most pickles are judged on crispness, flavor and color

Pickles same size

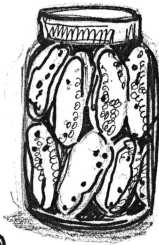

Butters: smoothness, color, container, label, consistency, texture

Jellies: clearness, color, consistency, flavor, package

CONNIE AMOS
LOUISVILLE, KENTUCKY

FIRST PLACE, CUCUMBER RELISH
KENTUCKY STATE FAIR

CUCUMBER RELISH

4 cups ground unpeeled
    cucumbers
1 cup ground green pepper
½ cup ground red pepper
3 cups ground onion
3 cups celery, diced fine

¼ cup salt
3½ cups sugar
2 cups white vinegar
1 T. celery seed
1 T. mustard seed

Combine all vegetables—sprinkle with salt, let stand 4 hours. Drain thoroughly, press out liquid. Combine sugar, vinegar, and celery and mustard seed. Bring to boil, stirring to dissolve sugar. Stir in vegetables, simmer 10 minutes. Pack in jars and process in water bath 10 minutes.

 "For one of the Kentucky State Fairs, I made petit fours. The car was full with other entries, so I held them in my hands. Getting out of the car I flipped them upside down on the concrete. They were a loss to me but the ladies at the fair said to enter them anyway. So I did. To my surprise they still won Third Place."

Besides cooking Connie also does cake decorating and candy making. She even teaches a children's cake-decorating class for Louisville Parks and Recreation Department.

IDA B. ARMSTRONG
LOUISVILLE, KENTUCKY

DILL PICKLES

Use small pickling cucumbers or split large ones and make slices. Brush clean, wash, and scald cukes. I bring water to boiling and let cukes remain for about 1 minute. Remove and place in jars along with 1 small garlic clove, 1 small red pepper, and a sprig of fresh dill. Boil 2 quarts of water, 1 quart of vinegar, and 1 cup of salt. Pour over pickles and tighten lids. I usually turn upside down and let stand until next day. I have used dill seeds when out of fresh dill. Also, I put more red pepper in some for those who like a hot mix.

Ida Armstrong learned to cook from "mother, mother-in-law, and aunts," and she's been cooking for 35 years. She describes her kitchen as "average, American," and she cooks for two now that her three children are grown.

BEULAH ARTHUR
CLINTONVILLE, WEST VIRGINIA

BEULAH'S COLE SLAW DRESSING

1¾ cups sugar
1 T. cornstarch or flour
1 T. salt
1 T. dry mustard

4 eggs
1 cup milk
½ cup butter
1 cup vinegar

Beat eggs well and add to dry ingredients. Add milk, butter and vinegar. Cook in double boiler until thick.

Beulah Arthur taught math for 35 years, and often made cakes for some of her students. Doesn't that sound like a sweet way to learn numbers?

She says, "I learned to cook in my mother's kitchen. Mostly by following directions she gave me from her bed when she was ill. I made Mother a birthday cake at age six."

CARMEN GAYE BARRETT
PALMER, ALASKA

CURRANT JELLY

3½ qts. currants	1 box Sure-Jell
1½ cups water	7 cups sugar

Mix currants and water in large pan. Cook until all berries are broken or until mixture boils for 10 minutes. Stir occasionally. Place in jelly bag or tie up in cheesecloth and squeeze out juice.

Measure juice into pan and measure sugar into bowl, using same measuring cup. Mix Sure-Jell into juice. Bring juice to a hard boil quickly, stirring occasionally. Add sugar at once. Bring to full rolling boil, stirring continuously. Pour into boiled jelly jars. Cool about 1 minute, spoon off jelly foam, and seal.

Yield: 8½ cups

See Carmen's sister, Denise Barrett, with a prizewinning recipe for Snickerdoodles (page 309).

TROPICAL PARADISE CONSERVE

3 cups tart apples	1¾ cups orange pulp
3 cups crushed pineapple	1 cup flaked coconut
2 cups sliced papaya	6 cups sugar
2 cups water	

Wash, core, peel, and slice apples; slice papaya. Combine apples, papaya, orange pulp, pineapple, and water. Cook 10 minutes, then add coconut and sugar. Bring to a boil, stirring frequently and slowly until the sugar is dissolved. Cook rapidly for 15 to 20 minutes, stirring often. Pour boiling hot conserve into sterilized jars and seal.

Yield: about 3 pints

MARIE'S CORN RELISH

2 dozen ears of corn (cut off corn)	1 oz. mustard
1 qt. ripe tomatoes (cut up)	¼ cup salt
1 ground green cucumber	¼ tsp. paprika
2½ cups sugar	1 tsp. turmeric
1 qt. vinegar	1 qt. ground onions

Combine and mix all items and boil for 45 minutes.

CHILI SAUCE

25 solid red tomatoes	½ tsp. allspice
5 large onions	3 T. salt
3 bell peppers (red)	1 tsp. cinnamon
3 bell peppers (green)	¼ tsp. red pepper
3 cups sugar	½ tsp. black pepper
3 cups white vinegar	1 tsp. celery seed

Chop vegetables, stir in other ingredients, and cook. Stir in last stage to keep from scorching.

Yield: About 6 quarts

"Small and inadequate," Marie Bigler says of her kitchen, but that hasn't prevented her from winning top honors "in bottled fruit, jams, jellies, pickles, and canned meats at the Utah State Fair in various years."

She told us that she learned to cook "at home in Tropic, Utah, trained by my mother, an excellent cook." With 68 years' cooking experience, she tells a story on herself that only another cook can appreciate—her worst mistake, she says, was "trying to put a lattice top on a rhubarb pie."

In 1977 Marie won the Ball Corporation $50 award for the most outstanding entry of home canned foods using an original recipe (Tropical Paradise Conserve).

PATRICIA BOOTH
PLACERVILLE, CALIFORNIA

FIRST PLACE, PICKLES
FIRST PLACE, FUDGE
EL DORADO COUNTY FAIR

DILL PICKLE CHIPS

18–20 lbs. cucumbers
(medium size)
1–2 lbs. red onions
6 cups vinegar
¾ cup granulated salt
¼ cup sugar (white)
9 cups water

2 T. pickling spice
2 tsp. mustard seed
per jar
1 clove garlic per jar
3 heads dill plant per jar
1 tsp. dill seed per jar

Wash and scrub cucumbers. Drain and slice into approximately ¼-inch slices (discard ends). Cover in brine (½ cup salt to 1 gallon water—you'll need about 2 gallons total). Let stand 4–6 hours.

Combine vinegar, sugar, water, and pickling spices and heat to boiling. Pack cucumber slices into clean, hot quart jars. Add mustard seed, dill plant and seed, and garlic to each jar, then cover with the hot vinegar mixture to ½-inch of top of jar. Adjust lids. Process in boiling-water bath for 20 minutes. (Start processing time as soon as jars are placed in boiling water. After 20 minutes remove jars and tighten seals if necessary.) Set jars upright 2 inches apart on wire rack to cool.

"My hobbies are all related to homemaking, with cooking being my favorite pastime (closely followed by eating, ha, ha). I have been cooking since I was just a kid. My dad was a professional chef for years and my mother could hold her own in cooking with lots of Old Country dishes handed down to her from her family, who immigrated to this country from Russia."

NORA BUSKIRK
LITTLETON, COLORADO

**FIRST PLACE, JUNIOR DIVISION,
FRUIT LEATHERS
BEST DISPLAY, DRIED FOODS**
COLORADO STATE FAIR

FRUIT LEATHER

Spread plastic wrap over cookie sheet with sides. Be *sure* to overlap.

Use about 2 cups of fruit pulp. You may add sugar if pulp is too sour.

Spread ¼-inch thick on cookie sheet. (It's very important to get it as even as possible.)

Dry several hours on lowest oven temperature. It's done when you can peel it off the plastic wrap.

NOTE: Nora says that this Fruit Leather is "great for a nutritious snack."

Seventeen-year-old Nora Buskirk says, "My mom first taught me how to cook when I was in elementary school. Through the years I've taken all of the cooking courses I could, both in school and out."

She has taken to cake decorating in a big way. Once Nora made a wedding cake that served 375 people! She is planning to attend the National Cooking Institute, and is well on her way to being a professional cook right now.

Cooking in "an average electric kitchen (but no microwave!)," Nora Buskirk has taken top honors for several years at the Colorado State Fair. She warns that her recipes are for high altitudes.

MAUDIE CRAIG
LAWRENCEBURG, TENNESSEE

BLUE RIBBON, PICKLES
AND RELISHES
MIDDLE TENNESSEE FAIR

SANDWICH SPREAD

12 green peppers (sweet)	1 pt. prepared mustard
12 red peppers (sweet)	1 T. flour
12 green tomatoes, medium size	1 qt. salad dressing (not
5 onions, medium	mayonnaise)
3 cups sugar	½ cup salt

Cut vegetables, let stand in salt water overnight. Drain and grind in food chopper; drain again. Put in stainless steel pot and add all the other ingredients except salad dressing. Cook 10 minutes after it begins to boil, stirring often. Remove from heat, add salad dressing, mix well, and fill sterilized jars. Process in boiling water 5 minutes.

Yield: about 8 pints

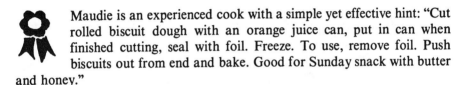

Maudie is an experienced cook with a simple yet effective hint: "Cut rolled biscuit dough with an orange juice can, put in can when finished cutting, seal with foil. Freeze. To use, remove foil. Push biscuits out from end and bake. Good for Sunday snack with butter and honey."

BOB DAVIS
DES MOINES, IOWA

BEET JELLY

6–7 medium large beets,
    skinned and cubed
2½ cups water
2 T. lemon juice (strained)

3½ cups sugar
1 envelope "certo" fruit
    pectin

Place cubed beets and water in saucepan and boil until about 2 cups of liquid (beet juice) remain. Strain beet juice through cloth and put 1¾ cups in large kettle (4- to 6-quart). Add lemon juice and sugar. Place kettle over high heat and stir with metal spoon until mixture comes to full boil. Add fruit pectin. Bring to a full rolling boil stirring constantly and boil hard 1 minute. Remove from heat and skim off foam. Pour quickly into sterile jelly glasses and seal at once with paraffin or sterile lids.

Yield: 3–4 8-oz. glasses of jelly

NOTE: "I kept adjusting sugar and juice quantities trying to get a good jelly. [At the Iowa State Fair] the judge noted that my gooseberry jelly was the best jelly in the fair that year."

GOOSEBERRY JELLY

2½ qts. hard ripe gooseberries
Water
6½ cups sugar
2 envelopes fruit pectin

Stem and slightly crush gooseberries. Place in large saucepan, cover with water. Place over high heat and bring to a boil. Boil about 10 minutes. Strain juice. Place 4 cups strained juice in large kettle (6-quart minimum). Add sugar and bring to a full rolling boil, stirring constantly, and boil hard 1 minute. Remove from heat and skim foam with metal spoon. Quickly pour into sterile jelly glasses and seal.

Yield: 7–8 8-oz. jelly glasses

Here we have a champion cook who was discriminated against. Way back in 1948, when he was fourteen, Bob was denied ribbons and premiums because of a "women only" rule. Now he has returned to competition, winning sweepstakes and ribbons galore. As he told us, "I have only cooked in competition the last three years (other than 1948) and all my entries have been in the Iowa State Fair competition. There are several ladies who are regular competitors at the fair who have won many more ribbons than I, however, I like to think my percentage of wins is well above average. Also, I believe my percentage of wins in the higher-ranking places is above average. This year, if memory serves me correctly, I won forty-three ribbons, including 4 sweepstakes, with forty-two entries."

He says about his Beet Jelly recipe, "I won second place with this. My fifteen-year-old daughter used my recipe and beat me!"

Bob Davis told us, "The fair started a beet jelly class in 1978 and I couldn't find a recipe so I developed this one. My sixteen-year-old daughter Karen won first place with it."

JANICE DELONG
PEACH BOTTOM, PENNSYLVANIA

FIRST PLACE
SOUTHERN LANCASTER COMMUNITY
FAIR, PENNSYLVANIA

PEACH OR PEAR BUTTER

Take pound for pound of peaches or pears and sugar. Cook fruit alone until soft; add half the sugar and stir for ½ hour; then add the remainder of the sugar, and stir. Cook for 1½ hours. Season with cloves and cinnamon. Pour into jars and seal.

If your butter starts getting thick before 1½ hours is over spoon small amount on saucer and place in refrigerator for a minute or two. If it doesn't run on the saucer when you take it out it is done.

RED OR YELLOW TOMATO PRESERVES

1 lb. red or yellow tomatoes, peeled and sliced	¾ lb. sugar
	½ lemon

Peel tomatoes and cut into thin slices. Add sugar and let stand one hour. Add thin-sliced lemon and rind. Cook until the tomatoes are clear and the syrup is thickened. Pour into jars and seal.

Try Janice's Homemade Potato Chips (page 87).

MARIAN EASTHAM
SAN JACINTO, CALIFORNIA

APRICOT AND ORANGE MARMALADE

3¼ cups ground apricots,
    unpeeled
2½ cups ground oranges

½ cup lemon juice
8 cups sugar

Combine apricots and oranges—add lemon juice. Mix and add sugar. Cook over high heat, stirring constantly, for 4 minutes. Remove from heat after mixture comes to full boiling point and skim foam to prevent floating fruit. Pour into prepared glasses.

Yield: 3 pints or 5–6 half-pints

Marian Eastham has been cooking "since I was married in 1931." Now a widow, she is a champion cook—many times a prizewinner. "I have never taken less than second in any Fair," she told us. She takes advantage of living in San Jacinto, famous worldwide for dates.

"They grow over 100 kinds of dates in Coachella Valley. Three quarters of the dates sold in the world are grown in Coachella Valley. They are hand pollinated. Harvest is in September and fall months. I use dates the year round. I keep mine in the refrigerator, but do not freeze them."

Marian told us a little about the apricots grown in the area: "They used to grow more twenty years ago, but the water situation and more retired people living here in San Jacinto Valley in mobile homes have taken out so many trees. This year there were only 790 acres of apricots."

DORIS EWY
HALSTEAD, KANSAS

BREAD AND BUTTER PICKLES

4 qts. sliced unpeeled
   cucumbers
6 medium white onions,
   sliced
½ cup pickling salt
Cracked ice

5 cups sugar
4 cups cider vinegar
2 T. mustard seed
1½ tsp. turmeric
2 tsp. celery seed

Combine cucumbers, onions, and salt. Cover with cracked ice; mix well. Let mixture stand 3 hours; drain well. Combine remaining ingredients; pour over cucumber mixture. Bring to boiling. Pack cucumbers and liquid into hot jars, leaving 1-inch headspace. Adjust lids. Process in boiling-water bath 5 minutes.

Yield: 8 pints

We also have Doris's Refrigerator Rolls (page 127).

VIOLET GRICE
GILA BEND, ARIZONA

BARBECUE SAUCE

1 tsp. salt
1 tsp. chili powder
1 tsp. celery powder
¼ cup Worcestershire sauce
¼ cup brown sugar
1 cup ketchup

1 tsp. barbecue powder
3 T. minced onion
1 tsp. garlic powder
¼ cup vinegar
2 cups water
Few drops Tabasco (optional)

Simmer until thick.

Yield: 1 pint

Try Violet's Grits and Cheese (page 90), and Summer Sausage (page 35).

STRAWBERRY PRESERVES

Hull and wash 2 quarts fully ripened berries. Crush berries in a heavy enamel-ware kettle so that each berry is reduced to pulp. Measure—you want 4½ cups, so add water if you are a little short. Add 1 box Sure-Jell. Bring to boil. Add 7 cups sugar. Bring to rolling boil. Boil 1 minute. Remove from heat and pour into clean, sterilized glasses. Cover with paraffin seal at once. (Be sure to watch closely so it doesn't burn.)

Mrs. Heer learned to cook "in my mother's kitchen by helping." Now she cooks just for her husband and herself, but with four children grown and married and six grandchildren she sometimes cooks for a crowd, and really enjoys it.

She had a bad experience three years ago when her pressure cooker exploded and she was burned. It didn't stop her from canning, though: "the next season I got a new canner and canned as much as before."

BETTY HIATT
OAKDALE, CALIFORNIA

BLUEBERRY-PEACH JAM

1 pt. basket of fresh blue-
    berries
Elberta peaches

1 pkg. fruit pectin
5½ cups sugar

Put blueberries into blender and purée. Add enough peaches to fill blender. Put in deep kettle, and add fruit pectin by sprinkling and stirring in. Bring to hard boil, add sugar. Bring to full rolling boil and boil 1 minute. Skim, pour into jars, and seal.

Yield: approximately 7 half-pint jars

Betty said: "The first time I cooked rice as a bride, I poured the boxful into water in a small pan. As it expanded I got a larger pan and a larger pan and—finally ended up with a dishpan full of rice."

Betty says she learned to cook "the hard way, in my own kitchen after I got married." She cooks for four now, in her well-equipped compact kitchen. Betty gave us some of the most interesting, original recipes in our book—a No-Cook Pumpkin Pie, a Bar B Q Beef recipe that serves 100, and Homemade Mincemeat. She also told us, "The past few years we have had our own cows and plenty of milk. I have enjoyed experimenting in cheese making. It's fun to have my own cheese waxed and aging in the refrigerator. I wanted to enter my cheese in the fair, but they had no category for it."

Betty describes how she came up with this recipe: "I had a lot of Elberta peaches when I lived in Denair, California. I canned peaches, froze peaches, dried peaches and had them fresh. I made peach marmalade and ginger-peach jam and was looking for another way of putting up the excess peaches when I made this recipe up in order to have a different flavor. The jam takes on the blueberry flavor. The family has enjoyed this recipe."

Try Betty's Homemade Beef Jerky (page 36), Barbecue Beef (page 36), Pumpkin Pie (page 284), and Peach Pie (page 284).

LAURA HYNEK
LINCOLN, NEBRASKA

GRAND PRIZE, JAMS
GRAND PRIZE, COOKIES
NEBRASKA STATE FAIR

PINEAPPLE-ZUCCHINI JAM

2 cups crushed pineapple
    (in its own juice)
1 cup grated zucchini
1 box Sure-Jel

4½ cups sugar
¼ cup candied cherries, cut
    in small pieces

In pan put pineapple, zucchini, and Sure-Jell. Stir. Place on heat and bring to boil. Boil 1 minute, stirring. Add sugar with cherries. Bring to boil and boil 1 minute, stirring constantly. Skim off foam. Place in pint jars and seal.

Yield: 2 pints

STELLA JEZEWSKI
DETROIT, MICHIGAN

RED TOMATO MARMALADE

12 cups red tomatoes, peeled
and cut up into small
pieces
2 oranges, cut up

2 lemons, cut up
10 cups sugar
2 T. whole cloves
6 T. broken cinnamon sticks

Tie cloves and cinnamon sticks in a cheesecloth. Add sugar and boil on high heat. Cook 50 minutes. Stir almost all the time. Put in jars. Seal and put in water bath for about 10 minutes.

To make jelly strain about 3 cups of marmalade, add 1 cup more sugar and 1 bottle Certo, and bring to a rolling boil. While hot put in jelly glasses or jars. Seal with wax or covers.

Try Stella's Poppy Seed Cake (page 236).

LUCILLE JOHNSON
VALE, NORTH CAROLINA

JIFFY APPLE-QUE SAUCE

½ cup cooking oil
¾ cup chopped onion
¾ cup ketchup
¾ cup water
⅓ cup lemon juice
3 T. Worcestershire sauce

2 T. prepared mustard
3 T. sugar
2 tsp. salt
½ tsp. pepper
1 cup applesauce

Sauté onions in cooking oil until transparent. Combine remaining ingredients, except applesauce, and add to the first mixture. Simmer for 10 minutes, stirring occasionally, then add applesauce and simmer for 5 more minutes. This may be kept in a jar in the refrigerator for up to 4 weeks. The applesauce makes this sauce cling to meat much better than regular sauce does, and it's good on any kind of meat.

MRS. FLOYD KEENER
LINCOLNTON, NORTH CAROLINA

FIRST PLACE, MISCELLANEOUS
CATEGORY
APPLE DISH CONTEST
VALE, NORTH CAROLINA

APPLE CHUTNEY

15 ripe tomatoes	1 tsp. cinnamon
8 apples	½ tsp. cloves (ground)
5 onions	½ tsp. dry mustard
2 cups sugar	2 tsp. celery seed
1 pt. vinegar	1 sweet pepper
2½ tsp. salt	¼ tsp. black pepper

Wash and peel apples. Cook till tender, add sugar, and continue cooking while getting the vegetables ready.

Wash, trim, and cut up tomatoes, onions, and pepper. Put through food grinder or blender. Combine vinegar and remaining ingredients and vegetables. Add to apples and continue cooking for 2 hours or until thick, at low heat, stirring occasionally. Seal and process in hot-water bath for 10 minutes.

Yield: 4 pints

Mrs. Miles J. Larkin
Douglas, Wyoming

KOSHER PICKLES

Wash small cucumbers. Put 1 dill head in bottom of jar, and clove of garlic. Pack cukes firmly in clean jars, add another head of dill on top, and ⅛ teaspoon alum. Bring 3 quarts water, 1 quart vinegar, and 1 cup salt to a boil and pour over cucumbers. Seal.

Mrs. Larkin has been a sweepstakes winner with her flowers at the State Fair. She's been cooking "over 50 years" and says she learned "by practicing."

Cathleen MacGavin
Casper, Wyoming

ORANGE MARMALADE

Remove skins in quarters from 3 oranges and 2 lemons. Shave off as much white as possible. Grind skins in coarse food grinder. Add 1½ cups water and ⅛ teaspoon soda, bring to boil, and simmer covered 20 minutes. Chop peeled fruit, add pulp to undrained, cooked rind. Simmer covered 10 minutes. Measure 3-cup mixture into larger saucepan, add 5 cups sugar, mix well. Over high heat, bring to rolling boil 1 minute, stirring constantly. Remove from heat, stir in ½-bottle liquid fruit pectin. Stir and skim full 7 minutes to prevent floating fruit. Ladle into glasses, cover with hot paraffin.

Yield: about 5½ cups

PEACH JAM

Chop and peel 4 cups (3 pounds) fully ripe peaches or put through blender.

In *large* saucepan, add to ¼ cup lemon juice and 7½ cups sugar. Bring to rolling boil and boil 1 minute, stirring constantly. Remove from heat, add ½-bottle liquid fruit pectin. Stir, skim for 5 minutes to prevent floating fruit. Ladle into glasses, cover with hot paraffin.

 Cathleen said she taught herself to cook, mostly by watching her dad cook pies and jellies at home. She has been cooking for 22 years, and cooks for three every day.

BARNIE I. MCBEE
COMANCHE, TEXAS

BAR-B-QUE SAUCE

2 medium-size onions,
  chopped
¼ cup of cooking oil
Juice from ½ dozen lemons
3 No. 303 cans tomato sauce
¼ tsp. garlic powder
1 cup Worcestershire sauce
1 T. chili powder

½ cup cider vinegar
¼ cup mustard
1 12-oz. bottle ketchup
¼ cup brown sugar
Salt and pepper to taste
2 cups black coffee (approximately)

Cook onions, oil, garlic, and chili powder until light brown. Add the rest of ingredients. Cook slowly for 45 minutes. Add black coffee to thin and flavor. Swab meat with sauce when ⅔ cooked.

Yield: 1 gallon

Barnie is a champion cook whose kitchen is a "350 gallon butane tank made into a Bar-B-Q pit mounted on a two-wheel trailer."

Barnie has some advice for you Bar-B-Que cooks: "Don't burn your meat." This is important if you're doing what he does—cooking for crowds of 150 to 200 hungry folks.

ELIZABETH MEITNER
FERNDALE, CALIFORNIA

FIRST PRIZE, JAMS AND JELLIES
HUMBOLT COUNTY FAIR,
CALIFORNIA

STRAWBERRY JAM

1⅞ cups crushed fruit	½ bottle fruit pectin
2 T. lemon juice	2 T. lemon juice
3½ cups sugar	

Prepare fruit, crush completely. Measure berries into large saucepan with lemon juice and sugar. Mix well.

Place over high heat, bring to full rolling boil, and boil hard 1 minute, stirring constantly.

Remove from heat; *at once* stir in pectin.

Stir and skim for 5 minutes to cool slightly and prevent floating fruit. Ladle into glasses. Cover at once with ⅛-inch hot paraffin.

Try Elizabeth's Applesauce Cake (page 249).

MRS. OSWALD MYRAN

WESSINGTON SPRINGS,
SOUTH DAKOTA

BLUE RIBBON
SOUTH DAKOTA STATE FAIR

WATERMELON PICKLES

Prepare rinds and cut in chunks. Cover with hot water and boil till they can be pierced with a fork. Do not boil too long—they should not be soft. Drain well. For 7 pounds of fruit make the following syrup:

7 cups (3½ lb.) granulated sugar	¼ tsp. oil of cloves
2 cups vinegar	½ tsp. oil of cinnamon

Let stand overnight in syrup. Second day reheat syrup and pour back over pickles and let stand overnight. Third day reheat syrup and rinds and pack in jars and seal.

Yield: 7 pints

BEET PICKLES

Boil beets in water till skins slip off easily. Cut in chunks or slices and set aside. Cook the following a short time:

1 cup brown sugar	1 cup water
1 cup white sugar	1 tsp. salt
2 cups vinegar	

Add beets to syrup and simmer about 10–15 minutes. Put in jars and seal.

Try Mrs. Myran's Honey Graham Bread (page 139) and Fudge (page 378).

CLARA E. NALL
ELIZABETHTOWN, KENTUCKY

FIRST PRIZE, PEAR PRESERVES
AND APPLE JELLY
FIRST PRIZE, BREAD AND
BUTTER PICKLES
KENTUCKY STATE FAIR

BREAD AND BUTTER PICKLES

25–30 medium-sized pickling cucumbers	5 cups cider vinegar
8 large white onions	5 cups sugar
2 large green peppers	2 T. mustard seeds
½ cup salt	1 tsp. turmeric
	½ tsp. cloves

Wash cucumbers and slice as thin as possible. Chop onions and peppers and combine with the cucumbers and salt; let stand 3 hours, and drain. Combine vinegar, sugar, and spices in a large preserving kettle, bring to a boil. Add drained cucumbers, heat thoroughly, but do not boil. Pack in hot sterilized jars and seal at once.

APPLE JELLY

Apple jelly may be made from parings and cores of tart apples used in other canning. Discard all imperfect parts. Cover with water and cook until fruit is quite done, strain twice. Add ¾ cup sugar to 1 cup of boiling juice. Boil rapidly to jelly stage. Pour into sterilized glasses. I don't know how long to boil. Never did time it.

PEAR PRESERVES

1 qt. pears (sliced or chopped)	1 cup water or juice
1½ cups sugar	2–3 slices of lemon, if you wish

Pare fruit (if hard, cook until tender in water). Make syrup of liquid and sugar, add fruit to partly cooled syrup, and bring gently to boil. Add lemon, if desired. Boil rapidly until clear and tender. Cool rapidly. Stand in syrup to plump. Pack into jars and add reheated syrup. Seal immediately. Watch that it doesn't stick. Burns easily.

Select small, young beets, cook until tender, dip into cold water, and peel off skins. Slice or leave whole. Make syrup:

2 cups sugar
2 cups water
2 cups strong vinegar
1 tsp. cloves
1 tsp. allspice
1 tsp. cinnamon
1 thin-sliced lemon

Pour over beets and simmer 15 minutes. Pack into sterilized jars and seal.

NOTE: I put 1 cinnamon stick in each jar.

Clara Nall wins blue ribbons in every class she enters. Or so it seems—at the Kentucky State Fair she won with Bread and Butter Pickles, Pear Preserves, Apple Jelly, a dried Thanksgiving centerpiece, and a baby quilt! She has been winning for years, yet she told us, "Now, I don't think I'm all that good—maybe I just had good luck."

Clara is seventy-seven and was raised on a small farm; she's the "fifth from top of seven children, six girls, one boy, all living."

Clara poses a cooking riddle. "I made an old-fashioned custard pie. I poured the ingredients into an unbaked crust. When I took it from the oven, the crust was on top. Custard was on the bottom. (It was eatable.) What happened?"

SYLVIA A. NELMS
MUSTANG, OKLAHOMA

FIRST PLACE, MIXED PICKLES
STATE FAIR OF OKLAHOMA

MIXED PICKLES

2 lbs. mixed vegetables:
Onions (boil, remove outer skin)
Cauliflower (blanch for 2 minutes)
Raw cucumbers, peppers, celery, and carrots

Boil the following brine and pour over vegetables in crock:

1 qt. water
½ cup vinegar
1 cup pickling salt

Let set overnight keeping vegetables below liquid level.

Drain off brine in the morning and cover with cold water. Let set overnight. Drain off water. Pack the vegetables into clean, hot, sterilized jars. Boil the following and pour into jars:

1 pint water
1 pint vinegar
1 T. sugar

Adjust lids. Process for 10 minutes.

PICKLED PEPPERS

4 qts. peppers	2 T. prepared horseradish
1½ cups salt	10 cups vinegar
4 qts. water	2 cups water
2 cloves garlic	¼ cup sugar

Cut 2 small slits in each pepper.

Dissolve salt in 4 quarts water. Pour over peppers and let stand 12 to 18 hours in a cool place. Drain. Rinse and drain thoroughly.

Combine remaining ingredients; simmer 15 minutes. Remove garlic.

Pack peppers into hot, sterilized jars. Seal. Process pints 10 minutes in boiling-water bath.

Sylvia cooks for her husband, her young son, and her little baby daughter. Her husband is a builder and built their house, so Sylvia got the kind of kitchen she wanted—contemporary with orange accents, and all modern appliances. She even has a large pantry for her pickles and canned goods.

Sylvia gives credit to her husband's mother for teaching her to can, "and also my grandmother," she says. She is a good student, for her canned peas and canned squash have both won blue ribbons at the State Fair of Oklahoma.

She advises others, "After cooking vegetables in syrup for pickles, be sure and strain the syrup to remove loose pieces of pickle and also remove spices, which can discolor the pickles."

ROY PARISH
BROOKLYN, NEW YORK

DILL PICKLES

25–30 5- or 5½-inch cukes	1 T. salt to each jar
3–4 fresh dill heads to each jar	4 cups cider vinegar
2–3 garlic cloves to each jar	3 qts. water

Put all but cukes in pot and bring to a boil. Slowly pour boiling-hot pickling liquid over cucumbers in sterilized jars, leaving ½-inch head space. Let stand until cool. Make sure lids are on tight. Put in cool place. Ready to eat in 5 days.

Roy has been cooking since he "learned from my mother, who is a good German cook. When I got married, I had nine children. My kids love to cook. Now I have ten grandchildren!"

His cooking advice is, "Take your time and relax and enjoy it." (Maybe that's how he got all those kids, too.) Roy told us that once "My cold-pack pickles blew up after standing for awhile. It scared the hell out of me."

Roy has these hints about making pickles:

Use clean quart jars. Boil lids and leave lids in boiling water until ready to use.

Slice cucumbers into spears. Fill jar with spears but do not over pack. Fill with hot liquid. Make sure you use fresh garlic and dill. Use pure granulated noniodized table salt, not iodized.

Use apple cider vinegar.

Make sure the area where you are working is very clean.

Use wet cloth to clean jars after filling and make sure the lids are on tight. When cool store in cool place, such as basement.

CATHERINE LARKIN PEXTON

DOUGLAS, WYOMING

FIRST PLACE, LIME PICKLES
WYOMING STATE FAIR

RIPE CUCUMBER RINGS

Peel 1½ gallons ripe cucumbers, slice ½-inch thick. Scoop out seeds, leaving a ring. Cover with water to which 2 cups hydrated lime have been added. Soak 24 hours, stirring occasionally as the lime settles to the bottom.

Wash cucumbers thoroughly in 3 or 4 waters to remove all lime deposits. Cover with cold water and let soak 3 hours. Wash well again. Cover with the following solution:

1½ qts. vinegar	½ tsp. oil of cloves
8 cups sugar	½ tsp. oil of cinnamon
1 tsp. salt	

Let stand 12 hours, then simmer for about 30 minutes or until rings become clear. Let stand 24 hours.

For the next 2 days, drain the syrup and add 1 cup sugar each day. Bring to boiling point and pour over rings.

The third day, heat entire batch to boiling point. Place rings in sterilized jars. Cover with hot syrup and seal.

NOTE: Usually the ripe cucumbers are larger than a quart jar (wide-mouthed) and only the smaller rings will fit in whole; the others must be cut.

Cucumbers are ripe when the skins turn completely yellow. In Wyoming it requires a whole growing season for the cucumbers to ripen—so keep a special section of your cucumber patch for the ripe ones.

Cooking in her large kitchen, Catherine Pexton has the space to prepare food "for receptions and teas for up to 150 people." She advises cooks to be flexible. "When making something for the first time, follow the recipe. The second time make the changes which you feel are necessary. Many recipes need changing either for taste or texture."

See Catherine's Applesauce Cake (page 252).

JEAN PREWITT
PALMER, ALASKA

BLUE RIBBON PREMIUM
FIRST PRIZE, CONSERVES
ALASKA STATE FAIR

RHUBARB CONSERVE

Slice 3 quarts rhubarb and 3 whole oranges. Add ½ pound dates (cut up), ½ pound raisins, 1 teaspoon salt, and ½ cup water. Cook until tender and then add 5 cups sugar. Cook until thick. Store in hot sterilized glasses and seal with lids.

NOTE: I personally don't care for all the orange rind, so after it is cooked and thick, I remove some of them before sealing into the jars.

Although her kitchen is only 6x12 feet, Jean Prewitt manages to cook for four as well as coming up with prizewinning jams and jellies.

Her parents were "original colonists of Alaska." She married at seventeen and had seven children—learning to cook by "trial and error, those that turned out became my standbys."

BREAD AND BUTTER PICKLES

4 qts. sliced cucumbers	⅓ cup *plain* salt
6 medium white onions, sliced	3 cups cider vinegar
	5 cups sugar
1 green pepper	1½ tsp. turmeric
1 sweet red pepper	1½ tsp. celery seed
3 cloves garlic	2 T. mustard seed

Wash cucumbers thoroughly, slice ³⁄₁₆-inch thick, add onions, peppers cut in narrow strips, garlic cut in small pieces. Sprinkle salt over layers as you work. Mix 2 trays of ice cubes through pickles, 1 tray on top. Let stand 3 hours. Ice is what makes pickles crisp. Drain thoroughly, discard salt water. Combine vinegar, sugar, spices. Add cucumber mixture and heat just to boiling. Ladle hot pickles in hot jars and seal. Let stand 1 month before using to allow time to marinate.

Yield: about 4 quarts

Nellie won an all-expenses-paid trip to Pittsburg for her husband and herself with these Bread and Butter Pickles. She also won a blue ribbon for her Jam Cake (see page 254) at the Kentucky State Fair. She has been cooking since she was a little girl growing up on a farm.

PHYLLIS RAML
GOODWIN, SOUTH DAKOTA

HOME CANNING AWARD
SOUTH DAKOTA STATE FAIR

SHORT-CUT CHILI SAUCE

---

3 qts. peeled and chopped
    tomatoes
3 cups chopped celery
2 cups chopped onion
1 cup chopped green pepper
¼ cup salt

2 cups sugar
¼ cup brown sugar
1½ tsp. pepper
1½ tsp. mixed pickling spices
1 cup white vinegar

Combine tomatoes, celery, onion, green pepper, and salt. Let stand overnight. Drain in colander, but do not press vegetables.

Place vegetable mixture in a large kettle and add sugar, brown sugar, pepper, mixed pickling spices tied in a cheesecloth bag, and vinegar.

Bring to a boil; reduce heat and simmer, uncovered, for 15 minutes.

Ladle into jars, seal. Process in a boiling-water bath for 10 minutes.

Yield: 5½ pints

See Phyllis's Pumpkin Pudding Cake (page 255).

STRAWBERRY JAM

2–3 cups large strawberries
4 cups sugar
1 pkg. pectin

Mash berries first, then measure. Boil pectin about 3 to 4 minutes, pour over berries and sugar. Stir for about 5 minutes. Pour into sterilized jars, or into cartons to put in freezer.

Marjorie Renaux says the worst mistake she ever made cooking was "my first roast chicken—I did not know the chicken had to be cleaned. I just washed it off and used safety pins to close the opening. Needless to say it never was served."
Now Marjorie wins prizes and we have this blue-ribbon recipe.

VIRGINIA LEE SKRZYNIARZ
NEW BALTIMORE, MICHIGAN

DILL PICKLES

Sort cucumbers according to size. Feel for soft spots—do not use those with bruises. Lay cut-up cukes by layer with crushed ice for approximately ½ hour—this will give you crisp pickles.

Be prepared before actual canning—your time frame is important.

Rinse pickles with cold water after the icing process. Let stand.

Wash jars in hot soapy water—rinse very well, till jar squeaks. Place jars on cookie sheet in 200-degree oven to keep warm till use.

Boil hard for 5 minutes in large pot:

3 cups white vinegar	6 T. salt
3 cups water	1½ tsp. mustard seed

Do one jar at a time. Place 2 dill tops and 2 garlic cloves in bottom of jar. Pack cukes (uniform size) tightly into jar. Pour liquids into jar. Push wooden spoon down inside of jar to release any air bubbles. Place prepared lids and rims onto jar tightly.

With tongs, place jar in boiling water, making sure to have jar covered. Leave for 10 minutes—this process is the water-bath method.

Remove gently with canning tongs, being very careful. Place in a well-lighted and ventilated room, but not near a direct draft. Too-quick cooling could tamper with the processing. Keep children away, because of extreme heat of jars.

Cooling will take several hours. When cool to the touch, check for depressed lid, indicating correct processing. Check color for any discoloration. Liquids should appear pleasantly clear. Then check by use of touch for breakage or nicks, which can occur during processing.

Store in dark, cool area. Again avoid drafts, a heat vent, or extreme changes in temperature. After 1–2 weeks check again for quality assurance. Label and date.

Yield: 3–4 quarts

"I invited my best friend over to help can peaches. We had her eighteen-month-old daughter and my two-year-old son, on a hot summer night. Well, eight hours and five cases of peaches later, we were exhausted. We never ate a bit of the peaches. We gave them all away—the memory of that night did not allow us to have a taste for peaches again. Probably we'll never can together with the kids till they're eighteen years old or more."

Virginia says, "There are no short-cuts to canning/preserving. Follow every direction as if your family's life depended on it—because it does."

RUTH STURDIVANT
TIFTON, GEORGIA

FIRST PRIZE
GEORGIA PEANUT COOKING CONTEST

HOLIDAY CRANBERRY SAUCE MOLD

1 6-oz. pkg. strawberry jello
1 T. unflavored gelatin
½ cup boiling water
1 5½-oz. can crushed pineapple (juice and all)

1 16-oz. can whole cranberries
1 orange peel (grated)
3 T. sugar
1 cup peanuts (roasted and
  chopped)

In large bowl, dissolve jello and gelatin in boiling water. Add pineapple and mix well. Chill until jello is nearly set. Add whole cranberries, grated orange peel, sugar, and peanuts. Pour into mold and chill until firm. Serve as garnish with holiday turkey.

Yield: 12 servings

 Ruth told us about a time that she mistakenly used plain flour instead of self-rising flour to make biscuits for a family reunion breakfast. The biscuits were "a disaster. This happened when I had been a recent winner in several recipe contests. I had to take lots of teasing."

Ruth spends a lot of time in her cheerful, sunny kitchen, and it is here that her family, husband, and two daughters like to eat their meals. People like to visit in her kitchen, perhaps because Ruth adds that extra ingredient, the same extra she puts into her cooking—"tender, loving care." And she never overcooks.

Ruth learned to cook by absorbing "ideas and techniques in my mother's kitchen." She adds, "I actually learned to cook as a necessity for my husband and daughters, who love good food."

TOMATO PRESERVES

2¼ cups ground ripe tomatoes
4 T. lemon juice
¼ cup boiling water

⅛ tsp. salt
1 pkg. pectin
3½ cups sugar

Peel tomatoes, cut out stems and hard cores, put through grinder. Measure pulp, lemon juice, water, and salt into large kettle, add pectin. Bring to boil. Add sugar. Again bring to boil. Boil 4 minutes, skim, and pour into sterilized jars. This makes a firm preserve.

Marilyn Thom learned to cook when she joined 4-H in Iowa, where she was raised. She cooks for her husband and four children.

Her microwave is her favorite appliance. "Sure would hate to do without it. Exploded a lot of eggs in it for a while."

HEIDI WAGNER
PALMER, ALASKA

OVER-ALL WINNER,
JAM AND JELLY
GRAND PRIZE,
OPEN COMPETITION
ALASKA STATE FAIR

HOW TO PREPARE JAM AND JELLY

Prepare glasses. Wash glasses and lids, sterilize and drain. Use ripe fruit, prepare as directed. Measure ingredients. Use 8-ounce measuring cup and level measures for both fruit and sugar. Measure sugar, set aside. Measure fruit into 8-quart saucepan.

To cook your jam. Mix Sure-Jell with fruit. Place on high heat and stir until mixture comes to a hard boil. Add sugar. Bring to a rolling boil. Boil hard for 1 minute, stirring constantly. Remove from heat. Skim off foam with metal serving spoon.

To seal. Quickly ladle into the hot jars, leaving ⅛-inch at top. Wipe tops of jars with clean damp cloth. Cover with lids, following manufacturer's directions. Process in boiling water 5 minutes from when water returns to boil. Cool.

RHUBARB-STRAWBERRY JAM

1 lb. red rhubarb   1 qt. strawberries

Chop or slice unpeeled rhubarb into large pan. Crush ripe strawberries until they have changed to pulp. Mix rhubarb and strawberries together. To every 4 cups of mixed fruit add 1 box of Sure-Jell and 5½ cups of sugar.

RASPBERRY JAM

2 qts. of raspberries

Crush berries, one layer at a time. Sieve part of the pulp. To every 5 cups of berries add 1 box of Sure-Jell and 7 cups of sugar. Makes 8¾ cups of cooked jam.

BLUEBERRY JAM

1½ qts. wild blueberries   1 lemon

Remove stems before thoroughly crushing ripe wild blueberries, one layer at a time. Add 2 tablespoons of lemon juice to 1½ quarts of berries. To each 4 cups of fruit add 1 box Sure-Jell and 4 cups of sugar. Makes 7 cups of cooked jam.

RED CURRANT JELLY

3½ qts. of currants

Crush ripe red currants. Add 1½ cups of water and simmer, covered, 10 minutes. Place in jelly bag, squeeze out juice. To each 6½ cups of juice add 1 box of Sure-Jell and 7 cups of sugar. Makes 8½ cups of jelly.

GRAPE JELLY

1 pt. of bottled juice

Add 1 cup of water to 1 pint of bottled grape juice and mix thoroughly. To every 3 cups of juice add 1 box of Sure-Jell and 3½ cups of sugar. Makes 4½ cups of cooked jelly.

RED RASPBERRY JELLY

2½ qts. of raspberries

Crush thoroughly ripe berries. Place in jelly bag and squeeze out juice. To every 4 cups of juice add 1 box of Sure-Jell and 5½ cups of sugar. Makes 6 cups of cooked jelly.

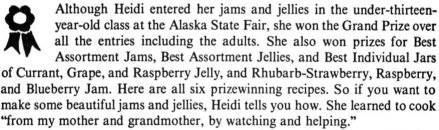 Although Heidi entered her jams and jellies in the under-thirteen-year-old class at the Alaska State Fair, she won the Grand Prize over all the entries including the adults. She also won prizes for Best Assortment Jams, Best Assortment Jellies, and Best Individual Jars of Currant, Grape, and Raspberry Jelly, and Rhubarb-Strawberry, Raspberry, and Blueberry Jam. Here are all six prizewinning recipes. So if you want to make some beautiful jams and jellies, Heidi tells you how. She learned to cook "from my mother and grandmother, by watching and helping."

Heidi told us about a funny, lucky incident: "I was making a combination jelly of raspberry juice and orange juice. The recipe called for a 6-ounce can of frozen juice and I put in a 12 ounce can by mistake. It never did gel, so I entered it in the fair as syrup and won first prize. I was shocked!"

MARGE WALKER
INDIANAPOLIS, INDIANA

ANTIPASTO

1 qt. water
1 qt. cider vinegar
1 lb. celery, sliced
1 lb. small onions, peeled
1 lb. carrots, scraped and
  sliced
1 lb. cauliflower, cut into
  small chunks
1 lb. wax beans, cut in 1-inch
  pieces
3 qts. tomato purée
2 cups olive oil
1 T. black peppercorns

½ lb. small mushroom caps
1 6-oz. can ripe olives
1 7-oz. jar green olives,
  drained
1 16-oz. jar sweet pepper
  rings, drained
12 sweet cherry peppers
1½ qts. red wine vinegar
1 T. salt
3 T. sugar
1 14-oz. can artichoke hearts,
  drained

Bring water and cider vinegar to boil; add celery, onions, carrots, cauliflower, and beans; boil for 10 minutes. Drain; let stand covered overnight.

Combine tomato purée, oil, and peppercorns, simmer 10 minutes. Add vegetable mixture, mushrooms, olives, pepper rings, cherry peppers, vinegar, salt, and sugar. Simmer 10 minutes longer.

Ladle into hot clean jars, leaving enough space to put one artichoke heart in each jar. Add artichokes; seal and adjust lids and bands. Process in boiling-water bath 30 minutes. Serve with thinly sliced salami or pepperoni and cherry tomatoes.

Yield: 7 quarts

 "I'm forever searching for new and old cookbooks. One would be surprised at some of the wonderful old cookbooks I have found at flea markets," says active cook Marge Walker. She advises beginners "to stick with the recipe at first to gain experience, and then they will eventually feel free to use their own ideas."

A real champion, Marge told us, "Although this year I won 35 ribbons, including 11 blues, 3 sweepstakes, and the Ball Corporation Special Award, I am still proud of my very first ribbon in 1974—it was for third place."

Try Marge's Honey Newtons (page 348).

THE WHITTAKER FAMILY
MRS. RAWDY WHITTAKER
LOUISVILLE, KENTUCKY

CHERRY, PINEAPPLE, AND APPLE CONSERVE

2 qts. pitted cherries	8 cups sugar
2 cups diced apples	½ lb. blanched English walnuts
3 cups pineapple (run through	(optional)
a food chopper)	

Mix cherries, apples, pineapple, and sugar. Let stand about 12 hours. Cook until thick. Add nuts, chopped fine. Pack hot into clean, hot Ball jars and seal immediately.

Shirley Whittaker, daughter of prizewinning cook Mrs. Rawdy Whittaker, told us about her mother because, she says, "I know my mother will never take the time—so I will do it for her.

"Mother is a very unusual person. She taught school for 39 years, kept house, brought up two children, and ironed seven white shirts a week for my dad because he was a school administrator for 49 years. Mom and Dad will be having their fiftieth wedding anniversary in June of 1982. We are really looking forward to this occasion. Dad, seventy-six, and Mom are both in exceptionally good health. They have a huge garden and all kinds of fruit trees on their almost-one-acre lot here in Louisville.

"Mother had never entered projects in the fair till she retired in 1974. Once she started we couldn't slow her down. She pickles, cans, bakes, and makes beautiful quilts and other kinds of handwork. I think she could be labeled a workaholic.

"She and Dad do everything together. He digs the holes and she drops in the seeds. She fills the jars and he tightens the lids. My sister and I help with the organization of the entry blanks, and the taking to and going back to get the entries before and after the fair. Last year she won 17 ribbons, the year before she won 15, and so on.

"Mom learned to cook by taking home ec classes in high school and college. I think she learned a lot from my grandmother, who was also a wonderful cook, as are her three sisters. However it all happened she has been cooking since she was eighteen when she had to drop out of her senior year of high school to stay at home and help keep house for her mother and father when an older brother fell from a tobacco barn and permanently damaged his left arm. She finished her high school senior year in college and continued from there.

"Her kitchen is rather large, comfortable to work in, and Dad sees to it that she has the latest in everything to work with. He takes great pride in her accomplishments. They have loads of company all the time and Mom cooks constantly. If Mom and Dad are home alone, she still cooks new things and takes some to the neighbors to sample. My sister and I live four miles away and are home on weekends to share in the goodies."

GLORIA PECK
BETHANY, OKLAHOMA

In addition to her prizewinning recipes Gloria sent us this.

RECIPE FOR A GOOD DAY

Take two parts of unselfishness and one part of patience. Work together. Add plenty of industry.

Lighten with good spirits and sweeten with kindness.

Put in smiles as thick as pudding, and bake by the warmth which streams from a loving heart.

If this fails to make a good day, the fault is not with the recipe, but with the cook.

HINTS

Here's how Gladys Green of Union Grove, Wisconsin solved the persistent problem of carrying goods to the fair: "I have two cardboard boxes with hand space for carrying. Each box has a wooden shelf I put on four metal glasses. They can be double-decker and I can get all food entries in these two boxes."

From Deborah Buxton, South Lyndeboro, New Hampshire

"ALTERNATIVE" PIE CRUSTS

Whenever I have leftover cookies that have gone stale, I use them to make "alternative" pie crusts. All you need to do is crush the cookies to fine crumbs. Add 1 stick margarine to 1½ cups crushed cookies, and about ¼ cup of confectioners sugar. If the cookie is vanilla, you might add 1 teaspoon cinnamon. Mix well and put in a 9-inch pie pan. Bake approximately 12 minutes, cool, and add a favorite filling. Suggested cookies for pie crusts: Hydrox cookies, vanilla wafers, pumpkin cookies, mint cookies.

Here is another favorite:

OAT CRUST:

1¼ cups rolled oats
⅓ cup brown sugar
½ cup melted margarine
⅓ cup wheat germ or bran or chopped nuts

Mix all ingredients together. Bake at 350 degrees 10–12 minutes.

From Georgia Ann Effenberg, Oconto Falls, Wisconsin

Put garlic cloves into a box of iodized salt, shake, and let stand for several days. You will then have a whole box of garlic salt for flavoring soups, salads, and meats.

From Robert Davis, Des Moines, Iowa

When cooking in competition (especially) pay attention to minor details and spend a few extra minutes to make your product extra attractive. Make your entry the one that catches the judges' eyes. Be original as possible and yet stay within the rules. If your entry is the best looking it becomes the entry the others have to beat for taste, etc.

When cooking pies I try especially hard to be original. This applies to filling and crust treatment. Judges usually don't have 10 to 20 pear or pineapple apricot pies to compare but sometimes they do get a number of cherry or berry pies. I've used orange-crunch topping on pumpkin pies, cut cheese slices on one-crust pies, and a part lattice, part solid crust combination on a fruit pie; just to be different.

When making preserves, forget that spoons were ever invented and remove the word *stir* from your vocabulary. Use saucepans for cooking and shake the contents.

With canned goods, beginners should get a good canning book and follow directions for preserving strictly. All cooks should use extreme care. Carelessness can result in poisoning.

APPENDIX

———————•———————

TABLE OF STANDARD LEVEL MEASURES AND WEIGHTS

3 tsp.	equals	1	T.
2 T.	equals	⅛	cup
4 T.	equals	¼	cup
8 T.	equals	½	cup
12 T.	equals	¾	cup
16 T.	equals	1	cup
1 cup	equals	½	pint
2 cups	equals	1	pint
4 cups	equals	1	quart
4 quarts	equals	1	gallon
16 ounces	equals	1	pound
1 cup liquid	equals	8	ounces (fluid)
2 T. liquid	equals	1	ounce (fluid)
1 Jigger	equals	1½	ounces (fluid) or 3 T. liquid

TABLE OF PRACTICAL METRIC CONVERSIONS

Volume (workable approximates)

Teaspoon, **tsp**; tablespoon, **T**; fluid ounce, **fl.oz**; pint, **pt**; quart, **qt**; gallon, **gal** (all non-metric forms = established U.S.A. and Canadian measures); milliliter, **ml**; cubic centimeter, **cc** (1 **ml** = 1 **cc**); liter, **l**.

¼ tsp = 1.25 ml

½ tsp = 2.5 ml

1 tsp = 5 ml

1 T (½ fl.oz) = 15 ml

2 T (1 fl.oz) = 30 ml

¼ cup (2 fl.oz) = 60 ml

⅓ cup (2.7 fl.oz) = 80 ml

½ cup (4 fl.oz) = 120 ml

1 cup (8 fl.oz) = 240 ml/0.24 l.

1½ cups (12 fl.oz) = 360 ml/0.36 l.

2 cups (16 fl.oz/1 pt) = 470 ml/0.47 l.

4 cups (32 fl.oz/1 qt) = 950 ml/0.95 l.

2 qt = 1.90 l.

3 qt = 2.85 l.

4 qt (1 gal) = 3.8 l.

*   *   *

100 ml = 3.4 fl.oz

500 ml = 17 fl.oz

1 l. = 1.06 qt

1.5 l. = 1.59 qt

2 l. = 2.12 qt

5 l. = 1.30 gal

Weight/Mass (workable approximates)

Ounce avoirdupois, **oz.av**; gram, **g.**; pound, **lb**; kilogram (1,000 **g.**), **kg**.

½ oz.av = 14 g.

1 oz.av = 28 g.

4 oz.av (¼ lb) = 113 g.

8 oz.av (½ lb) = 226 g.

12 oz.av (¾ lb) = 340 g.

16 oz.av (1 lb) = 454 g./0.454 kg

1½ lb = 680 g./0.680 kg

2 lb = 908 g./0.908 kg

5 lb = 2.27 kg

10 lb = 4.54 kg

*   *   *

100 g. = 3.5 oz.av

1,000 g./1 kg = 2.2 lb

2 kg = 4.4 lb

5 kg = 11.02 lb

10 kg = 22.04 lb

Temperature

Fahrenheit, **F.**; Celsius (Centigrade), **C.** (rounded to nearest digit).

F.	C.	F.	C.	F.	C.	F.	C.	F.	C.
0	−18	80	27	195	91	275	135	425	218
10	−12	100	38	205	96	300	149	450	232
20	−7	145	63	212	100	325	163	475	246
32	0	165	74	220	104	350	177	500	260
40	4	185	85	238	114	375	191	525	274
50	10	190	88	240	116	400	204	550	288

INDEX

STATE/TOWN INDEX

For a listing of recipes and the pages on which they appear, see the Subject Index, which begins on page 454.

PENNSYLVANIA
Ephrata
Mrs. Richard Ritter, 340
Pat Roth, 258
Gloria Shober, 200, 380
Franklin
Billie Lou Solle, 298
Lancaster
Esther Sangrey, 261
Peach Bottom
Janice DeLong, 87, 412
Quarryville
Florence May Kreider, 241
Ronks
Juliann F. Bloom, 311

RHODE ISLAND
Providence
Elizabeth Hughes, 176–77
Saunderstown
Helen Handell, 283

SOUTH CAROLINA
Columbia
Rachel S. Cole, 274–75

SOUTH DAKOTA
Bryant
Mary Prouty, 198, 338
Goodwin
Phyllis Raml, 255, 435
Wessington Springs
Mrs. Oswald Myran, 139, 378, 426
Wolsey
Joyce Dubois, 321

TENNESSEE
Calhoun
Ruby Isenhower, 39
Copperhill
Catherine Burger, 24
Delano
Lora M. Creasman, 174
Ethridge
Dawn C. Hill, 285–86
Lawrenceburg
Ann Campbell, 122
Maudie Craig, 409
Flossie Wilder, 160
Seymour
Joy S. Jones, 375

TEXAS
Athens
Ginger Morton, 69
Linda Martin, 107
Ballinger
Joanne Cheshier, 85
Jo McMillon, 14
Comanche
Barnie I. McBee, 424

Murchison
Diane Milner, 45, 95

UTAH
Logan
Val Crowley, 15
Salt Lake City
Marie Bigler, 405–6

VERMONT
St. Albans
Mae E. Manning, 186–87
Craftsbury Common
Marian Urie, 98
Underhill
Marie Puttlitz, 143

VIRGINIA
Danville
Helen T. Williams, 74
North Tazewell
Shreda Dye Jones, 237–38

WASHINGTON
Asotin
Marie Snow, 73, 343
Dayton
Sally Penner, 140
Pomeroy
Jeanine Richardson, 46
Steptoe
Cloy Harvey, 17
Toppenish
Doria Gauthier, 33–4, 129

WEST VIRGINIA
Clintonville
Beulah Arthur, 403
Iaeger
Syreda G. Tye, 264
Lewisburg
Janet K. Lyons, 246
Leora McClung, 331
Peggy Stuart, 345
Neola
Sara C. Bodell, 58
Renick
Zelda Kershner, 184
Sinks Grove
Carol Spence, 342
Summersville
Cindy Stalnaker, 381
Union
Betty Dransfield, 219
Williamsburg
Mrs. A. G. Sykes, 300

WISCONSIN
Alma
Bessie M. Secrist, 97

SUBJECT INDEX

For a state/town listing of cooks and the pages on which their recipes appear, see the State/Town Index, which begins on page 449.

Yankee Noodles, 361
Yeast Bread, 160
Yogurt or Sour Cream Raspberry Bars,
  314
Yogurt Bread, Strawberry, 199

Zucchini
  Bread, 193, 201
  Brownies, 326
  Carrot Bread, 169
  Pineapple Jam, 418